Ace of Hearts

ACE of HEARTS

The Westerns of Zane Grey

by Arthur G. Kimball

Texas Christian University Press
Fort Worth

Library of Congress Cataloging-in-Publication Data

Kimball, Arthur G.
Ace of hearts : the westerns of Zane Grey / by Arthur G. Kimball.
p. cm.
Includes bibliographical references and index.
ISBN 0-87565-121-6
1. Grey, Zane, 1872 – 1939 — Criticism and interpretation.
2. Western stories — History and criticism. 3. West (U.S.) in literature. I. Title.
PS3513.R6545Z73 1993
813′.52 — dc20 93-7024
CIP

Book design and woodcut by Barbara Whitehead

For Mother and Dad

Contents

V The Dream

Introduction

In this time of a "shrinking world" and international interdependency, it might interest the reader to know that a book about an American western writer has a Japan connection. I was teaching at Yokohama's Kanto Gakuin University when I received a summer research stipend to purchase the novels of Zane Grey and relevant critical and background material. The university was encouraging research at the time and I happened to have chosen a paperback anthology of western short stories for a seminar I was offering; my Japanese students, I hoped, would respond with interest to the western.

An earlier impetus for the study also arose in connection with a teaching experience when, as I note in the opening chapter, I decided some years earlier to introduce a Zane Grey western into an American literature survey course. At that time I discovered the available criticism to be both scarce and skewed; there wasn't much around, and what there was seemed inadequate for my teaching needs. Evidently those needs found their way to the surface when Kanto Gakuin University passed the word that funds were available for summer research projects. The present study eventually resulted.

This book is not an attempt to rehabilitate Grey in the sense of trying to make him out an unappreciated talent, nor does it have an overriding thesis to establish. Rather, it is an attempt to offer a fresh reading based on all fifty-six of Grey's westerns, something most critics have not attempted. If there is a central thrust it concerns the importance of Grey's erotic love plots (as the title, *Ace of Hearts* suggests), where seduction, in one reading, can be seen as a metaphor of unrestrained economic activity, and erotic desire an ironic source of violence.

Other emphases — other ironies — include the disturbingly ambiguous nature of "law" as Grey portrays it, and the equally disturbing and ambiguous presence of his Native Americans. The significance of these and other emphases and ironies emerges in the way they undercut the novels' surface affirmations (and those of some critics).

Though the subject matter inevitably overlaps and intertwines, I felt I could deal best with Grey's major features within a five-section framework. In section I, "The Formula," I try to set Grey within a general critical context (1: The Critical Setting), briefly survey criticism from the earliest reviews to the current situation (2: The Critics), and then focus in some detail on a particular misreading concerning an alleged Grey "formula" (3: Re-Branding).

Section II, "The Land," deals with the way Grey uses external (and sometimes internal) landscape, including the slippery concept of "nature," first with the neglected area of overland travel (1: The Trek), then with the way Grey endows his West with "spirit" (2: The Mystery), next the way the land affects characters (3: The Shaping), and finally a specific feature of the landscape (4: Sunset).

In Section III, "The Lovers," I examine the characteristics of Grey's heroines and heroes (1: The Ace & King of Hearts), and the ways their erotic encounters comment ironically on American values (2: Sagebrush Sex).

"The Law," Section IV, focuses on Grey's ambiguous portrait of the concept of justice, especially as it appears in the form of conflicting forms of "law" (1: "Lawlessness"), its embodiment in one internalized form (2: The Code), the ambiguous role of the "wanted" man (3: The Outlaw), and the action which necessitates law (4: The Violence).

Finally, in Section V, "The Dream," I attempt to show how Grey presents, and at the same time undercuts, the notion of an American dream, first in the form of an appealing literary package (1: The Frontier Idyll), then in terms of his use of Indians (2: Native Americans). In the concluding chapter (3: Roundup), I re-emphasize my major themes and findings.

For the reader's convenience the Appendix, which follows the publication order printed in Kenneth W. Scott's reference guide, *Zane Grey: Born to the West,* suggests major themes, plot elements, and a highlight or two for each of the fifty-six works. A "key" for each novel is included — a word, name, symbol, or theme, etc. — which is idiosyncratic, merely an item which helps get a handle on that particular book. Sketchy, selective, and inevitably slanted, these summaries nevertheless invite certain observations.[1]

The Formula

I

1
The Critical Setting

Attempting a critical foray into the fictive land of Zane Grey is like walking into a cowtown for a sociable drink only to learn some notorious gunmen are already entrenched there, well-heeled and waiting, on the lookout for brash strangers who may not know the rules. Russel Nye's smoking gun, in a chapter appropriately titled "Sixshooter Country," from *The Unembarrassed Muse* illustrates:

> The purpose of the popular Western novel is to entertain, and it is effective only in so far as it succeeds in doing so. It is written neither to shock nor titillate; it is neither myth nor epic nor multileveled symbolic narrative. It is an adventure story, good or bad only as it succeeds or fails to come alive as adventure and communicate the Western experience accurately and honestly. Fashionable academic criticism, beginning about 1945, saddled the Western novel with hero myths, fertility rites, quests, ritual killings, and phallic symbolism, very nearly smothering it in a fog of footnotes.[1]

Similarly, Don D. Walker, himself a major contributor to western literary analysis, takes aim at "Quantitative Analysis," "Finding the Mythic Hero," and the penchant for formulaic reductions:

> In the laboratories which pass for halls of humane learning, vast numbers of popular Westerns have been stripped down to their essentials and these given structural neatness as a formula. I cannot now imagine how anyone could have ever thought this process of reduction was literary criticism.[2]

Despite these strictures, critics continue to call for and produce more and closer readings, some even in the above "forbidden" areas. As for Grey, Cynthia S. Hamilton writes that he is an important writer because "in Grey's work, more than in that of any other western-writer of the period, one begins to glimpse the assumptions and implications of the genre."[3] She is right, and for other reasons as well.

Although Nye's grasp of Grey is one of the most perceptive, his pronouncements on what the popular western novel is not are too dogmatic and limiting. As to myth, for example, Richard Etulain in a comprehensive bibliographical essay notes the contributions of Max Westbrook, stressing "the Jungian and mythic quality of western literature," Richard Slotkin's *Regeneration through Violence: The Mythology of the American Frontier, 1600 – 1860* (the title speaks for itself), and Henry Nash Smith's "emphasis on symbol and myth" which has "broadened interpretive approaches to Western literature."[4] Again, Nye says the popular western is not written to titillate, but Grey's, at least some of them, certainly were. Not only to titillate, of course, but Grey knew how to tickle the ids of his era and did it, "shrewdly," in fact, as Nye himself admits a few pages before his strictures in an amazingly accurate summary: Grey, he says, "combined adventure, action, violence, crisis, conflict, sentimentalism, and sex in an extremely shrewd mixture, adding just enough history, scenery, and seriousness to give it the unmistakable stamp of a Zane Grey story."[5] Also, Nye's criterion for success, to "communicate the Western experience accurately and honestly" begs the question and opens a very large can of western worms. What is the authentic western experience? Critics are still debating the answer.[6]

Walker's critical complaint about formulas is more formidable; the reduction, as he puts it, of a book to skeletal bones of formula may indeed squeeze out the work's individual life. And yet even here critics have found fruitful ground. In the same bibliographical essay, Etulain cites John Cawelti's *The Six-Gun Mystique,* noting that Cawelti's thesis "asks readers to take seriously the conventions of the formula western and to scrutinize carefully the components of the formula to see what they reveal about a society that produces and reads Westerns."[7] In Cawelti's view, a reader conscious of formulaic features can gain insight into American culture. These and other critical approaches, Etulain shows, have made literary criticism of the western a vital force; they demonstrate the need for an ongoing critical effort.

Cawelti's point about society urges a closer look at Zane Grey in particular, since a writer as enormously popular as Grey in the 1910s and 1920s both reflects and shapes values. Mody Boatright makes the case for the "reflection."

> If the writer seeking a mass audience is to be successful, he must present his characters in relation to the beliefs and values that this audience holds. This does not mean that he must relate them to a consistent social philosophy. For the intellectual constructs of philosophers, historians, and other learned men become fragmented, broken into myths, symbols, and slogans, and reach the masses as a series of tenets and attitudes often inconsistent with each other. It is by appealing to these attitudes, which he may in fact subscribe to, that the writer makes his characters emotionally satisfying to his audience.[8]

Among these "beliefs," "values," and "attitudes" that Grey caters to are, for one, reaction to disturbing complexities of modern life. According to Robert G. Athearn, "during the days of World War I and shortly thereafter, Zane Grey answered the emotional needs of Americans who wanted to look back, if only a few years, to the 'old days' when life was simpler."[9] Cawelti agrees, but goes further than Athearn's emphasis on escapist nostalgia: "Grey made of the West a magical enclave where the strains and uncertainties of a modern urban industrial culture could be temporarily forgotten," Cawelti says, "and where the truth of wild nature turned out to be not the meaningless Darwinian jungle but an uplifting and elevating moral force." More, Grey's fictional world is "a means of exploring and coping with the threat of a meaningless universe," where he seeks to imagine "an image of heroism and a vision of relation between the sexes that would bring some kind of meaning out of a world of violence and chaos."[10]

Thus readers, troubled by urban changes, immigration, sectional rivalries, mechanization of industry, evolutionary thought, and the seeming loss of values following the War could, while retreating to the magic western enclave, find certain values reaffirmed. Specifically, in Grey's case, Nature becomes not just dog-eat-dog, but a challenging, regenerating force (for characters who respond to it), rugged competitive individualism heroically prevails over evil, and happy marriage follows an idyllic romance of "true love."[11] For Cynthia Hamilton, Grey's heroine in this happy marriage will be a "traditional homemaker-helpmate" characterized by "chastity, cloistered unworldliness and moral purity, ultimate obedience, and the abnegation of an independent self in the service of husband and family."[12] To the extent these or other alleged affirmations have an impact on readers — and response to Grey suggests they do — they both shape and reflect American culture. Thus, for example, Carlton Jackson cites an appreciative reader's letter asserting that *The Shepherd of Guadaloupe* "shows this isn't an entirely Synthetic Age."[13]

Another reason for a closer reading of Grey is that his novels contain ambiguities and ironies — most of them unintentional — that comment still further on American culture and its values, in some cases undercutting and calling into question the surface value affirmations. The "unintentional" is a subjective judgment based on Grey's failure to capitalize on these ironies thematically or artistically. In any case, the presence of these features is one more, perhaps the most important, reason for a careful reading of individual works, heeding Walker's warning about cases where there is "too little chance for a book to be considered as a *book,* with a unique oneness of its own."[14] In short, one has to move from the general to the particular, from the formulaic bones to the fleshing out of a given novel. Boatright makes a significant point in noting that the mass-audience writer may not present "a consistent social philosophy," and the "intellectual constructs" of various authorities may become "fragmented, broken into myths, symbols, and slogans, and reach the masses as a series of tenets and attitudes often inconsistent with each other."[15] If some of our values thus appear "inconsistent," as Boatright suggests, we ought to examine how and why.

One such inconsistency or ambiguity, noted by different critics, arises out of one of the basic formulaic elements which characterize not only Grey novels but a large number of westerns, namely, the clash of violence in a lawless realm. Cynthia Hamilton spells out the problem.

> Not surprisingly, the lawlessness is often viewed with ambivalence: detrimental to society in general, it tests a man's true worth, both morally and competitively. The result is a contradictory impulse to perpetuate lawlessness while eliminating it; to take the law into one's own hands, meting out extra-legal revenge to reassert the importance of virtue.[16]

Cawelti approaches the same issue from a slightly different point of view; the reader of "popular escapist fantasy" can find a resolution: "resolving in fantasy the ideal of peaceful progress toward civilization and the impulse toward lawless freedom and aggressive violence."[17] Cawelti hints of other ambiguities too when he later characterizes Grey heroes as having a "mixture of maturity and innocence, of experience and purity, of shyness and latent violence," and Grey's descriptions "a surface concern for verisimilitude, mixed with a deep religiosity and sentimentalism."[18]

Still other ambiguities and ironies, peculiar to Grey and varying with individual novels, also argue for the need of close reading. One, for example, is that Grey further complicates the already complex problem of aggressive violence and lawlessness noted by Hamilton and Cawelti. Another is his ambiguous use of "nature," as in *The Vanishing American*. Still others involve double standards in dealing with outlaws (*Forlorn River, The Lone Star Ranger, Sunset Pass*), the ironic notion of possession (*Heritage of the Desert*), and, especially, the role of sexual passion (*The Border Legion, Wildfire*). A reader looking for Cawelti's "fantasy resolution" may not want to bother about or even notice such ironies but they are imbedded in the text nonetheless, and they comment not only on Grey as writer, but on the values he ostensibly affirms, complicate one's understanding of those values, and sometimes subvert them, hinting at possible flaws in the American dream. In fact, and in spite of the critics' generalizations, social commentary abounds in Grey's novels (*Riders of the Purple Sage,* for example).[19]

2
The Critics

In Kenneth W. Scott's *Zane Grey: Born to the West, A Reference Guide,* a reader finds summaries of reviews and critical commentary on Grey from the publication of *Heritage* in 1910 through 1977.[20] Most of the reviews comment superficially, in part because the critique is brief, sometimes because the reviewer is prejudiced. In general, they represent the fluctuations of a manic-depressive chart, peaking with accolades about vivid description, an authentic West, and "continual suspense," and bottoming out with charges of crudest melodrama, contrived plots, and, in the words of one, "maudlin mush."

The earliest of Scott's review samples for *Heritage* comes from the *New York World* of September 18, 1910. Under "A New Writer's Fine Novel," the anonymous reviewer praised Grey's sympathetic picture of Mormon life, vivid description, and lack of sentimentalism and concluded that it had been "a long time since so good a novel of the Southwest in its wild, rough days" had appeared. *Heritage,* and the famous *Riders* which followed got Grey off to a start high on the chart.

A decade later, Grey was a wealthy writer of bestsellers, but the critical downside was apparent. Commenting on "Current Taste in Fiction," John Wolcott viewed Grey among the popular writers who "have never had any sort of respectful treatment from criticism." Actually, the ambivalence continued. In 1921 Grey was for one writer an author who could create a character (Hell-Bent Wade of *The Mysterious Rider*) who ranks "but little below Cooper's Leather Stocking," while another, writing in the Boston *Evening Transcript,* saw the same novel as a "glorified penny dreadful," but acknowledged grudgingly it would undoubtedly become a best seller. Perhaps no one better illustrates the positive and negative poles, to say nothing of the vagaries of taste, than Eugene Manlove Rhodes, who claimed in "The West That Was" (*The Photodramatist,* September 1922) that *Riders* and *Rainbow Trail* were Grey's best novels, while he detested *To the Last Man* and said that in *The U.P. Trail* Grey "foozled one of the finest opportunities ever missed by any American writer."

1930 marked twenty years of Grey's association with *Harpers.* The twenties had roared for Grey too, at least in terms of sales. *Publishers Weekly* for March 1927 said that among popular writers of fiction for the years 1919 through 1926 Grey ranked first. Critical assessments continued to manifest extremes, however. One 1930 reviewer saw *The*

Shepherd of Guadaloupe as "Grey at his best," but Fred Lewis Pattee in *New American Literature, 1890–1930*, relegated Grey to the "bottom layer variety of fiction."

Another decade and Grey was dead, his literary reputation nearly so. Among the obituaries for 1939 appear charges that, beyond his descriptive powers and ability to create suspense, critics "would concede little else of literary value,"[21] that his more than fifty novels were judged bad by "any accepted literary standard,"[22] and that it was "difficult to imagine any writer having less merit in either style or substance than Grey and still maintaining an audience at all."[23]

For Grey, the shootout at the pass may have arrived in 1970, a year that marks the publication of several serious studies on the man and his work. In the intervening decades (1939 – 1969) his reputation remained low, including scathing comments by James Folsom (*The American Western Novel,* 1966) who found it "galling" that "the epic of America" had "not Homer but Zane Grey as its chronicler." But 1970 somewhat redressed the balance. Kenneth Scott published a sensitive article, "*The Heritage of the Desert:* Zane Grey Discovers the West," Richard Etulain in "A Dedication to the Memory of Zane Grey, 1872 – 1939" called for "more consideration of Grey and his writings,"[24] Frank Gruber published his biography, *Zane Gray* and in *The Unembarrassed Muse,* Russel Nye, after discussing a number of western writers, said it remained for Grey to "put together everything that had been done and do it better than anyone before him and most of them after him."

Since that banner year major treatments of Grey include Carlton Jackson's useful *Zane Grey* (1971), the brief but comment-full study *Zane Grey* by Ann Ronald, John Cawelti's essential *Adventure, Mystery, and Romance* (1976), and, more recently, Candace C. Kant's richly informative *Zane Grey's Arizona* (1984), and two 1987 studies, Cynthia Hamilton's keen and thought provoking *Western and Hard-Boiled Detective Fiction in America* and Christine Bold's study of popular western fiction from 1860 to 1960, *Selling the Wild West.*

3
Re-branding

One semester I decided to introduce a western into the required reading of an American literature survey course. Why not? Each time around I changed two or three novels anyway, mostly to keep myself stimulated and I thought the students might enjoy it. As a teenager I had read some of Zane Grey's books: *Heritage of the Desert, Riders of the Purple Sage,* and the title for some reason I remembered best, *To the Last Man.* At the bookstore I searched *Books in Print* and found nearly a full column of paperback westerns under "Grey." I pondered, then settled on *Code of the West* and placed the order. The title had a kind of representative ring to it, I thought, and the idea of the "code" intrigued me as a teaching point.

When Grey's turn rolled around in mid-semester, I did what small-college teachers confronting a heavy teaching load and a maverick text usually do: I rustled for the library. I needed material so I could "get up on" Grey and pose as an enthusiastic advocate of the American western. The library's holdings were one slim volume and one pamphlet. But small is beautiful, especially if one is desperate. I found very little specifically about *Code of the West,* but eagerly copied the "formula" which one of the authors maintained *Heritage of the Desert* presents "in its purest state," — a formula "most of his novels used." Call it "Formula 1." According to Ann Ronald:

> An Easterner — that is, an innocent — arrives in the West. He, or she, has been a failure in the past and seems unprepared to meet the challenges ahead. The land at first seems harsh and unforgiving — the sun is too hot, the canyons too deep, the peaks too rugged, the rivers

> too swift. Problems are compounded by the appearance of evil, of men who live by their guns and who care nothing for the rights of others. Gradually, however, the neophyte becomes a man. Rather than be beaten by the environment, he learns to conquer the elements, and in doing so he acquires a deep appreciation for the land. Rather than see innocent people tormented by evil, he learns to fight and to protect those he has come to love. The West, seeming almost a Garden of Eden, becomes a proving ground for man. Here he loses his innocence and gains knowledge. In Grey's words, the hero learns "the heritage of the desert" exactly as the author did on his first trip with Buffalo Jones, and exactly as he hopes the reader will do while reading each of his novels.[25]

I confess. I retailed this to the students as "classic Grey," a venial sin for which I hope to atone.

Actually, some of the formula's broad features at first seemed applicable to *Code of the West,* though its central thrust remained misplaced. The character Georgiana Stockwell did come from the East, and was "unprepared" — at least for Grey's brand of western moral behavior. But Georgiana was hardly an "innocent"; she was in fact an "outrageous flirt," a post-war, precocious new American type, whose pink knees and flapper ways threatened to create havoc among the cowboys. Nor was she a "failure" — she was all too successful in the East (everybody loves her, her mother writes) — except in the sense that such "modern" women, in Grey's eyes, might be termed failures. Her weakness, as her sister Mary chides her, is rather ignorance of western men and western mores: "I tell you they have a savageness in them, a strength born of this wilderness, a heritage from fierce, ruthless, natural men. And they have a code of honor that no woman can risk breaking." (p. 78) For the most part these "ruthless" men keep their guns holstered in *Code of the West,* though it is the fistfightingest of all Grey's novels, thanks in part to Tuck Merry, a trickster-like ex-marine and ex-sparring partner of Jack Dempsey, who plays a substantial role in the working out of the plot. Georgianna fights too — a tongue-lashing of the villain, Bid Hatfield, at the book's climax — but she hardly has to "learn"; she's scrappy and game from the beginning, as when she goes along with Cal Thurman's hoax to outwit the tease-loving Thurman cowboys shortly after her arrival.

Such details aside, the critic's formula fails to mention the novel's central feature: the romantic love-plot. Another critic — Gary Topping — agreed with the first. Ann Ronald's account "describes the plot aspect of the Grey formula concisely, and serves as the basis for his own," he wrote. Grey's novels have a "stifling predictability," Topping wrote, and offered this summary ("Formula II"):

> An Eastern dude comes West and sheds the superficialities of his Eastern cultural background, finding physical health, moral strength, philosophical enlightenment, or true love. Once the names of his characters, the specific geographical setting, and the exact nature of the Easterner's problem are established, often the only interest remaining is to find out which of the stock catalysts Grey will use to effect the cure: stampede, Indian attack, kidnapping, exposure to the elements, and so on.[26]

Though shorter than and ostensibly based on the first critic's, the second commentary differs in emphasis; with the addition of "or true love" Topping includes the element — so central to Grey's westerns — as one of the possible "finds" of a heroine or hero. His summary also stresses "cure" whereas the first critic emphasizes the West as "a proving ground for man."

Where did these critical formulations arise? Probably in part from concern with Owen Wester's earlier *The Virginian*, which stressed East-West confrontation, and partly perhaps from Frank Gruber, the devoted Grey biographer whose 1970 volume offers high praise though only sparse literary commentary. *The Heritage of the Desert,* Gruber says, "was the forerunner of all of Zane Grey's Western novels. In it he set the pattern that he was to follow for so many years. It is the story of John Hare, an Easterner, suffering from tuberculosis who has gone West, hoping to cure his tuberculosis — or die." The novel, he adds, "has in it all of the elements for which Zane Grey became famous later, including a magnificent horse, Silvermane."[27]

In any case, none of these approaches proves adequate. *Heritage of the Desert* aside, "most" of Grey's novels do not focus on an easterner come West; when one adds other features of these critical accounts, the number of novels to which the "formula" applies shrinks even further. Grey's love plots as often as not involve two westerners. When easterners are involved, they are not always "innocent," let alone failures in the past who seem "unprepared to meet the challenges ahead," as the first critic maintains. Patricia Edgerton of *The Deer Stalker* is "young and in perfect health," and although she has been part of the New York set, she is "not of it." (pp. 38, 44) Warren Neale of *The U.P. Trail* is "a New Englander of poor family, self-educated, wild for adventure, keen for achievement, eager, ardent, bronze-faced . . . a young man of twenty-three with strong latent possibilities of character," who has been "the most daring and successful of all the men picked out and put to perilous tasks." (pp. 13, 14) Terrill Lambeth of *West of the Pecos* is from the South, but can "stick like a burr on a horse" and "throw a lasso." (p. 4) The list goes on.

The best way to determine the elements that put Grey on the bestseller list for ten years and made him a rich man and a western writer worth studying for what he reveals willy-nilly about American culture is to do what any number of Grey protagonists do — make a trek. A brief survey of the Grey canon of fifty-six westerns establishes the groundwork — a skeleton framework at least — for a revised formula. As with any number of Grey's range-riding cowboys, to learn where the stock is, one has to spend considerable time riding the canyons and brakes. The misbranded cattle and stray mavericks show up most often down in those individual draws. It's time to get out the real ZG branding iron.

First, for Grey, self-professed writer of "romances," the love plot is clearly central. Unlike "Formula I," which has only an oblique reference to "those he has come to love," and "Formula II," for which true love is an optional find, romance proves the *sine qua non* of Grey's western novels. In fact, nearly a third of them have a second romance; in a few cases (*Riders of the Purple Sage* and *Wilderness Trek*) the two are nearly equal in plot significance.

More surprising, in view of the two "Formulas," in two-thirds of Grey's westerns the female or male protagonist and, usually her or his lover, are from the West. This in itself disqualifies the initial formulaic claim — an easterner come West. Pressed further, the formulas apply to fewer and fewer of Grey's narratives. For example, Formula I's easterner is "an innocent" who "has been a failure in the past." Formula II's "dude" sheds eastern "superficialities." Among these easterners, Marian Warner of *The Vanishing American* has come West from Philadelphia influenced by a letter from Nophaie, the Indian she will later marry. In that long letter Nophaie writes, "You were different from most of the white girls. I loved you at sight and respected you when I knew you. I stopped drinking for you." Marian herself says, "I am my own boss. I've always dreamed of love with honor." And soon after her arrival at the desert post, good Mrs. Withers tells her, "You're young, healthy, strong. You've got a mind." (pp. 15, 19, 45). In short, Marian is anything but a failure.

Again, Ernest Selby of *The Dude Ranger* (conceding Iowa to be "East") learns he has inherited an Arizona ranch from his uncle, talks it over with his parents, and heads west with "a growing elation." In comical but gutsy fashion he immediately displays his courage, taking on two would-be outlaws. (pp. 5 – 6, 16 – 18) Nothing suggests he has in any way been a failure. Of course he's a "tenderfoot," as are virtually every one of Grey's easterners, a neophyte who needs to learn and adapt to western ways. Gary Topping, creator of Formula II, though purportedly accepting Formula I assertions, nevertheless makes an important distinction, using "dude" and omitting the telltale and inappropriate "failure." For a dude or tenderfoot is not a failure, and Ernest Selby, like most of Grey's easterners, displays courage early in the novel — often with his fists — as does Missourian Jim Traft of *The Drift Fence*. Jim has "from knee-high listened to stories of Indian fights and road-agents, gunmen and rustlers," and also comes West to run a ranch (which his uncle will leave to him). He was "making good money when your letter came," he tells his uncle, but jumps at the new opportunity. He's an awful tenderfoot, as he admits, but no failure.

Among the other easterners, two gritty young people star in *Wyoming*. Andrew Bonning admits to his father that he has "failed in business," but adds, "Confinement strangles me somehow. . . . And, Dad, to come clean — I hate modern business methods." His destined mate, Martha Ann Dixon, with "nagging at home," "fumbling passes" from lecherous men, and finding "the proms, the formals, the movies," have all "become stale and unprofitable," hitchhikes across the country. Even if one concedes a measure of "failure" for these problems — and Grey would not have considered either attitude failure — the additional qualification of Formula I, "seems unprepared to meet the challenges ahead," doesn't apply; Andrew flattens a hobo who has seized Martha Ann, and Martha Ann herself kicks a would-be seducer nearly senseless. They are surely prepared to meet challenges.

One needs to ask what constitutes "failure." For Grey's eastern protagonists certainly not moral fortitude or physical courage; they soon demonstrate both. Glenn Kilbourne of *Call of the Canyon* has gone west a physical "wreck of his former sterling self" having been shellshocked and gassed in World War I, hardly an indication of failure; he has regained health and adapted to a rugged life of hard work as the novel opens. His lover, Carley Burch, has "a real heart," her aunt says, underneath the "blase ultra something" that seems her only flaw. She has "gone in for Red Cross relief work with more sincerity than most of her set." (pp. 8, 14, 18) Kansan Paul Manning of *Black Mesa,* already wealthy, rescues a friend from jail and comes west to ranch after a grievous love relationship.

Inescapably, even with concessions concerning "failure," the initial assertions of the two "Formulas" prove inapplicable to the overwhelming majority of Grey's books. Unfortunately, those initial misreadings skew what follows. None of Grey's western protagonists, for example, needs "to become a man" (Formula I), only, occasionally, to regain strength. Nor do they need to "acquire a deep appreciation for the land," because they already have it. The easterners will acquire the appreciation. They will, in fact, often experience a spiritually rejuvenating "call" (like Carley Burch and Marian Warner) from canyons or hills; the westerners will show their appreciation by responding in some way, perhaps stopping on a ridge to admire the grandeur or even, in the case of some gun-slinging heroes, notice the flowers — a touch, of course, never associated with a bad hombre.

And the failure to accord romance its central place results in an important omission: neither formula mentions the erotic appeal of the stories, a feature Grey develops in connection with his lovers and heightens in seduction threats posed by the villains, especially in the form of abductions. In half of Grey's plots the villains make off with either the heroine or another important character; in approximately another fourth there is a confrontation with an overt sexual threat from the outlaw such as ripping a blouse. Occasionally a female victim has been sexually forced and a child results (Lucinda Huett of *30,000 on the Hoof,* Gekin Yashi of *The Vanishing American,* Louise Belmont of *Black Mesa*). As titillation, Grey's suggestive incidents and dialogue may be tame by current standards and his characters — the good ones — prudish, but readers, beginning in 1910 with the appearance of *Heritage of the Desert* and continuing on through the 1930s and beyond, obviously responded to the appeal, as did the filmmakers, for whom Grey's romantic plots furnished the stuff of an astonishing number of oaters.[28]

The erotic accounts for only one part of Grey's appeal. Another is the land, and Formula II does a better job in emphasizing its importance. One can scarcely overstate the significance of the land for Grey; his romantic protagonists are bound to it, react to it emotionally, make their living on it, most often on a ranch, and make treks, often long and arduous, across it. In nearly two-thirds of Grey's narratives at least some major action takes place on a ranch. Consequently, a good deal of action involves saving the ranch from outlaws and corrupt cowmen whose lawlessness — rustling, robbing, cheating — threaten the outfit with bankruptcy or outright takeover. Even in novels not featuring a ranch the protagonists often look forward at the end to starting one as the culmination of a dream (see, *Wilderness Trek, Thunder Mountain, Fighting Caravans*). A ranch represents the ideal way to enjoy that sense of liberation, space, beauty, and renewal associated with Grey's West.

Whether or not the setting is a ranch, the protagonists — as if to demonstrate the West's imprint on character — spend time trekking back and forth across the land. In a few of the novels a long cross-country journey even forms the narrative spine (*The U.P. Trail, Western Union, Wilderness Trek, The Trail Driver*). Short or long, the trek over (and sojourn on) the land will evoke the proper response from and have a salutary effect on the protagonist trekker, healing if need be (as in *Call of the Canyon, The Shepherd of Guadaloupe, Rogue River Feud*), "calling," especially to easterners, and satisfying all.

Grey does have action, trek-slowed though it may be, and that action or "adventure" forms the third major component of his tales. Before the romantic protagonists can marry, as they inevitably do, they must overcome the opposition within a lawless environment. A major problem will be sexual threats posed by the villains. This means chases, rescues, escapes, and confrontations, to say nothing of the doubts, jealousies, and misunderstandings which often preoccupy Grey's lovers. The bad hombres pose other problems too, and the protagonists will certainly have "to fight" (Formula I) to counter the rustling, robbery, deceit, and other intimidation. Grey's novels portray a lot of violence: knockdown drag-out fistfights, man-to-man shootouts, lynchings, and pitched battles. When the smoke clears, the romantic pair end married and prosperous.

Among the action-accompanying sources before that happy ending occurs, two others — Indians and horses — figure prominently for Grey. Biographer Gruber mentioned Silvermane, Mescal's splendid horse in *Heritage of the Desert*. From Silvermane on, special horses often clatter importantly through Grey's books. Usually the "good" people — either protagonist or the rancher — own one or more super-horses (*Majesty's Rancho, Wilderness Trek, Wildfire*) and several of the novels deal with wild horse hunting (*Forlorn River, Horse Heaven Hill*); they contribute, sometimes in a major way, to the action. Indians are harder to formulate. Grey runs the gamut in using them, from stick-like stereotypes who attack caravans (*The Lost Wagon Train, Fighting Caravans,*) to secondary but significant role-players (Nas Ta Bega of *The Rainbow Trail,* Sosie of *Wild Horse Mesa,* Magdalene of *Captives of the Desert*), to the fullblooded and fully-developed hero (Nophaie' of *The Vanishing American*), often with an underlying irony.

It is time to re-brand. Label it "Formula ZG," and to rival claimants say only, "Go for your gun."

Formula ZG goes like this:

A romantic adventure story set in the West. Two westerners, often two couples, find true love, marriage, and, unless they already have it, wealth, after overcoming obstacles in a lawless environment (which has other "laws"). Some protagonists are from the East. The majestic western land confronts them: beauty, vastness, physical challenge, renewing spirit, and fresh start; they respond, westerners demonstrating appreciation and the fitness for survival demanded, easterners and scarred others soon acquiring those traits. Outlaw violence also confronts them: rustling, cheating, gunplay, and threats of seduction, the latter enhancing the erotic appeal; they respond with fists and guns. Splendid horses frequently aid the protagonists. Indians, either as enemies or victims, often constitute a disturbing presence.

This is vintage Grey if one insists on a formula, though it is no substitute for close reading of individual novels. Nor can one, in light of such reading, agree with Formula II's statement about "stock catalysts" and "the only remaining interest." Grey's plots do have considerable "predictability," especially in the kidnappings and happily married endings — after all, that's what a formula is all about. But considering his enormous output of over two books a year plus short stories and articles for over thirty years, Grey shows considerable variety within his chosen genre (enough, it seems, to confuse critics at times).

The Land

II

1
The Trek

"Since the land is often a character in the Western novel, as well as setting, it cannot be taken lightly." The phrase is John Milton's. Later, he adds clarifying details: to be authentic, the western must be "a novel of the land, a novel in which the land actually becomes a character, a force to be reckoned with, part of the conflict as well as background." In works by accomplished writers a reader will find "landscape as character, landscape as shaping force, landscape as agent."[1] Describing just how this comes about in a given work becomes a challenge — easier said than done. And setting aside for a moment the question of just how well Grey achieves these goals — a question involving taste and judgment — no one can deny the sheer acres of fictive space he gave to the land. Nor can one doubt the exhilaration and motivating power of his first real experience with it accompanied by Buffalo Jones: "We shall start in a day or two. We travel with the Mormons for a hundred and eighty miles. . . . We reach Jones's ranch in four days," he wrote to his wife, Dolly. "Then we work around the north rim of the Canyon, where we shall camp. . . . I am positively quivering with joy at the prospect of the trip. I have lost all my blues and I'm actually happy."[2] Like Grey, this section starts with the trek, for though commentators have duly noted Grey's prose descriptions, virtually no one remarks his extensive use of ordinary journey across the land.

Both mini-treks and maxi-treks cross Grey's pages, particularly in the novels with desert settings. The trek is one device by which he can attempt to give an authentic ring and verisimilitude to what he admits are romances. Grey usually lists actual places — most of them places he has visited — to underscore this.[3] In *West of the Pecos,* Terrill Lambeth gets her first view of country that will be her home. "The river changed its course with Horsehead Crossing, but soon veered back to its main trend southward. . . . She had loved the river bottoms of the Red, the Sabine, the Brazos, the Colorado, and the San Saba," Terrill thinks, but "this Rio Pecos, for all its pale silver gleam, its borders of white and green, seemed cold, treacherous, aloof, winding its desolate way down into the desolate unknown." (pp. 49 – 50) This bit of geographical authenticity also anticipates the treachery she will encounter, and perhaps evokes sympathy for her adventure into a wild and unknown future.

Aside from those works already mentioned (*Wilderness Trek, The Trail Driver*), which are in subject matter extended "treks," Grey's hands-down champion trekker is Jim Slone of *Wildfire.* Slone starts his quest for the red stallion on page fifty-three, soon dismounting to study the wild horse's tracks:

> A little sand had blown into the depressions, and some of it was wet and some of it was dry. He took his time about examining it, and he even tried gently blowing other sand into the tracks, to compare that with what was already there.

Ten pages later he faces a dangerous cliff:

> This trail was passable, even though choked with snow. But the depth beyond this wall seemed to fascinate Slone and hold him back, used as he was to desert trails. Then the clean mark of Wildfire's hoof brought

> back the old thrill. . . . There was no stopping. Once started, the horses had to keep on. Slone saw the impossibility of ever climbing out while that snow was there. The trail zigzagged down and down. (p. 63)

A few pages — and a long time — later, Slone presses on:

> By and by only isolated mescal plants with long, yellow plumed spears broke the bare monotony of the plateau. And Slone passed from red sand and gravel to a red, soft shale, and from that to hard, red rock. Here Wildfire's tracks were lost, the first time in seven weeks. (p. 67)

Twenty pages into his trek:

> At last from the height of a slope Wildfire appeared, looking back and down. Then he was gone. Slone plodded upward. Long before he reached that summit he heard the dull rumble of the river. (p. 73)

And thirty:

> Slone sat astride Nagger in the mouth of this pass — a wash a few yards wide, walled by broken, rough rock on one side and an insurmountable slope on the other. (p. 83)

Slone's super-trek ends with the capture of Wildfire on page ninety-nine.

A long trek in *Desert Gold* nearly rivals Slone's. Yaqui, an Indian riding on the super-horse Blanco Diablo, leads Richard Gale, the beautiful Mercedes, and others in a flight from the pursuing Mexican bandit, Rojas:

> For once Belding's great white devil had met his master. He fought rider, bit, bridle, cactus, sand and yet he went on and on, zigzagging, turning, winding, crashing through the barbed growths. (pp. 162 – 163)

Helen and Bo Rayner prove game in *The Man of the Forest* when they no sooner arrive in the West than they have to endure a long trek on horseback to Milt Dale's mountain retreat:

> "Faster you come the better," called Roy. Helen could not see the sense of that, but she tried. Roy and Bo had dug a deep trail zigzag up that treacherous slide.(p. 109)

Or John Hare, in his quest for Mescal in *Heritage of the Desert,* riding on Silvermane and following the dog, Wolf, into the arid waste:

> . . . and Silvermane followed never lagging, sure-footed in the dark, faithful to his master. . . . In and out, round and round, ever winding, ever zigzagging. (p. 207)

Or Marian Warner's twenty-five page trek in The *Vanishing American,* which proves her "no tenderfoot," Withers says, after a familiar description:

> Down and down she zigzagged, growing out of breath. The slope of boulders sheered out, affording less precipitous descent. Stones as large as houses lay everywhere. (p. 72)

So the reader — zigzagging down countless pages of Grey's western panoramas along with the protagonists, or "up," as with Nophaie, Marian's lover, who climbs "in a long slant, up the brown, smooth incline, veined and striped, and around the headcorners, and back to a long slant in the other direction, up and up by these zigzag courses." (pp. 216–217)

The argument that such lengths are inevitable, given the terrain Grey chooses, doesn't hold; the novelist, like the cameraman, always has the option of a judicious "cut." In *Shadow on the Trail,* Wade Holden has already made a considerable trek to escape Texas Rangers when he finally arrives at the rim of Doubtful Canyon, site of the Pencarrow ranch. He pauses to absorb the maze of canyon branches. A movie version might cut to the ranch at this point, especially in view of the excitement there: a group of bad hombres confronting Pencarrow and his family. So might a novelist. Grey instead chooses to bring Holden down with three pages of description along a trail which is "steep and rough, full of loose rock, and zigzagged down weathered slopes that groaned and slid under his horse." (p. 104)

These acres of description enable Grey to achieve other ends as well. For one, he intends the reader to feel the land, not only in terms of the red shale and steep canyon, flora and fauna, but in a somewhat realistic sense of the time all that western space takes when one travels it, and of its demands on body and spirit. *Wildfire* proves the extreme, but Grey wants to convey something of the effort, patience, and tedium involved, a sample at least of these weeks hero Slone spends tracking the horse.

As with Marian Warner and the Rayner sisters, as well as Slone, the trek also indicates character. Since it demands much, the land reveals whether the eastern tenderfoot is game or not. Westerners like Slone are already tough. Their encounter with the land reinforces their potential for heroic action. The male protagonist of *Wyoming* demonstrates his toughness with his fists early, but still needs to feel the land as challenge. A week of range-riding fills the bill:

> That first week of torture in the saddle sweated and bled all the softness and the indolence, and most of the morbidity, out of Andrew Bonning. He had welcomed the trial; never for a single moment had he quit. From the very first he had sensed something vastly healing in this elemental contact, in this driving of spirit and flesh. (pp. 97 – 98)

Of course the trek often issues in action beyond that of the trek itself, especially when the journey involves escape, chase, and rescue. Or, more simply, even a scouting expedition. When Dodge Mercer heads into the hills to hunt for a still where "white mule" is brewed in *The Arizona Clan*, he is shot in the back. (p. 67) During Kent Wingfield's trek to find the Hole in the Wall Gang in *Stranger from the Tonto* he buys Lucy Bonesteel's fine black horse, Spades (earlier stolen), kills a gang member and wounds another (they suspect him with regard to Spades), and does the same with three Paiutes — killing one, wounding two — who try to seize the animal along the trail.

And sometimes, besides the touch of authenticity, reinforcement of character, and dramatic action, one uncovers a fringe benefit, an irony which enriches the narrative. *Wildfire* illustrates this and a good many other Grey features. One of them is the appeal of the horse in Grey's horse operas. An early reviewer was right when she called the book "polyangular," and said it was "a many-sided novel."[4] For one thing, it continued the presentation of superhorses begun with Grey's first three successes, *Heritage of the Desert, Riders of the Purple Sage,* and *Desert Gold.* Grey's own love of the animals shows through, embodied in Silvermane, Black Star, Night, Wrangle, Blanco Diablo, and others. These fine animals embody the traits Grey would have external nature foster: spirit, courage, endurance, physical strength, and a grace indicating nobility. Grey suggests the half-mythic status of these beasts at the end of *Wild Horse Mesa.* Caught and then released by Chane Weymer, Panquitch goes off into the sunset: "The lilac haze lent him unreality, but the uplift of his head gave him life." (p. 34) Lovers Chane and Sue Melberne make him even more; they sentimentalize and internalize, Sue saying, "He's like my heart or something in my blood." Chane replies dreamily — and intriguingly — "You are Panquitch and I am Wild Horse Mesa." (p. 365) Evidently her heart will now run wild through his.

Wildfire adds still more, Slone's captive stallion carrying irony, symbolic significance, and a unifying role in the plot beyond that of any other of Grey's supersteeds. To start with plot, Wildfire is the object of Slone's search, the occasion of Slone and Lucy meeting, the secret "wild card" entry in the Bostil race, the symbolic focal point of Bostil's obsession concerning fine horses, a major link with Joel Creech and his father, a tie-in for the minor role of the outlaw Cordts, and a major actor in the book's climactic second "race."

But the grand stallion also becomes the source of ironic and symbolic appeal, features linked, it turns out, with the character of Joel Creech. Though *Wildfire* ended as number three best seller of 1917, early reviews were mixed. Most considered the novel inferior to *Heritage of the Desert* and *Riders of the Purple Sage,* but entertaining, and, according to one, contained "unsurpassed moments of thrills." But for a reviewer in the *New York Sun* it was "marred by the dictates of the modern school of Brutality," and Joel Creech was "a repulsive maniac."[5] Creech is one of Grey's most impressively drawn villains, his "repulsive" deeds less gratuitous than those of most other Grey badmen. Crazy, yes, for his mind "snaps" during the course of the story, but Grey early on anticipates and prepares plausibly enough for what follows. Joel comes from across the tracks — the Colorado River in this case — and lives with his father, "a poor sheepherder and horsetrader." (p. 9) Blue Roan and Peg, two fine horses, are sources of pride for Joel and his father, and not surprisingly they dream obsessively of forcing a race with rich Bostil, owner of Bostil's Ford (river crossing) and Sage King, another superhorse. Bostil himself has an obsession with horses: "Whenever Bostil could not get possession of a horse he coveted, either by purchase or trade, he invariably acquired a grievance toward the owner." He sees the two potential rival horses and plots to get them "because he coveted them and because he feared them." (pp. 8 – 9) Grey, of course, destines these twin obsessions to clash.

Joel's infatuation with Lucy Bostil complicates the matter, doubling old Bostil's fears, since town rumor speculates about a romance, though Lucy insists she has only been kind to Joel out of pity. In a telling simile, Grey links these passions and in doing so hints of Wildfire's symbolic role; the outcast horse thief, Cordts, wants Bostil's horse Sage King, with "the passion of a man for an unattainable woman." (p. 10)

Grey's description of Joel points up his oddity:

> . . . a tall, lean young man, stoop-shouldered and bow-legged from much riding, with sallow, freckled face, a thin fuzz of beard, weak mouth and chin, and eyes remarkable for their small size and piercing quality and different color. For one was gray and the other was hazel. There was no scar on his face, but the irregularity of his features reminded one who knew that he had once been kicked in the face by a horse. (p. 38)

Brain damage? Speculation? Grey doesn't say. In any case, Lucy is both sympathetic toward but uneasy with Joel. Perhaps her sympathy stems in part from knowledge of her own father's quirk. Trouble begins early when, as Lucy reports, she and Joel meet, quarrel, and she tells him to "go wash his dirty face." Later she sees him doing it, bathing in a creek. He invites her to come for a nude swim and, embarrassed, she grabs his clothes and with Joel's horse following her, takes the clothes ten miles down trail. Joel ends up covering himself with adobe mud to prevent sunburn and runs into town "foamin' at the mouth like a winded hoss!" a rider says. Joel feels humiliated, doubly so since the cowboys have "conniption fits" laughing and scrub him raw getting the mud off. (pp. 15 – 16, 24 – 25)

When they next meet, at the Colorado River crossing, Joel complains of his humiliation. She replies, "If you hadn't taken it so hard they'd have let up on you." Joel responds:

> "Mebbe I might have stood that. But they taunted me with bein' — loony about you."
>
> Joel spoke huskily. There was no doubt that he had been deeply hurt. Lucy saw tears in his eyes, and her first impulse was to put a hand on his and tell him how sorry she was. But she desisted. She did not feel at her ease with Joel. (pp. 39 – 40)

To add injury to insult, a cowboy named Van knocks Joel down and kicks him for threatening to repay Lucy in kind — for stealing her clothes so she'll have to run home naked. Joel tells Lucy he is "no good in Bostil's Ford" anymore, that before, he could get a job and credit when he needed it, but now he "can't get nothin'." Pathetically he adds, "I'm no good! . . . I'm no good! An' it's your fault!" Chagrined, Lucy asks what she can do and Joel says marry him. She refuses, they quarrel, he grabs her, and they fight; "Joel could not hold Lucy, but he tore her blouse into shreds. It seemed to Lucy that he did that savagely." She lashes his face with a heavy leather quirt and rides off to his threat — which anticipates the novel's climax: "I'll lay fer you — an' I'll strip you — an' I'll tie you on a hoss — an' I'll drive you naked through Bostil's Ford!" (pp. 40 – 43) In this extended dialogue and confrontation, Lucy's emotions range from sympathy and pity to guilt, fear, contempt, and finally, rage. Thus Grey, in the first forty pages of his novel, creates a relatively complex character in Joel Creech.

The development of Joel Creech also underscores the role of passion, one of the "wildfires" so central to the narrative.

At the end of his long trek after the stallion, Slone captures the horse by setting fire to dry valley grass to drive the animal to the narrow outlet where he can rope him: "'Wildfire!' exclaimed Slone. "That word was a favorite one with riders, and now Slone used it both to call out his menace to the stallion and to express his feeling for that blaze, already running wild." (p. 86) As it turns out, that "menace" and "running wild" prove ironically prophetic. When the river floods, Bostil cuts the cables and sets the boat adrift, both ruining Creech, who is out of feed, and dooming the trader's race against Sage King. Bostil looks into his own soul: "it was a gulf like this canyon pit where the dark and sullen river raged. He shrank at what he saw, but the fires of passion held him fast." (p. 164)

They grip Slone too on the day when, burning with love, "the touch of her, as he lifted her to Wildfire's saddle, had made a madman out of him," and he had swept her into his arms and "kissed the sweet, parting lips till he was blind." (p. 207) Wildfire, one notes, is catalyst for this "madness." To compound the irony, Joel at one point visits Slone and, though Slone pities Joel and starts out being friendly, he loses his temper, knocks Joel halfway out the door, and kicks him the rest of the way when he hears Joel's repeated threat: "I'm a goin' to ketch Lucy Bostil an' strip her naked, an' when I git through with her I'll tie her on a hoss an' fire the grass! By Gawd I am!" He does. After the incident, during which he has called Joel "crazy," Slone cools down and thinks — in view of what Joel has told him, namely, that Bostil was the one who cut the river cables, and that Slone himself was "gone" over Lucy — young Creech may not be so crazy after all. (pp. 216 – 219)

At the climactic finish, the pathetic Joel deliberately fires the grass in the wild hills where he and his father have taken Lucy after abducting her. In the course of the narrative Joel has changed from mildly eccentric to aggressively hostile to frantically mad. His father has grievance enough against Lucy's father, but relents and tells Joel he is returning both Lucy and the prize Bostil horses. The loss of Lucy is more than Joel can stand at this point, and "the final thread which linked his mind to rationality" stretches and snaps. He grapples with his father, shoots him, strips Lucy to the waist, and they fight savagely. Then he ties her to Sage King and sets fire to the grass.

Not with dry cedar sticks as Slone has done earlier, but with a phallic gun. He puts the gun down in the grass and fires. Is this Grey's intent? He features the gun's erotic potential elsewhere (*Riders of the Purple Sage, The Border Legion, The Vanishing American*). In any case, the context renders it an appropriate reading. Denied, Joel's desire turns to madness and proves death-dealing. There is just enough truth here to make the reader pause, despite the melodrama which follows. Slone arrives on Wildfire as the blaze starts, rides over Joel, killing him, and races after Lucy. Wildfire the horse in effect kills Creech, then must outrun wild fire. He does, finally bringing about the race of races overtaking and thus defeating Sage King so that Slone can rescue Lucy. But the great red horse has run himself to death and dies.

Appropriately, passion "running wild" is the real destroyer, its consuming nature suggested in both blazing grass and wild stallion which become, in part, its symbols. Desire run amok must burn itself out, prove lethal, self-destruct. Fittingly and ironically then, the fiery stallion which Slone tames, and first brings Slone and Lucy together, becomes agent for the death of Joel Creech who, with his gun, starts the blaze. In light of events, Grey's title takes on added significance and wildfire — as horse, blaze, and passion — remains one of his most intriguing books.

In one form or another Grey's pages inevitably describe or otherwise comment on the landscape and the men and beasts who populate it, especially on the land as challenge — swollen rivers, sandstorms, quicksand, stampedes. Grey also strives for verisimilitude to portray some ostensibly "real" side of the West. To take but one memorable example, in *Western Union* the West-wise Vance Shaw saves hero-narrator Wayne Cameron and the telegraph crew from a buffalo stampede. He directs the men to soak the two oldest wagons with oil and put them at the tip of a V-shaped wedge. When the buffalos thunder in, the men fire the two wagons, then all shoot to pile up as many dead animals as possible in front of the flaming wrecks. Cameron describes the results.

> And suddenly the center of that advancing line sustained a staggering shock and disintegrated, huge black shaggy forms hurdling high to fall and slide and others as if by magic taking their places until the augmenting pile encroached upon the burning wagons, bumping them to send aloft showers of sparks from the burning canvas. My faculties, my blood, almost my heart itself, had stopped with that first shot. . . . (p. 208)

They succeed; the herd splits and roars by on either side. Exciting, intriguing, and "real" enough.

2
The Mystery

But Grey makes multiple use of the land; realistic at times as with the trek, he also endows it with mystery. For critic Ann Ronald perhaps the "ultimate appeal" of Grey's novels is "his own special bend of pantheism." She cites Grey's 1924 article, "What the Desert Means to Me," to show the "truth" of existence as Grey sees it, namely, that "in nature there exists a spirit which manifests itself in scenery of intense beauty."[6] The "ultimate appeal" of "pantheism" is arguable, but the mystical quality of the land emerges as one of Grey's most characteristic traits. And this spirit-filled land does more than just "manifest" itself; it "calls," awakens to new opportunity (sometimes even to a spiritual rebirth), evokes a wide range of responses, and sometimes, if one considers the context and subsequent events, becomes an ironic reference point.

Shefford, the protagonist of *The Rainbow Trail* goes to Arizona on a quest to rescue Fay Larkin. A failed minister, he not surprisingly thinks of the awesome desert country in partly Biblical terms:

> The desert and the stars and the wind, the silence of the night, the loneliness of this vast country . . . these somehow vaguely, yet surely, bade him lift his head. They withheld their secret, but they made him a promise. . . . And it was at this moment that Shefford, divining whence his help was to come, embraced all that wild and speaking nature around and above him and surrendered himself utterly. . . . He seemed to be born again . . . ready to trust what yet remained a mystery. (p. 39)

More than halfway through his adventure, the mystery begins to clarify. The Indian Nas Ta Bega has taught him about the desert's sublimity, and Fay has given him purpose, he realizes, and thinks, "In my hunt for a lost girl perhaps I wandered into a place where I shall find a God and my salvation." (pp. 140 – 141) Near the end of the narrative he can pretty well articulate the mystery:

> There was a spirit in the canyon, and whether or not it was what the Navajo embodied in the great Nonnezoshe, or the life of the present, or the death of the ages, or the nature so magnificently manifested in those silent, dreaming, waiting walls — the truth for Shefford was that this spirit was God. (p. 226)

It has led Shefford to a comprehensive spiritual point of view: "Life was eternal. Man's immortality lay in himself. Love of a woman was hope — happiness. Brotherhood — that mystic and grand 'Bi Nai!' of the Navajo — that was religion." (p. 226)

Most of Grey's characters don't press for such a definitive outlook; they're content to let the land remain a vague, mysterious evoker of feeling. A sunrise brings Hetty Ide of *Nevada* "wholesomeness and sweetness of nature, the exquisite beauty of woodland and wasteland at the break of day, and a marvelous, inscrutable, divine will" pervading the wilderness scene. (p. 173) For Kurt Dorn of *The Desert of Wheat,* the golden fields point to "something measureless and obscure, infinite and universal." (p. 344) And Katherine Winfield of *Captives of the Desert* feels the mystery almost as a divine assault:

> This desert solitude . . . did something to one, something inexplicable; it drew one's narrow soul out from oneself, and poured in something big. . . . Tears came too, and a strange yearning. Was it the desire to be in tune with the Infinite? Was it self trying to meet God? Was it God trying to storm her soul? (p. 26)

More likely it is her budding love for the hero, for Grey is neither a profound nor systematic thinker regarding matters of the "spirit," and Russel Nye is right in asserting that he included just enough of such seriousness to give it a peculiar Zane Grey stamp.

One had best read close and mind context with Grey. In *Stairs of Sand,* Adam Larey's friend, Merryvale, also ponders the "mystery" of the land. He hears the lonely wail of a wolf and thinks that man too is an animal, subject to the same physical laws, including the "instinct to preserve life and produce it." (p. 80) Then he wonders, "Yet what of the beating of that colossal heart — the spirit which enveloped the desert and the night, and reached to the whirling stars and into the void beyond?" The chapter ends, and the question goes unanswered, but Merryvale seems to have found his answer by the novel's climax. As he watches Adam and his brother struggle, he realizes he has "existed for this, prolonged his life for it," kept his own heart beating so he could stop Guerd's, which he does, with his revolver, "once — twice — through the heart." (p. 252) In short, what Nye would likely consider a shrewd touch of religiosity proves an ironic touch as well: nature's colossal beating heart beats away, but Guerd's stops.

For Ruth, Adam's lover (earlier forced to become Guerd's wife), the mystic experience has a different outcome. Running as a leitmotif through the novel, Ruth's "stairs of sand" derive on a literal level from the shifting dunes surrounding Lost Lake oasis, scene of her misery. As symbol, they represent the trials she must endure to deal with her fate, as Grey, seemingly ill at ease with symbols for the most part, persists with the "stairs" throughout the book. They remain a negative image for three-fourths of the narrative, seeming, to Merryvale, a mockery: "Who could surmount that sliding stairway? Up and up, toiling, dragging, panting, fighting, only to find it false!" (p. 132), a fear echoed by Ruth herself who finds it impossible not to see in it "the stairway of her imprisonment, the barrier and gateway to her freedom, the deceit and allurement and pang and uncertainty and strife of love, love the slipping, sliding footsteps of her fate." (p. 198) Even after Guerd's death Ruth fears she has failed, has made Adam kill his brother: "Oh my stairs of sand! I climbed only to fall — only to fall!" Adam sees it differently. She has toiled up the stairs and "reached the heights." He explains that Merryvale killed Guerd, and that he loves her "with all the passion and strength that the desert has given" him. It proves enough and the book's final desert image reflects the positive turn:

> The mood of the desert was changing. A mellow light tempered the ghastliness. The white wracks of dust had settled. Nature had ended her harsh audit for the day. . . . Mystical, beautiful, illusive, beckoning, the dunes of sand stepped up to the infinitude of blue. (pp. 253 – 254)

But the pious and inscrutable "mystery" of the desert here is an open secret; Ruth enjoys the final vision of her stairs in the very visible and earthy arms of her lover who carries her outside to witness the sunset.

But Grey persists in and obviously likes this kind of sentiment. Inhabited by quasi-religious mystery or "spirit" — his most frequent name for it — the land will often "call," if not to a new birth, then to new hope and opportunity. Madeline Hammond hears the call in *The Light of Western Stars*. Newly arrived in the West and enroute to see her brother, she feels "the insistence of familiar yet baffling associations." The white stars, she finds, have "called strangely to her or haunted her." (p. 55) For Helen Rayner it comes as she looks down the valley of the Rio Grande in *The Man of the Forest:* "it was there; the open, the wild, the beautiful, the lonely land; and she felt the poignant call of blood in her — to seek, to strive, to find, to live." (p. 41) But westerners hear it too. Lucy Bostil's call opens *Wildfire,* and for Ida Blaine of *Forlorn River* it is almost literal: "Moreover, as she gazed intently, these mountains of gray, with the shadows of purple in the clefts, seemed to call to her. It was a distinct sensation almost like an audible voice. The beckoning hills!" (p. 29)

Tough cowboys hear it too, like Chane Weymer for whom

the titular land of *Wild Horse Mesa* speaks with Biblical overtones: "It was as if he had been arrested by a prophetic voice that bade him give heed. He could not grasp the vague intimation as a warning; it was rather a call which urged him to come, to seek, to labor, to find." (p. 4) Lynn Weston of *Boulder Dam* also hears it (p. 48), as does Richard Gale, a tough ex-football player (played for Stagg), and the hero of *Desert Gold* listens: "A voice that he had never heard called him to see, to feel the vast hard externals of heaven and earth, all that represented the open, the free, silence and solitude and space." (p. 48)

Coming, as it sometimes does, with quasi-spiritual overtones, Grey's "call" undoubtedly appealed to many readers. After all, Christianity "calls" to faith, brotherhood, and service; the writer of the first Gospel asserts that "many be called, but few chosen"; Paul tells the church at Thessalonica he prays they'll be worthy of their calling; and the old hymn refers to "God calling yet."[7] But with or without their pseudoreligious tropes, Grey's calls undoubtedly appeal, subliminally, if not overtly. Who doesn't want to be one of the elect? Readers could be born again through Grey's landscapes along with the protagonists.

Like Harriet Lindsay, who gazes at the "magnificent eastern front of the Rocky Mountains" in *Raiders of Spanish Peaks:* "Greater than amaze and ecstasy something had birth in her. The thing she had waited for all her life seemed to be coming — the awakening of a deeper elementary self." (p. 134) Or Keven Bell, who feels it in the river in *Rogue River Feud* (p. 25), or Andrew Bonning of *Wyoming* who finds it, "inscrutable," in the "purple immensity" of the spreading range (p. 52), or, in *Wanderer of the Wasteland,* young Adam Larey, who feels the "grand wild" desert "will do something wonderful — or terrible" with him. (p. 15)

And of course the call may be to the promised land of the long-cherished ranch, as with newlyweds Panhandle Smith and his bride, Lucy, who find it after their troubles have ended: "And see the open canyon with the cedars scattered?

What a place for a ranch. It has been waiting for us all these years. . . . And so on into the rich grass where no wheel track showed — on into the sage toward the lonely beckoning walls." (*Valley of Wild Horses,* p. 200)

As often as not the land's mystery and purpose will come both literally and emotionally as a "peak" experience, heroes and heroines gazing in awe from some crest or other high point. Chane Weymer's view of Wild Horse Mesa (which opens the novel) is a first for him: "Chane had never before seen it from so lofty and commanding a height as this" (p. 1), and in *Stranger from the Tonto* Kent Wingfield climbs out on the Utah upland to a mind-staggering panorama so awe inspiring that he is momentarily stunned. (p. 60)

More especially, the lovers often share these views from the top. The experience may serve as confirmation of their love, as it does for Keven Bell and Beryl Aard of *Rogue River Feud* when they climb to a ridge and confront a "riot of yellow, of scarlet, of orange, of cerise, of purple." (pp. 149 – 151) Or Lark Burrell and Stan Weston of *Horse Heaven Hill,* who survey a fifty-mile expanse below. Stan recalls with chagrin how his fiancee, Marigold, had sat with him on the same spot mocking him with "Ain't nature grand?" At novel's end Stan and Lark share another peak; they look down from the divide and watch the mountain range bulge out of the desert, Lark's ranch and horses mere specks.

More frequently, the shared view foreshadows the true love whose course is still a bit muddied, though the reader, along with the purple sights and pungent smells, can imagine the tinkle of wedding bells. Sterl Hazelton and Leslie of *Wilderness Trek* surmount a ridge and look down into "the magnificent mountain pass" through which they've come. Aroused by the scene and Leslie "pressing close to his side," Sterl seizes the initiative, as Grey's impulsive cowboys often do, and obeying the "convulsion" in his breast and "hot gush of blood," kisses Leslie passionately, again and again until her cool, quivering lips warm up. (pp. 82 – 83) Scenes like this support a critic's claim about Grey's vivid nature descriptions indicating "displaced passion," though this is true only in certain cases.[8]

Cal Thurman of *Code of the West* abstains from amorous advances — he thinks he's in enough trouble with Georgiana already — though aroused by a double view: the sweeping valley below and the sight of Georgie emerging with the top button of her blouse torn off and neck exposed from the climb through the brush. He has to settle for a "thrill" that her response is awed silence. (pp. 96 – 97) Again, Thad Eburne and Patricia Edgerton of *The Deer Stalker* crouch "like eagles upon a mountain crag" one afternoon on the rim "where a lone giant pine" rises from its mat of needles "on the very edge of the chasm." Their nesting time has to wait a while yet, but the occasion inspires Thad to the first of several marriage proposals, though he has known her only ten days. (pp. 145 – 147) For John Hare of *Heritage of the Desert,* the view from the top brings certainty "of Mescal's love, of the things to be!" (pp. 90 – 91)

Grey certainly felt his mystery-permeated landscapes would have appeal. Did he believe in this "spirit?" Perhaps. He says so in his "What the Desert Means to Me" article. In any event, his letters indicate that he found the western land stunning. "Arrived at El Tovar this morning, finding the canyon lost to view in clouds," he wrote to Dolly. "Towards evening it revealed itself in the glory of the sunset. It is a second inferno, stupendous, awe-inspiring, glowing with fiery colors."[9] Like his characters, he sometimes climbed for inspiration. Some dozen years later he could still write, "This morning I got up at six-thirty and climbed the mountain. It was foggy, but the hills and slopes were clear. I was elated. I thrilled. I felt it all so poignantly, and I came back with the intention of working hard."[10] The awe and the thrills found their way into countless pages of the novels.

3
The Shaping

In his important study of the western, John Cawelti says Grey portrays the West "as distinctive moral and symbolic landscape with strong implications of regeneration or redemption for those protagonists who can respond to its challenge by recovering basic human and American values.[11]

Yes and no. First, miles of Grey's prose provide what in John Milton's words western writers often do, "a romantic perspective: . . . unbearably beautiful, or terribly harsh and violent, for its own sake or as a mere backdrop."[12] Romantic, yes, but often neither distinctively moral nor symbolic. Second, not all of Grey's protagonists need to "recover" values. Some do, including the embittered war veterans, but Larch Burrell, Jim Slone, Chane Weymer, Ben Ide, Edd Denmeade and the like already display solid values. But "respond to its challenge" remains valid, for Grey's characters certainly respond, and for some the land does prove "regenerative" or even "redemptive." For others it has other effects, all sorts of them.

They're apt to turn introspective, for one thing. Faced with troubles, Virginia Lundeen of *The Shepherd of Guadaloupe* turns to nature for "strength and endurance." She slips away from her friends to a favorite viewpoint: "So, through the purple depths and the colorful desert, and the infinite nothing of distance, she peered into her own soul. Long she gazed, with wide eyes, and then with eyes tight shut. She saw the same with both." What she "sees" amounts to a level-headed assessment of her situation. She is twenty-two, wants to live her own life, wants love and children, cannot sacrifice herself to marry the villain Malpass, and "with all her heart and soul" she loves Clifton Forrest, "and only through him could the fulfillment of life come to her." (p. 96) This desert-aided clarification soothes her and she returns to camp so glowing her friend Ethyl gasps: "You look strange, you're ripping! . . . You're the loveliest creature on earth." (p. 97) At the end of the novel she again looks to the desert, but this time introspection, philosophy and resolve are "mere thoughts." This time she looks not out from her "shrine" above, but up at it from below, "motivated now by the simplest and sublimest of emotions." She gazes at range and mountain and across "this strange empty colorful desolate void called desert. It had saved her lover." (p. 272) Married and joyfully awaiting her shepherd husband, Virginia's response to the land varies with the situation of her romance, first introspective, then sublimely happy.

The truth is, Grey offers a wide range of reactions to the presence of the land. *Robbers' Roost* illustrates. Early in the novel Jim Wall responds to his surroundings with apprehension. After supper he strolls out of camp "to where the canyon opened upon a nothingness of space." While he meditates in the gathering darkness he feels "an inexplicable reluctance to go on with this adventure." His soul feels "clamped," and he envisions himself "in the shape of a naked man, driven to and fro across the sand and the rock, tormented by horrors that were not physical, tortured by a spirit within." (p. 34) Later, he lags behind his companion trying "to grasp the spectacle that his eyes beheld," a spectacle so powerful "his sensations were not his to control." (p. 39) Still later, his enthusiastic description of the area surrounding the Herrick ranch surprises Helen; she doesn't expect a gunman to have any "appreciation of nature." Jim responds with a touch of sarcasm:

> "A common mistake, Miss Herrick. Nature develops the men who spend their lonely, hard, bloody lives with her. Mostly she makes them into beasts with self-preservation the only instinct, but it is conceivable that one now and then might develop the opposite way." (p. 82)

Facing the "hell" of a shootout at Robbers' Roost, Jim feels that if he were to die that day he would not have fully realized the earth's "sublimity, its mystery, its solemn warning, its inscrutable promise." (p. 176) But even after surviving together with Helen, he finds the shaping land threatens to do him in. He rides on, aware that "the terrible nature of the desert, and another storm at hand, were wearing away even his indomitable spirit." (p. 219)

Jim's responses to the land run the gamut from apprehension, to awed appreciation, to a sense of its mysterious purpose, to near despair at its harshness. He even adds a butte which has become his personal symbol:

> Far out there on a plain rose the butte which had influenced him from afar. . . . It had typified not only freedom, but for him the unattainable. His idle, dreaming thoughts . . . had made of this rock thing a goal. And now not only was it a possession of magnifying vision, but something he had attained symbolically. (p. 235)

This shapes him in every way, he says. As he looks at his butte, at the slow upheaval of the mountain burning "to flaming saffron, which merged into blue, and that to violet, and through all the darker shades, up and up the swelling slopes," he concludes:

> the Nature or the Omniscience that had made it was responsible for him, for his unwelcomed birth, his wayward boyhood, his footsteps that partook of evil, and the maturity that had seen his moral collapse and his victory. He had looked upon a physical thing that typified his conception of himself. (p. 235)

There's not much one can add; for Jim Wall the land is the "Allshaper," including the final sunset and "a glorious cloud-pageant over Wild Horse Mesa and the canyon brakes of the Dirty Devil," which find him happily united with Helen. (pp. 239 – 240)

Given the range of Jim's responses, reactions of most other characters will more than likely find in them something similar. Most will share Jim's awed appreciation. Jim Traft of *The Drift Fence* staggers to find Arizona has "claimed him." (pp. 170 – 171) Similarly, Lincoln Bradway of *The Maverick Queen* looks at the Wyoming hills and finds his love of the "cleansing wilderness" returning. (p. 187) Janey Endicott, alone among canyon walls, grows "pensive, dreamy, absorbed and happy" in *Lost Pueblo.* (p. 100) And tough Jim Slone of *Wildfire* chokes up, finding his "sight dimmed, blurring the spectacle" of the canyon, and his eyes "filled with tears." (p. 62)

Others, again like Jim Wall, turn to the land in time of trouble. Gang leader Jed Stone of *The Hash Knife Outfit* reveals his "badness" to be only skin deep. As he strolls under "great checker-barked junipers" in a canyon of the Yellow Jacket, he feels the loneliness. Like Jim Wall, he has a premonition, one it turns out, more accurate than Wall's. Jed feels the long, notorious life of the Hash Knife has about run its race. He continues around the high bank of the beautiful glen and ponders sadly the loss of his dream of honest ranching. The effect: "From that hour Jed Stone was more than ever a preoccupied man, wandering around the canyon . . . towards betrayal of those who trusted him." (pp. 90 – 92) Hetty Ide (*Nevada*) too has troubles. While her gaze strains "on and on, and ever upward to the purple ranges lost in the rosy pearly clouds of hot afternoon," she confronts "the staggering truth" that the man she loves may be "a consort of rustlers, a bloodthirsty killer, a terrible engine of destruction." (pp. 170 – 171) In those troubled moments, neither Hetty nor Jed Stone finds much immediate relief, so that the land acts mainly as catalyst for their thoughts. That catalytic power nearly brings Patricia Edgerton of *The Deer Stalker* to her knees when she first views the Grand Canyon. For her the land operates as liberating force, bringing hope: "I feel on the threshold of a new life," she exclaims. (pp. 41 – 43)

But for others the landscape proves anything but hopeful. In *Stairs of Sand* Merryvale feels the desert's shaping influence and along with it a stifling depression. As he stands in darkness "peering away down the starlit aisles which ended in obscurity," he thinks the desert "a Collosus [*sic*] of natural elements in process of decay, dying through the ages, destructive, terrible, dominated by the spirit of the sun." (p. 99) That same sun hangs over a winter scene in *30,000 on the Hoof* as Lucinda Huett watches the drifting snow: "During these winter months that ghostly wind had been the cruelest of Lucinda's trials. She hated it. She feared it." She ponders the lives of women before her who have come to "this devastating West." They too would have had to "become hardened to meet the callousness and brutality of the wilderness." (pp. 65 – 66) For people like Lucinda and Merryvale, the land forces one to endure in order to survive.

For still others — quite a few of them — the land will direct their thoughts to the one they feel is their true love. Brazos Keene of *Twin Sombreros* seeks out the land "to have it out with the dark forces" he feels have motivated him to kill two men and wound Bess Syvertsen. Like Hemingway's Nick in "Big Two-Hearted River," Brazos heads for the hills to gain healing through his senses. He builds a rough shack under the pines by a brook, listens to the wind, brook, and coyotes, feels the cool air, and chops piles of wood. Then, after some healing weeks, he begins to frequent "places that fascinate him," a sunny swale, a rocky glen, and, especially, "a lofty promontory." He doesn't know why. Later, he begins to understand. "He gathered from all his vigils up there that he had found a strength to lose himself in solitude and be at peace should his dream of love fail him." (pp. 165, 169, 171 – 172) The repeated slope-gazing turns out to be because of June Neece.

Brazos is not alone in finding the landscape an indicator of his beloved. Cal Thurman of *Code of the West* turns to "the favorite place of his boyhood," and its checkered juniper tree, "sturdy and gnarled, old and gray." It bends over him "with the lesson of its struggle," then its loneliness speaks to him: "the black depths of the canyon jungle called him in the name of primitive men." All about him breathes an "insidious whisper — to go claim his mate." (pp. 149 – 150) He does. Again, the beautiful heroine of *Riders of the Purple Sage* has long turned to her Utah hills in good times and bad. The opening of the novel finds her at one of the worst; Elder Tull, an evil Mormon, confronts Jane along with a band of men and threatens to whip her friend Venters:

> Once more her strained gaze sought the sage-slopes. In her extremity she found herself murmuring, "Whence cometh my help!" It was a prayer, as if forth from those lonely purple reaches . . . might ride a fearless man . . . who would hold up a restraining hand in the faces of her ruthless people. (p. 7)

Sure enough, hell-bent and wearing "black leather," Lassiter rides in just in time to thwart Tull and be Jane's champion. The "shape" bestowed by the sage slopes proves to be a tough and handsome gunman, her future lover.

This melange of interactions between landscape and character constitutes a shaping, of course. Environment inevitably exerts a shaping force whether it is under the Tonto Rim or in one of the concrete and glass canyons of New York. At one point Grey must have wondered about this phenomenon, and he gave one kind of answer in the guise of Paul Manning's thoughts in *Black Mesa:*

> Places were the most vital and compelling things in the world, next to human life. . . . Whatever happened to people — birth, growth, trouble, defeat or success, love, passion, joy, loss, death — all were vitally affected by the part of earth in which they took place. A new respect was born in Paul for the wide earth. (p. 38)

Grey himself was shaped by the West enough to want to set his romances there. He wanted to convey some of his own awe at the vastness, beauty, and harshness of the landscape. In a number of ways, then, he made the land a "character," or in John Milton's words, "a shaping force." Grey, of course, becomes the ultimate shaper, including so much about the land that it in turn shapes the characters, becoming part and parcel of their fate.

Grey's first relative success, *Heritage of the Desert,* suggests the characters have a special "heritage" in the land, and a good deal of irony surrounds that desert territory.

Critical appraisals of *Heritage of the Desert* are for the most part inadequate, and sometimes downright misleading. They ignore key elements of the irony which underlies much of the work's appeal. A reader needs to probe into the nature of this "heritage."

In the opening chapter, "The Sign of the Sunset," a company of Mormons finds the sick John Hare and saves him from the outlaw Dene. Hare tells his rescuers a few brief facts: he is twenty-four years of age, his parents are dead, he comes from Connecticut, and he has traveled West because the doctors said he couldn't live in the East. He gets a job with a big cattle company but is unjustly accused as a spy, threatened by a man named Chance, and then flees, loses his way, and wanders until he drops where the Mormons find him. The Mormons see Dene and his band in the distance, assume they are after Hare, and August Naab, the leader, says if Hare and Naab's adopted half-breed daughter, Mescal (Indian mother, Spanish father), will pretend to be sweethearts, the approaching outlaws may pass by. Dene and Chance soon show up, and Chance brazenly looks about the Mormon camp but dismisses the figures of Hare and Mescal huddled in the shadows as "sparkin'," and the outlaws leave as Naab had hoped.

For Ann Ronald, a sunset in the middle of this chapter — between the Mormon discovery of Hare and the outlaws' departure — "implies all the things a Grey Western environment accomplishes during the course of a novel."[14] Fairness to both Grey and Ronald requires the full passage:

> The desert, gray in the foreground, purple in the distance, sloped to the west. Eyes keen as those of hawks searched the waste, and followed the red mountain ram-

> part, which sheer in bold height and processional in its craggy sweep shut out the north. *Far away little puffs of dust rose above the white sage, and creeping specks moved at a snail's pace.*
>
> *"See them? Ah! then look, August Naab, look in the heavens above for my prophecy," cried Cole, fanatically. "The red sunset — the sign of the times—blood!"*
>
> A broad bar of dense black shut out the April sky, except in the extreme west, where a strip of pale blue formed background for several clouds of striking color and shape. They alone, in all that expanse, were dyed in the desert's sunset crimson. The largest projected from behind the dark cloud-bank in the shape of a huge fist, and the others, small and round, floated below. *To Cole it seemed a giant hand, clutching, with inexorable strength, a bleeding heart. His terror spread to his companions as they stared.*
>
> Then, as light surrendered to shade, the sinister color faded; the tracing of the closed hand softened; flush and glow paled, leaving the sky purple, as if mirroring the desert floor. One golden shaft shot up, to be blotted out by sudden, darkening change, and the sun had set. (pp. 2 – 3; author's italics mark portions which Ronald omits, substituting ellipses)

Ronald sees three "things" implied by "this particular setting." First, "it is a pictorial rendition of a specific place previously unfamiliar to both the main character and the reader," a "frontier" where the character can get a fresh start. Second, the setting is initially hostile "with the sunset suggesting a giant hand clutching a bleeding heart, and then as kindly, with the hand softening." This "is precisely how both John Hare and the reader will perceive the desert as the novel progresses," Ronald says. "Last — and this is how setting determines character — we learn the 'heritage of the desert.' Grey's description — a golden shaft blotted out by darkening change — parallels Hare's development. Innocence is replaced by experience," she adds, "and Hare becomes a man through his confrontations with nature."[15]

Flaws mar each of these observations. Grey in fact describes the desert here — gray foreground, purple distance, western slope, red mountain rampart and craggy sweep — quite generally. What is "specific" is the cloud formation at sunset, and Ronald omits all reference to the man, Cole, who points it out and fanatically interprets it, and to the "little puffs of dusts" (Dene and his outlaws) that occasion his anxiety. These are important omissions, for one of the functions of the passage is to suggest trouble and violence to come from the outlaws, thus whetting a reader's appetite, a function which Grey underscores with his chapter title.

One can also see this scene in the context of Grey's varied use of sunsets.[16] Later, on the trail, at "precisely the moment of sunset," the Mormons hold a simple ceremony of worship. A large group of Navajo friends are camped with them, "weapons laid aside." (pp. 37 – 38) Still later, at August Naab's shepherd camp, Hare nearly stumbles over Mescal watching a sunset and for the first time begins "to see in her a responsive being, influenced by his presence." (p. 78) At sunset, which becomes their meeting time, Hare and Mescal declare their love (pp. 89 – 90), and at novel's end the two reach the old camp on their honeymoon just as "the sun was setting behind the Painted Desert." (p. 297) Thus the first sunset, so ominous for Cole, ironically foreshadows happier events for the lovers. The Indian-Mormon harmony suggests additional irony.

For the Mormons, however, the early passage has grim significance. Cole's "prophecy" about the cloud shape which seems a menacing fist or hand and bleeding heart suggests violence, death, and suffering to come. One of the dead is Snap Naab, August's son, shot through the heart. Perhaps it suggests the general grief endured by the Mormons. Cole himself is killed by the outlaws, August Naab loses another son, and Bishop Caldwell's son has joined the outlaws and is nearly hanged. For the Mormon fathers, the bleeding heart is an apt symbol. Here too irony enters, for though August Naab loses two sons (he has lost five previously), they are partially replaced by Hare, who looks upon Naab "as a father," but rejects the Mormon faith. (p. 294) This underscores the changing nature of the frontier as well as the inefficacy of Naab's turn-the-other-cheek conviction. Hare agrees to "share alike" with Naab's remaining sons in work and profit, a non-Mormon becoming, in effect, a twenty-five percent shareholder with the remnant.

But the early passage has still other functions. Grey also makes intriguing use of hands and fists throughout his narrative, more than in any of his other works (with the possible exception of *Riders of the Purple Sage*). Early in the story the powerful August Naab disarms Dene, showing off his amazing draw, then doubles "his huge fist" and shows it before the outlaw's eyes. Later, "huge fist clenched," he expresses his anger and frustration on finding one of his waterholes plugged, and near the end he stands with "brawny fists" raised over the dead Holderness, enraged because he has been "robbed" of his revenge. (pp. 30, 125, 291)

Other variants of the hand imagery include "Naab's trick" (the lightning draw) used by both Snap and Hare, August Naab's arms raised in blessing at the wedding of Hare and Mescal, and the couple watching the sun set "with hands closely interwoven." Again, early in the novel Holderness slaps Hare, an insult later avenged when Hare slaps him back and finally kills him using Naab's trick. Still other examples include the handshake marking Hare's promise to the dying Dave Naab not to hang up his gun again, Mescal's "black and blue" wrists from Snap tying her too tightly when he abducts her, and the "long fingers, the sharp wart, the laced wristband" that save Paul Caldwell from hanging when he is identified as the one who set Mescal free. (pp. 27, 189, 247, 282, 296, 297)

For one thing, this potpourri of imagery supports the importance of Cole's observation in the early passage about "blood" and ominous events to come. In running the gamut of emotions — violence, anger, frustration, blessing, love, mercy — the hand and fist motif also contributes strongly to the pervasive irony in the novel, an irony which is linked to the tension between "the heritage of the desert" — Hare's lesson that he must "strike first and hard" — and the pacific desire of August Naab to live and love in relative isolation from the "world."

Ronald's claim that the first sunset "gives the character an environment where he can have a fresh start" also misses the mark.[17] Grey's "West" — mountain, desert, plain — generally proves reinforcing and sometimes regenerative for the good guys, but this particular setting focuses elsewhere. If Hare's fresh start literally occurs when the Mormons first find him, then the novel's fourth sentence provides an ironic setting: "The desert still stretched before him, the appalling thing that had overpowered him with its deceiving distance." (p. 1)

Two other settings in fact prove better candidates for Ronald's "frontier" in this novel. One is August Naab's "oasis," a likely place for a fresh start, an "oval valley, level as a floor, green with leaf and white with blossom, enclosed by a circle of colossal cliffs of vermillion hue . . . safe from the storms of the elements as well as of this world." (p. 50) As events — family strife, cruelty, murder — suggest, however, this idyllic setting is but one more source of irony. Another candidate is the shepherd camp in the hills where Hare actually regains his strength, learns to love Mescal, proves himself adept with a gun, and where they return for their honeymoon at the book's end.

Ronald's second function for the passage calls attention to the cloud "hand" clutching a bleeding heart and softening. "This is precisely how both John Hare and the reader will perceive the desert as the novel progresses. Increasing familiarity will make the land seem less harsh," she says, "and each succeeding step in the action will lead toward a fuller sense of its benevolence."

Well, readers are funny. They may not be as ready to jump

over this critical cliff as the sheep in the novel that leap to their death. In fact, three-fifths of the way through the narrative Hare is just beginning to learn. He stands with Eschtah, the Navajo chief, looking out over the Painted Desert where Mescal has escaped. At first only the scene's beauty moves Hare. Then he grasps "a little of its meaning": "It was a sun-painted, sun-governed world. Here was deep and majestic Nature eternal and unchangeable. But it was only through Eschtah's eyes that he saw its parched slopes, its terrifying desolateness, its sleeping death." (p. 183)

Sixteen pages later Hare begins his desert quest to find Mescal. He sees differently now. He does not see the "sharp peaks as pitiless barriers, nor the mesas and domes as black-faced death, nor the moisture-drinking sands as life-sucking foes to plant and beast and man" because he now expects to find his sweetheart alive. He now loves the desert "because it had not been a grave for Mescal, but a home." (p. 197) Nine more pages and Hare, parched and weary, sees something besides "benevolence" in the "stone-fettering grip of the desert," which has "opened wide to him, bright with its painted windows, inscrutable with its alluring call." Having bid him enter, it has now "closed behind him" and he looks upon it "in its iron order, its strange ruins racked by fire, its inevitable remorselessness." (p. 206) There may be a trace of Grey humor here, though half-buried in sand. In any case, Hare's experience is quite other than the critic's claim for an increasing familiarity where each step leads toward a "fuller sense of its benevolence."

In her last claim for the scene in the first chapter, Ronald says "Grey's description — a golden shaft blotted out by a darkening change — parallels Hare's development. Innocence is replaced by experience, and Hare becomes a man through his confrontation with nature." Hare learns a good deal, and gains much experience during the narrative, but even if one could accept "golden shaft" and "darkening change" as indicating "innocence" and "experience," Grey's description does not "parallel" Hare's development. Ronald omits Grey's "sudden" in her analysis, a telltale adjective which undercuts her interpretation. Hare's development is anything but sudden, as the Painted Desert rescue suggests, or an earlier passage when, while shepherding, Hare finds his love has ripened "through all the days on the plateau." (p. 89) Nor is he in need of "becoming a man." He has a problem to be sure; he is sick, his money has given out, and he is trailed by outlaws. But unless one takes the sickness as a metaphor of moral weakness — and nothing in the narrative supports that — he is already a "man" in every sense. In short, Ronald's analysis of this "particular setting" crumbles on close scrutiny.

Other readings do shed some light on *Heritage of the Desert*. Frank Gruber's biography of Grey summarizes the plot of the novel and says the story "has all the elements for which Zane Grey became famous later, including a magnificent wild horse, Silvermane." He adds virtually nothing by way of commentary, but his emphasis on the horse does highlight an important element in the novel.[18] Silvermane furnishes the means of escape for Hare and Mescal, and like other handsome animals in Grey's stories embodies western traits at their best — endurance, skill, intelligence, and loyalty.

Kenneth Scott's essay of 1970 is another, more penetrating matter. "The traditional elements of the Western story are given little play," he says, "The long chase, the shoot-em-ups, the last minute rescue are there, but not much space is devoted to them. The emphasis instead is on Hare's discovery that a life lived simply and naturally in the wilds is the most meaningful one." This is not the central emphasis, but surely it is an emphasis, one which Grey endorsed emotionally, one which shows in his prose. Scott is particularly taken with the character of August Naab, the figurative "New Eden" over which the god-like Naab rules, and the role of Eve (Mescal), the intoxicating spirit of the desert. He concludes that "perfect health, the wild beauty of the . . . desert, and the love of an innocent child of Nature form the rightful heritage of any man willing to forsake the effete East."[19]

That's an appealing package, but it falls short as commentary, for Scott does not follow up his Garden of Eden analogy to show the pervasive irony. Venomous spirits attack August Naab's "Eden" from within and without. The Mormon Garden proves ironic: Naab's rotten-apple son, Snap, brutally mistreats his wife and she dies; Mormon sons prove traitors (there is almost a Cain and Abel variant with Snap and Dave Naab, though Holderness actually kills both); deceit pervades the community. Perhaps Grey hints at the irony in this case with August Naab's too-ample graveyard and a description of the Colorado River as sliding onward "like an enormous slippery snake." (p. 51) There are too many deaths, too much violence, too much excitement to sustain Scott's emphasis on a life lived simply and naturally in the wilds, though it dangles as a hopeful dream. Even Hare's most idyllic moments with Mescal occur in the highlands, where he has been sent to kill coyotes, wolves, and bear and hone his shooting skills. Nor does Scott do justice to the love story, though he comes near Grey's eroticism when he quotes the passage where Hare "whirls in darkness" under Mescal's "intoxicating spirit."

Carlton Jackson's book-length study of Grey appeared three years after Scott's article. Jackson extensively summarizes the plot and says the "leading theme" is that "the gentle calling of religion could not destroy evil by a continual policy of appeasement toward bad men," a lesson August Naab at last comes to accept. Whereas Naab believed passive goodwill ultimately reigned supreme over evil forces, the desert taught "survival of the fittest for all the creatures who lived on it and man was not exempt from this requirement." Jackson also mentions a Good Samaritan theme and notes the "almost imperceptible change affecting Mormonism in the 1870s along the Utah-Arizona border." Again, he notes the "healing and edenic qualities of the West."[20]

There is little to quarrel with in this statement. The challenge of lawless men and evil to the Mormon religious community is, again, at least a major emphasis in the novel, and part of a larger context of theological, historical, and familial problems that provide one of the novel's distinctive features. But like Scott, Jackson fails to mention any irony in connection with his edenic West. "If there was a Garden of Eden in this country, Grey let his readers know that it was West of the Mississippi River," he says.[21] Naab's decimated family suggests otherwise.

Ann Ronald provides yet another perspective. "Essentially," she says, "in *The Heritage of the Desert* and in most other Grey books, we have a novel of education, one that initiates a character into manhood through a series of masculine rites and challenges." Hare observes the desert, sees the struggle for survival. "When he realizes that he, too, must fight not only the desert but also his fellow men, he has learned 'the heritage of the desert,' and he behaves accordingly." (This is more quicksand; what about Grey's female protagonists? And do Jim Slone, Larch Burrell, et al, lack "manhood" or "womanhood?" The problem compounds — misreading followed by over-generalization). Having raised the possibility of myth via "masculine rites" and "initiation," Ronald vetoes it. "Several key phrases that are appropriate to Grey's work — Garden of Eden, innocence and experience, survival of the fittest — might suggest a mythic pattern. But," she says, "the novels never rise to the level of myth because the formula, rather than setting the characters free, only binds their actions by restricting their choices. Life in a Zane Grey novel is too simple to create mythic patterns."[22]

A more recent critic disagrees. Christine Bold says "Grey repeatedly organized his fictional action into the sequence identified by Joseph Campbell as the 'monomyth,' the principle of action in all mythological tales. It consists of the progression, separation-initiation-return." Bold cites *The Rainbow Trail* as a "particularly neat" example, but acknowledges the pattern is not always as perfectly cyclical. She says *Heritage of the Desert* provides a variation where a circular movement takes place within the incomplete cycle. "At the center of *Heritage of the Desert,* the eastern hero, Hare, goes into the desert to save Mescal, the Indian heroine." He endures heat, sandstorms, thirst, and pain before he reaches the "goddess" and then returns through desert imagery "particularly close to Campbell's description of a dream landscape."[23] She might have added Hare's slaying of a totem bear (dragon) in order to rescue his "princess," and the symbolic "crowning" by Piute [*sic*] afterward: "Damn — Heap big bear — jack kill um — big chief!" (p. 86)

The possibility of mythic elements is intriguing but, as the comments of Ronald and Bold suggest, poses a problem in definition. Cynthia Hamilton acknowledges this. Aware that "myth" is a slippery term, she says "Grey assimilated the myths of his culture and used them to endow even the mundane aspects of his past with heroic import. In his fiction too," she adds, "Grey explored the ideological myths which provided a ready-made value structure and sense of identity, and used them to supply the 'answers' he sought." This act of faith eliminated any need to generate personal myths. Concerning *The Heritage of the Desert* she says, "Grey uncovered the value rift between social Darwinism and Christian humanism." She sees the last chapter of the novel as "an attempt to reverse the pessimism, to cover the hollowness of Naab's victory with the happy ending of Hare's and Mescal's honeymoon." Grey himself, she says, "is an almost perfect mirror of the contradictions of his society," who absorbed the values of conservative, small-town America completely and uncritically, and "swallowed the myths of his culture whole." In later books, she adds, he "solves" the rift by assigning passive moral perspective to women while allowing men to be active, aggressive, and "practical."[24]

Unfortunately, Hamilton's prose — "aspects," "ideological myths," "myths of his culture," for instance, to say nothing of "social Darwinism" and "Christian humanism" — are terms fuzzy enough to invite many a scholarly ambush. They confuse the myth issue, though she points to the importance of Grey as commentator on values. But if she does not solve the problem of myth definition, Richard Slotkin does, at least in his own terms. His two substantial and impressive works, *Regeneration through Violence: The Mythology of the American Frontier, 1600 – 1860,* and *The Fatal Environment: The Myth of the Frontier in the Age of Industrialization, 1800 – 1890,* confront the critic with provocative insights. As his titles indicate, "The Myth of the Frontier" is central; in Slotkin's words it is:

> arguably the longest-lived of American myths, with origins in the colonial period and a powerful continuing presence in the contemporary culture. Although the Myth of the Frontier is only one of the operative myth/ideological systems that form American culture, it is an extremely important and persistent one. Its ideological underpinnings are those same "laws" of capitalist competition, of supply and demand, of Social Darwinian "survival of the fittest" as a rationale for social order, and of "Manifest Destiny" that have been the building blocks of our dominant historiographical tradition and political ideology.[25]

And for Slotkin, the tales and frontier heroes who exemplify this myth and "laws" are inextricably bound to the fact of the Indian. As the earlier of these two works puts it, "The story of the evolution of American mythology is, in large measure, the story of our too-slow awakening to the significance of the American Indian in the universal scheme of things generally and in our (or his) American world in particular."[26]

Slotkin's "frontier myth" with its "ideological underpinnings" and Hamilton's emphasis on cultural values and value rifts bear on *Heritage of the Desert* and its irony. At the end of the novel, "the happy end," that Hamilton notes, one may see in the marriage, as Hamilton suggests, something of a cover-up, an attempt to "reverse the pessimism and cover over the hollowness of Naab's victory." Primarily, however, it is the logical end toward which the love plot moves. For Grey, self-professed writer of "romances," the love interest nearly always assumes major significance, a fact not stressed by most commentary. Hare and Mescal are paired from the opening pages; for much of the novel Hare is either with Mescal, seeking her in the Painted Desert, or trying to rescue her from the villains. If there is anything formulaic about Grey's love stories, it is the inevitable happy union.

The marriage also symbolically joins East and West, a commonplace of many westerns, including some of Grey's. Mescal represents Indian (Navajo) and Spanish (aristocracy — "of some rank"), a nice amalgam. As her name implies, Mescal also embodies some qualities of the desert and desert survivors: beauty, endurance, self-reliance, with a touch of Grey's mystical quality thrown in, "the somber, brooding strength of the desert" in her glance. (p. 78) Hare is an easterner, presumably Anglo (though his name, Hare, and preferred nickname, "Jack," suggest a well-known desert survivor also).

Mescal is part of Hare's "heritage." The chapter titled "Heritage of the Desert" states explicitly that Hare learns the lesson "to strike first and hard." He has to fight to keep his desert flower. But Grey adopted his chapter title for the novel as a whole, which suggests a wider significance. Hare's union with Mescal hints at a heritage of democratic levelling in the best of all possible American worlds: East, Spanish Southwest, Native American — in an idyllic western setting.

Hare's heritage includes more. The novel has two heroes, Hare and August Naab. Naab shows love, compassion, strength, endurance, capacity to heal, appreciation for the desert, and near prophetic powers of "sight." A kind of Mormon-Puritan projected into the far West, he has made friends with the desert "savages" and they live in harmony, ready to come to one another's aid. This is a rich "heritage" available to Hare from his adopted "father." A colossal figure, Naab's failure is his religious orientation, and Hare rejects that part.

He accepts another, less abstract gift, however, when he agrees to "share alike" in work and profit with Naab's remaining sons. This hints at an underlying irony almost ignored by critics. The comments of Hamilton and Slotkin nevertheless suggest the direction. The irony surfaces early in the narrative. After rescuing Hare, August Naab tells him, "You will come with me. It's a beautiful place, my Navajo oasis. The Indians call it the Garden of Eschtah." (p. 19) A reader at this point might well be unaware of the irony lying in ambush, implicit in "my Navajo"; Grey himself seems to have remained so. In any case, the point of ownership or "possession" arises.

A few pages later, the irony begins to compound with the introduction of the idea of law. Holderness offers Naab $10,000 for the water rights to Seeping Springs and Silver Cup. Naab refuses and Holderness tells him, "The land is owned by the Government," that the government won't let Naab have a monopoly, and that "no one man can control the water supply of a hundred miles of range." Naab counters, saying, "No men save Mormons could ever have made it habitable. The Government scarcely knows of its existence. It'll be fifty years before there's any law here. Listen. This desert belongs to the Mormons. We found the springs, dug the ditches. No man can come in here to take our water."

Why not? Holderness wants to know, since "The water doesn't belong to anyone." Naab replies that it is "Because of the unwritten law of the desert," and that "even an Indian respects desert law!" Holderness counters, "Bah! I'm not a Mormon or an Indian. I'm a cattleman. It's plain business with me." (pp. 26 – 27)

Three items — water, law, and the idea of ownership — mingle here in a confrontation shot through with irony. Naab's argument about Mormon ability is untenable, but he follows it with a squatter's rights or "finders-keepers" claim. Wily, obtuse, or both, Holderness says nobody can have a monopoly or control, yet offers $10,000 for exactly that. He also says the land is the government's. Nothing remains of the Indians' claim, it seems, but the names — Eschtah and Navajo. Further, Naab says there is no "law" operative, and yet in the next breath there is — an "unwritten law of the desert" — which means, he tells Holderness, that "you can't come in here and take our water . . . to supplant us" (exactly what the Mormons have done). He adds that even Indians respect this desert "law."

Holderness' candid reply, "It's plain business with me," is far more honest than the confused ramblings of Naab here, for one thing, and his "Bah!" has considerable justification; one might well ask an Indian about his "respect" for the "supplant" of Naab's desert law. Three pages later Naab invokes another law, God's, higher than man's: thou shalt not kill. As the chapter "The Heritage of the Desert," asserts, and the novel generally indicates, if thou wilt survive, thou darn well better; tooth and claw prevail. Shortly after this, Naab and his group pitch camp at a pond where cattle stand "up to their knees." Naab tells Hare it is "Seeping Springs" and "it's mine." He describes the area and says there are two valleys separated by a ridge, and "at the other end is Silver Cup Spring, also mine. Keep your eyes open now, my lad." (p. 43) The reader may well heed Naab's advice.

This early irony-ridden confrontation between Holderness and Naab over the water/law/ownership issue provides Grey with a rationale for a good deal of the action that follows. Holderness' men encroach on Naab by taking over and spoiling the water sources. Naab loses not only land but stock in the process when his thirsty sheep stampede to their deaths by plunging over a cliff. Naab has to buy more from the Navajos who in this fiction are spared further encroachment. Other exciting action — chase, kidnapping of Mescal, Holderness' killing of Snap Naab — also focuses around the waterholes.

The Navajos? Grey idealizes the Indians in *Heritage of the Desert*. He treats them sympathetically in that the chief, Eschtah (who incidentally has three wives — and thus a talking point with polygamous Naab), displays loyalty and wisdom; he has a long-standing bond of friendship and mutual trust with the Mormon leader. His tribe represents a back-up source of power for Naab, and at the end comes, unnecessarily, as it turns out, to Naab's aid. Other than that the Navajos live almost as if on a reservation, "on the other side" of the river, quietly and peacefully except for the brief associations with the Naab clan when Grey shows the men idyllically frolicking in "rude merriment around the camp-fire." (p. 46)

But when Eschtah displays his wisdom, irony again pervades Grey's scene. Late in the story, Naab confesses his troubles to Eschtah: his enemies, one a "chief" (Holderness), have killed his friends, stolen his cattle and water, and now he's had to bury another son. He wants Eschtah's advice. The chief obliges:

> "Eschtah respects his friend, but he has not thought him wise . . . Eschtah grieves. He does not wish to shed blood for pleasure. But Eschtah's friend has let too many selfish men cross his range and drink at his springs. Only a few can live on the desert. Let him who came too late go away to find for himself, to prove himself a warrior, or let his bones whiten in the sand. The Navajo counsels his white friend to kill." (pp. 256 – 257)

It is hard not to see the irony here. Evidently Naab did not come "too late" to claim his "Navajo" oasis. Eschtah's speech at the wedding of Hare and Mescal piles on the last ironic straw. Surrendering his earlier dictum that "white and red blood will not mix" (p. 179), the old chief pronounces his blessing on the new heirs to the enterprise.

Irony again enters, for the good guys here in fact do not engage in preemptive strikes; they wait for the enemy to attack first. Hamilton's comments on a "rift" in American values figure here, for August Naab's brand of "Christian humanism" (to use Hamilton's term) — a turn-the-other-cheek philosophy in this novel — fails as a means of dealing with the likes of Holderness and Snap Naab, who apparently listen to the desert's "strike first" advice. If these outlaws represent a kind of perversion of "social Darwinism" survival behavior, and if, as both Hamilton and Slotkin imply, that behavior links with "capitalist competition," then the "rift" between what Americans preach and practice becomes clear. In terms of the narrative, passivity doesn't stop the thieves and murderers.

Finally, Hare's heritage is twenty-five percent of Naab's rich oasis ranch. For Hare this means a "place" — a new home and a ready-made kinship group of good people. For August Naab the heritage looms as ambiguous. He gets rid of his enemies, but loses two more sons, and gets a gentile step-son, profit and loss of his ineffective moral and religious (and poor business?) stance.

But Grey's title suggests a heritage "of the desert" generally available to anyone: beauty, challenge (as in the Painted Desert rescue episode), and with idyllic niches like the Garden of Eschtah. In this sense the high desert country of the novel represents the West as a whole.

The ironies in this novel add to the reader's enjoyment. Since irony is rooted in contradiction, and contradiction produces tension, the result for the reader can be interest and excitement. For the critic it can add up to an awareness how in Grey's work, as Hamilton claims, more than in that of any other western writer of the period, one begins to glimpse the assumptions and implications of the genre.[27] For Grey purveys some of the "contradictions of his society" (Hamilton), and "laws" which comprise our frontier myth (Slotkin), and in doing so sometimes exposes their seamy side. A part of our heritage from Grey is the figure of the aging Eschtah ironically giving to his white brother a piece of desert advice he might better have heeded himself.

But at the end Eschtah blesses the newlyweds, says, "the kiss of the Flower of the Desert is sweet" and *Heritage of the Desert* ends happily.

Not surprisingly, the novel was a popular success.

4
Sunset

"In established Western typology," says Christine Bold, "the setting sun represents eternal life."[28] For James Fenimore Cooper maybe, but not Grey. Grey's sunsets, like his landscapes generally, have any number of uses, most of them a good deal more mundane. He exploited their beauty with his most vivid prose, used them as realistic settings for events, occasionally let them function as erotic substitutes ("displaced desire" in the critic's words), and sometimes, willy-nilly, allowed them to convey considerable irony.

Given the vastness of Grey's West, and the constant trekking required back and forth across it, one might expect a sunset to mark no more than the end of a day, time to rustle camp if one hasn't already. In *Fighting Caravans,* Buff Belmet and the others have driven the "old and familiar trail" day by day, "with the vast and sublime monotony of the plains on all sides, from rosy sunrise to golden sunset, on and on over the waving, gray and green, flower-dotted prairie." On November 19 they find a favorable camp site:

> Broken clouds in the west obscured the setting sun, but through the rifts poured a golden effulgence that painted the prairie. There was still a warmth in the air. Peace and quiet seemed to reign over the plains. Here and there, around their smoking camp fires, freighters sang and whistled at their tasks. (pp. 128 – 129)

As sunsets go, nothing special, though Grey's "seemed" has an ominous ring, for Comanches soon attack, upsetting that "peace and quiet." Later, a sunset marks Buff's nadir: "The sun was setting gold in the pass between the ranges, and to the east the gray obscurity hung like a pall over the void where the overland trail wound down into the Great

Plains. (p. 209) Again, as sunset nothing special, but the "like a pall" and "void" hint of the episode at hand. Buff has had a fight with May; now he finds her with a rival, Murdoch. Murdoch slaps Buff and Buff knocks him senseless. Still later, one more sunset — inconsequential in itself ("A golden glow from the setting sun mellowed the glade") — marks Buff's return to the Maxwell Ranch, which has reverted to the wild. He recalls the event when he fought Murdoch and left May "with a roguish devil in her dark eye," but he had not understood.(p. 289) A final sunset, however, finds all well. As with John Hare in *Heritage of the Desert,* Buff ends with his beloved "quiet in his arms" and sees "the golden afterglow" fade in the West. (p. 361) Sunsets here mark ordinary trail days, hint of Indian trouble, mirror the protagonist's feelings, and finally accompany the success of the love affair. *The Thundering Herd* illustrates similar variety (see pp. 57, 108, 327, 398).

Not all of Grey's vivid prose describes sunsets, but enough does to make them more than representative. Kalispel Emerson of *Thunder Mountain* ends up not with Sydney, as one at first expects, but Nugget, a dance-hall girl. At novel's end they leave Thunder City and Kalispel pauses in the pass to look back on the great landslide and what was once the roaring gold camp:

> The triangular side of the mountain, the rock face, gleamed with the gold of the sunset; and the dark earth grew rich in purple and lilac; the rolling terraces caught the tints of the sun like oncoming billows of surf burning with gold fire on their crests; the tilted houses . . . moved on under down-dropping curtains of rose light, while others floated on the lake, gray-sailed barks that grotesquely rode the shimmering water. (p. 177)

Grey runs riot with a sunset scene that Carley Burch of *Call of the Canyon* thinks is the West's "revenge"; she heads east after breaking her engagement with Glenn Kilbourne:

> Here the cloud mass thinned and paled, and a tint of rose began to flush the billowy, flowery, creamy white. Then came the surpassing splendor of this cloud pageant — a vast canopy of shell pink, a sun-fired surface like an opal sea, rippled and webbed, with the exquisite texture of an oriental fabric, pure, delicate, lovely as no work of human hands could be. It mirrored all the warm, pearly tints of the inside whorl of the tropic nautilus. (p. 226)

Aside from the elaborate prose, nothing of moment occurs here. Carley reacts to this "sunset transfiguration" with sadness, feeling that the West has "mockingly flung at her one of its transient moments of loveliness."

Sometimes Grey couples sunset and lovers in a scene with erotic overtones. *Nevada's* Hettie Ide rides into the woods feeling miserable, wanting Jim Lacy ("Nevada") but fearing he's an outlaw: "the thickets were on fire with golden and scarlet flame of autumn leaves; the westering sun caught the glint of falling leaf and pine needle." Nevada unexpectedly rides up and they talk. Grey, in a cute touch, has their horses promote the romance, acting while the lovers merely talk. "His horse, nosing Hettie's, brought Nevada closer to her, so that she might have touched him. This proximity bore upon her with incalculable influence." (p. 250) The horses' efforts pay off; when Hettie tells Nevada she loves him but thinks he must have someone else, he drags her from her horse, lifts her over the pommel, crushes her to his breast, and she finds herself "bent backward, blind and breathless, a victim of terrible devouring lips." (p. 253) Variants appear in *The Drift Fence* and *West of the Pecos*. In both, the heroine tends the hero's wounds at sunset with erotic results, Molly Dunn with Jim Trask, Terrill Lambeth with Pecos Smith (pp. 191 –193; 234 – 235 respectively).

Adam Larey of *Wanderer of the Wasteland* wanders enough to chalk up quite a few sunrises and sunsets in the long narrative. Adam leaves his ward, Genie, at a wild desert hot spring while he climbs a nearby crest to meditate: "The sun was westering when he descended the long, zigzag trail." He stops to pick up two beetles, intending to sneak up on Genie and drop them on her bare feet or book:

> Thus it happened that he did not look ahead until after he had straightened up inside the glade. All before him seemed golden gleams and streaks of sunset rose. The air was thick with amber haze. Genie stood naked, ankle-deep in the bubbling spring. Like an opal her slender white body caught glimmer and sheen. Wondrously transparent she looked, for the sunlight seemed to shine through her! (p. 356)

Nothing sexual happens here, except for the titillation Grey knows he'll achieve, but does earlier when Adam walks with a Mexican beauty, Margarita, at sunset and awakens "to the danger in this dusky-eyed maiden." (p. 27) His intuition proves right and later he succumbs, a rarity in Grey's fictions.

Soon after the episode with Maragarita, Adam flees for his life, thinking he has killed his brother. He reaches a road and falls exhausted.

> Presently he sat up to look around him. A wonderful light showed upon the world — the afterglow of sunset. Picacho bore a crown of gold. All the lower tips of ranges were purpling in shadow. To the southward a wide gray barren led to an endless bleak plateau, flat and dark, with dim spurs of mountains in the distance. (p. 61)

Nothing erotic here. Adam in fact despairs at the thought of becoming an outcast. Nor in the sunset he enjoys later with another desert wanderer, Dismukes: "A sunset, rare on the Mohave, glowed over the simple tasks of these men who in their wanderings had met again. Clouds hung along the mountain tops, colored into deeper glory as the sun sank." (p. 136) It marks a more positive time for Adam; he and Dismukes each see something in the other, Adam seeing a life-saver and teacher, and Dismukes seeing in Adam "the divine spirit of man rising above the great primal beasts of the desert, self-preservation and ferocity." (p. 137)

Later, erotic overtones again accompany the scene. Adam takes Madeline Virey to a Death Valley viewpoint: "Adam felt the lessening heat of the sinking sun. Half that blaze was gone. It had been gold and was now silver." (p. 203) Madeline returns speechless, and Adam goes to bed throbbing with the hope he can save this woman's "life and soul, and perhaps even her happiness." (p. 205) A few pages later he saves her from a fatal fall. This time it is sunrise, with "the east luminous and rosy, ethereal and beautiful momentarily brightening with a rayed effulgence that spread from a golden center behind the dark bold domes of the Funeral Mountains." Madeline, in his arms, wants time to stand still, but the unresponsive Adam can only wonder why. She says, "Wansfell, you are the only man I've ever known who could have held me in his arms and have been blind and dead to the nature of a woman." (pp. 214 – 215) This sunset-sunrise pair of scenes proves only an erotic tease.

As *Wanderer of the Wasteland* illustrates, and the earlier examples underscore, Grey does not use the sunset-sunrise consistently, but rather in a variety of ways — realistic setting with or without significant action, as vivid prose passage to highlight the West's beauty or mystical appeal, as erotic juxtaposition where lovers meet, and in combinations of these.

As in *The Rainbow Trail* when Shefford and Mary (really Fay Larkin) climb together in the hills outside the town where she is held in Mormon bondage to await being taken as a "sealed" wife. For Mary it is a moment of freedom; she runs ahead of Shefford, up the smooth stone to the "very summit" of the crest and stands there, "her arms wide, her full breast heaving, her slender body straight as an Indian's, her hair flying in the wind and blazing in the sun." She seems to embrace the West, to reach for something: "The sinking sun touched the rim of the distant wall, and as if in parting regret shone with renewed golden fire. And the girl was crowned with a glory." The description combines a real (more or less) sunset, lovers, mild eroticism, and an additional feature where the sun parallels Fay's feelings. "The sun sank swiftly, and instantly there was a change in the golden light. Quickly it died out. The girl changed as swiftly . . . the flush faded out of her face. The whiteness stole back, and with it the sadness." (p. 86) Grey's focus here is not on a vivid description of the sunset itself, but on a transfiguration of Fay Larkin.

But sometimes Grey's sunrises and sunsets suggest ironic developments, some perhaps intended by Grey, some likely not, though the "intentional fallacy" hovers over such conjectures. The ironic setting in *The Desert of Wheat* is obvious — farmer vigilantes break into the jail and seize the foreign agent collaborator, Glidden:

> A loop of a lasso, slung over his head and jerked tight, choked off his intelligible utterance. But as the silent, ruthless men dragged him away he gave vent to terrible, half-strangled cries.
>
> The sun rose red over the fertile valley — over the harvest fields and the pastures and the orchards, and over the many towns that appeared lost in the green and gold of luxuriance. (p. 219)

A bit heavy-handed, the "red" sun makes the valley fertile, but hints at the bloody deed enacted as, with "a ghastly, distorted face," Glidden hangs, bearing a frontier-days message: *"Last warning. 3 – 7 – 77."* (pp. 219, 221)

To the Last Man further illustrates, but here the sun joins other features of nature. Jean Isbel follows the trail of the gunman, Queen; the sun is setting:

> Early frost had touched the heights with its magic wand. And the forest seemed a temple in which man might worship nature and life rather than steal through the dells and under the arched aisles like a beast of prey. . . . It was a golden-green region, enchanting to the gaze of

> man. An Indian would have walked there with his spirits.
>
> And even as Jean felt all this elevating beauty and inscrutable spirit his keen eye once more fastened upon the blood-red drops Queen had again left on the gray moss and rock. His wound had reopened. Jean felt the thrill of the scenting panther. (pp. 119 – 120)

Grey's "felt the thrill" is in keeping with Jean's heritage. Half Indian, he has been summoned from Oregon early in the narrative to learn that his father expects him to be "the last man" of the blood-feud; he feels "the savage instinct of self-preservation bequeathed by his Indian mother, and the fierce, feudal blood lust of his Texan father." (p. 47) Later, during a siege, Jean sneaks up on one of the attackers, knife drawn:

> To kill this enemy of his father's was not enough. Physical contact had unleashed the savage soul of the Indian. Yet there was more, and as Jean gave the straining body a tremendous jerk backward, he felt the same strange thrill, the dark joy that he had known when his fist had smashed the face of Simm Bruce. (p. 127)

Still later, painfully wounded, Jean feels "all that was wild and savage in his blood and desperate in his spirit" rise up to make him "more than man and less than human." (p. 198)

This reversion to savagery motif, explicit in the above quotes and implicit in the novel's revenge theme, becomes especially ironic in view of the way Grey connects it with the landscape, though he seems generally unaware of the long tradition of "savage" in American literature and history.[29] He credits the "retrogression" (so Jean once calls it) as especially from "the soul of the Indian." The irony builds as Grey links the same savagery to Ellen Jorth via nature imagery. Thus while Jean carves up enemies, in Ellen's heart "a hidden gathering storm" gains force. At sunrise Ellen greets the "glorious burst of golden sun" with an intuition that it will bring "strange tidings." It does. Old John Sprague informs her of the bloodshed at the siege: two on the Isbel side dead, three on the Jorth. The connection between the carnage and Ellen's "storm" now becomes explicit; Sprague tells her how Jean has ripped Greaves with his bowie knife saying he was cutting him for *her,* and the news sends her riding into the woods with abandon: "Her hands could not stay on anything. They pressed her breast and flew out to caress the white aspens and to tear at the maple leaves and gather the lavender juniper berries, and came back again to her heart." (p. 156)

Soon twin storms break, Ellen's and the one in the skies. "Then a blue-white, piercingly bright, ragged steel of lightning shot down out of the black cloud." What follows is thinly veiled sexual arousal (pp. 167 – 168). Ellen experiences the beauty and inscrutability of nature, the sense of wildness, the instincts, the animal kinship, the "thrills," and the violent unleashing of emotions — the same imagistic "savagery" — that characterizes Jean's earlier knifing of Greaves. And this narrative link has another ironic connection in the secret of the Isbel-Jorth feud; Jean's father tells him when he arrives that he and Jorth long ago "both fell in love with the same girl." (p. 44) Grey's violence-and-irony-filled story emerges on more than one level as an "affair of the heart," and "nature," both external and internal, becomes an ambiguous amalgam with death-dealing, "savage" potential.

Not all of Grey's novels have such pervasive irony as *Heritage of the Desert* and *To the Last Man;* some have "small" ironies where a sunset (or "nature" in general) encourages a raised eyebrow. Holly Ripple's "knights" hang three outlaws in *Knights of the Range:* "Up he shot, six feet above the ground. And Britt turned away. Just then the sun rose, bright and red, over the eastern wall, and flooded the glade with crimson light. Shadows of the writhing victims danced across the sunlit rocks." (p. 238)

The Vanishing American is another matter. It illustrates nearly everything that characterizes Grey's use of the land

and nature: its sunsets, beauty, mystery, shaping effect on character, irony, and ambiguity. A close look teaches one to be judicious with generalizations. Marian Warner, midway on a trek into the desert highlands to meet the Indian, Nophaie, the man she loves, finds herself awed and moved by her first encounter with the majestic expanses of desert scenery:

> From this height Marian found the spectacle to be immense and baffling — league on league of gray-green desert — the red ramparts on each side of the portal to the Valley of Gods — and between these wide sentinels the pinnacles of grandeur and mystery and light — sacred to the Indian. She felt the uplifting of her spirit. Could anyone be dead to this? What was nature if not eternal? (p. 66)

Confronted by such spectacle, she asks questions. "Could anyone be dead to this?" Yes — the corrupt missionaries who control the reservation. "What was nature if not eternal?" Quite a number of things in Grey's narrative strategy. For example, after a sojourn among the silent walls of his canyon retreat, Nophaie says nature has "deluded him." (p. 214) It "does" even more, for in *The Vanishing American,* as much as any of his novels, Grey focuses on "nature": on external and internal landscape ("human nature"), creating a complexity critics have not yet adequately examined.[30]

Sunsets provide an entry point. Sunsets circumscribe the novel's major motifs — Nophaie's dilemma as a white-educated Indian, the love between Nophaie and Marian, and the plight of the "vanishing" Indians. Early in the narrative the child, Nophaie, seven years old, wanders through the sage tending a flock of sheep. In this pastoral, idyllic setting he feels "unconsciously and unutterably happy" because he is "in perfect harmony with the reality and spirit of the nature" that encompasses him. (p. 5) All around and above him, "in the great silence, in the towering barriers of stone, in the vast flare of intense sunlight, there seemed to be life in harmony with him, a voiceless and eternal life that he felt but could not see." (p. 7) The key word here is "seemed." Grey has the child observe a spectacular sunset:

> . . . there came a moment of marvelous transformation. The sun dipped its lower segment from under a white-rimmed cloud, firing the whole magnificent panorama with blaze of gold and rose and opal. A light that seemed a beacon of the universe burned across the heavens, clear to the east, where the violet and lilac haze took on a sheen of gold. Against the effulgence of the western sky stood up the monuments, silhouetted on that burnished brightness of sunset, black and clear-cut, weird and colossal, motionless and speaking gods of stone. (p. 8)

What "speaks," however, is a dog's warning bark, for a band of renegade whites rides up. They kidnap Nophaie, and the "marvelous transformation" ironically becomes the Indian's initiation into the world of the white man. This incident marks the "birth of a dark heritage of hate" in his heart. (p. 10) His joy in the lovely sunset, "nature" at Grey's vivid best, gives way to despair at "nature" of another sort, that of the greed-driven outlaws. Moreover, the silhouetted monuments are Indian gods, including the sacred Nothsis Ahn. Thus the irony compounds, for the sunset vision proves an ominous foreshadowing; the speaking gods obviously cannot speak out to save the vanishing tribe.

According to William Bloodworth, "Grey's heightened, romantic purple-prose perception of the land itself may generally be read either as displaced desire or as symbolic reflection of the strong sexual feelings of particular characters."[31] This generalization does not explain a passage like the ironic sunset which precedes the kidnapping of Nophaie, but does apply to some of Grey's narrative situations, and is closer to the mark with a second sunset that occurs when Nophaie tells Marian they will "watch the sun set over the desert." Sunset, he says, is "the fulfillment, the glory, the end of the Indian's day!" Marian is deeply moved:

> Every moment the spectacle changed, and out over the wasteland there was chaos of light and color. The purple shadows turned to black; the reds and yellows grew less intense. Vast rays of light slanted down from the broken sunset clouds. Marian's emotion increased with the growing transformation. (pp. 100 – 101)

Surely the occasion and description could suggest Bloodworth's "displaced desire" or "strong sexual feelings," and perhaps in part it does; it is a moment of intimacy between the lovers. But after the long watch Marian says, "I have seen. I feel all you feel. . . . Now tell me your trouble." He does — in the form of a confession of his spiritual distress: *"I am an infidel!"* — and shocks Marian speechless. (p. 102) This does not necessarily negate Bloodworth's suggestion, for one may read the action here as part of a pattern of erotic titillation, of the "turn-on turn-off" critic John Nesbitt suggests for Grey, but if so, and if the purple passage translates as "displaced desire," then Nophaie's response — repressed feelings channeled not into professions of love but into spiritual discontent — shows another intriguing variant among Greys's several uses of landscape in connection with character.[32]

And again there is irony. If the "fulfillment and glory" of the Indian's day proves a time of intense distress for Nophaie, for the Nopah tribe it signals disaster. Nophaie and Marian end the day (and the chapter) walking hand in hand through the darkness toward a campfire. As another foreshadowing, the sunset event does suggest a certain "fulfillment" for Nophaie, but only through being "absorbed" (as he later puts it) by Marian; for Nophaie's tribal brothers it means curtains, the "end of the Indian's day" in an ironic sense.

That day comes on the novel's final two pages when Marian and Nophaie stand in the doorway of their friend Withers' place and watch the Nopah Indian remnant "ride away into the sunset."

> It was a magnificent, far-flung sunset, the whole west flaming with intense golden-red that spread and paled far into the north.
>
> Against this glorious background the Indians were riding away, in dense groups, in long, straggling lines, in small parties, down to couples. It was an austere and sad pageant. . . . Shoie, the tongueless, was the last to depart. It appeared that he turned with gleaming visage and gesture of denunciation. (pp. 341 – 342)

For the Native Americans, this third sunset is anything but eternal life, to say nothing of glory, fulfillment, or desire. Shoie, the tongueless, and last Indian left on the horizon, provides the ironic component; reduced to silence and "bent in his saddle," his only means of protest, gesture, is rendered dubious by the vague "it appeared."

The second of these sunsets, the one watched by Marian and Nophaie alone, suggests — as do most of the examples in the section on "The Shaping" — some kind of interaction between external and internal nature and landscape. As with Nophaie, a character's response may be highly emotional. But such reactions need not always accompany external landscape; sometimes inner "nature" stirs as a result of some observed action. Thus, "displaced desire" operates in an erotic passage when Marian stops Nophaie from killing Morgan and Blucher, worst of the villains. Their crimes include the seduction of the young Indian woman, Gekin Yashi, and the murder of her father, Doetin, for opposing them. Nophaie, holding a gun, says he will kill the two in revenge for Gekin Yashi and for his own people. Marian's arguments against murdering them fail until she pleads with him to restrain "for the sake of her love." She prevails, and he hands her the gun. The violent scene which follows reflects sublimated desire:

> Trembling, Marian accepted the heavy weapon, wondering the while what he meant to do! She began to throb and thrill. His look, his demeanor, the very radi-

> ation of him had undergone a remarkable transformation. The deadliness, the something foreign in Marian's conception of him, had vanished. (p. 195)

A demonstration of Nophaie's skill and power in calculated violence replaces the "deadliness." First he attacks Morgan, launches his knee into the missionary's prominent abdomen, then assaults Blucher and knocks him down. Using the kicking ability acquired at Carlisle football, he repeatedly batters the men until they are bloody and nearly senseless.

The scene resembles a passage from *Riders of the Purple Sage* in several ways. Jane wants Lassiter's guns, ostensibly to keep him from killing more men, to save him "from more wickedness — more wanton bloodshed." Nesbitt, writing of Grey's "confused and uncertain purpose" with regard to "sexual interest" in his novels, cites this passage and says Jane's campaign "is fundamentally erotic" and that in this incident, as well as in the Venters-Bess plot, "Grey re-channels the interests from sex to violence." Nesbitt later adds that in other places in Grey's fiction "bloodshed is, interchangeable with sexual assault," but provides no examples.[33] In any case, the connection does show here. Both the Marian-Nophaie and Jane-Lassiter scenes feature a gun, a woman's "campaign" against killing, and heavy eroticism. In *The Vanishing American* violence is immediate, and Marian, holding the powerful symbol in her own hands, finds her desire triggered. She reacts to Nophaie's efforts in what makes a passable description of orgasm:

> Marian could not have cried out or moved to intercept him to save her life. She was in the grip of an absolutely new and strange and terrible spell. Nophaie no longer meant to kill; he meant only to hurt. And that liberated something deep in Marian's blood. It seemed to burst and shoot in fiery currents all over her. (p. 195)

Marian refers to this bit of sado-masochistic arousal in a Christmas letter to Nophaie. "I will never get over that day," she writes, "never will I trust myself again. If you were an Indian, I was a *savage*. I just swelled and tingled and burned with fiendish glee every time you kicked one of the — footballs." (p. 212)

For "savage" here read sexual desire. It is the same "savage" she arouses in Nophaie later in another scene of passion, an outdoor scene this time, which shows still more variety in Grey's combination of inner and outer landscape. Gekin Yashi, the young Indian woman seduced by Morgan, is dying of influenza. She has a baby, evidently Morgan's, but has subsequently married an Indian. Learning of her plight, Nophaie, Marian, and Withers set out to help. On the way Marian sees a "strange radiance" emanating from the snowflakes:

> Blue, white, gold! Or was it only the strange light? Marian had never seen the like. The sun was shining somewhere and through the marvelous moving veil of snow gleamed the blue sky. How unreal! Then it became a transparent medium, revealing the golden rims of the canyon above, and magnified a tower into a Babel of mosaics. Clearer, more amber, grew the light; and soon purple slopes of sage rose from the stream bed, to the snow banks under the cliffs. (p. 292)

Though not a sunset, the passage is vivid enough, and one might expect the critic's "displaced desire." The immediate context, however, suggests otherwise. In the next paragraph they find an Indian hogan; both Gekin Yashi and her baby are dead. Shocked, Marian gazes at the dead girl and wonders if it could be "the face of a sixteen-year-old." The change, she imagines, is not merely distortion from disease and death, for "her songs and dreams and ideals had died before her flesh," and Marian has the "distinct impression" that "the little Beauty of the Nopahs had found the religion of the white men as false as Hell," and had been "infinitely worse off for her contact with civilization." (p. 295) In short, by juxtaposing the beautiful natural scene with the ugliness of the white missionaries' deeds, Grey creates another scene of irony akin to that of the first sunset when white outlaws kidnap Nophaie.

Desire does arise, but only after this bit of polemic, the burial of the dead, and a total of five pages after Marian's "Babel of mosaics." Fears of the plague, Nophaie's presence, and his noble actions in carefully burying the dead according to Indian custom arouse Marian and she takes Nophaie's hand "endeavoring to quell her mounting excitation." Once again the sun appears, "momentarily, crowning the towers with gold." (p. 296)

There's nothing "displaced" about the desire which follows, one of Grey's most explicit scenes of passion. The sun may show its golden touch outside, but high winds are blowing within Marian. Nophaie presses her hands, his eyes dilate, and Marian throws her arms around his neck. This action "liberates and augments the storm in her breast" and she experiences a "mad moment" in which she does not know what she has done, but awakens to a terrifying consciousness that she has "inflamed the savage in Nophaie." He responds appropriately enough. He crushes her in his arms and bends to her face with "eyes of black fire":

> He did not kiss her. That was not the Indian way. Tenderness, gentleness, love had no part in this response to her woman's allurement. His mastery was that of the primal man denied; his brutality went to the verge of serious injury to her. But for the glory of it — the sheer backward step to the uttermost thrill of the senses — deep in the marrow of her bones — she would have screamed out in pain. For he handled her, bent her, swung and lifted her, and flattened her body as might have a savage in sudden possession of a hitherto unconquerable and unattainable woman of the wilds. (p. 297)

Marian obviously likes 'em rough. Nophaie throws her over his saddle "like a sack," and the erotic encounter, again with tantalizing sadomasochistic appeal, ends with the Indian panting in "husky, spent passion." (p. 297) Here the two "natures" — external and internal — symbolically merge in Grey's trope; at the moment of stormy passion Marian becomes a "woman of the wilds."

But Grey has still more variations to play on the theme of "nature" in *The Vanishing American.* A major plot interest concerns Nophaie's desire for spiritual wholeness. The quest, and a good portion of Grey's description of external landscape in the novel, involves two of his sojourns in the wilderness (chapters 15, 16 and 22 respectively). Nophaie feels he is an "infidel," without belief, caught between his Indian heritage and white education. On his first retreat, he establishes a refuge "in one of the almost inaccessible niches of his Canyon of Silent Walls." (p. 197) He explores the area feeling that the "dreaming walls" have a voice "for others beside the red man — for all of humanity." The time will surely come, he thinks, when they will speak to him. (p. 199) Nophaie comes to feel that a "hope" gestates within him, trying to be born. He wonders if there might not be "a spirit in nature infinite and everlasting." His stirring hope is "that he had really begun to hear the voices of the silent walls." (p. 202)

Once again a sunset furnishes an ironic backdrop. Breathing a prayer which begins "Glory of sun at dying day," Nophaie faces the "unattainable heights" of Nothsis Ahn, highest of the silent walls, and watches while the sun sinks in its miracle of transfiguration. "Life of color, spirit of glory, symbol of eternal change! This enchantment of a moment was the smile of nature." Two paragraphs later, the "smile" seems to have left. He stands before the "silent wall with a thousand walls" alone, "burden uplifted, with the passionless, pitiless, ruthless, all-pervading and all-concealing eyes of nature on him in his abasement." (pp. 206 – 207) Then an Indian messenger interrupts his stay with a letter from Marian. She says she will be happy to marry him and will wait and dream of him. (p. 214) His struggle now intensifies. Loneliness has augmented his desire for a mate. "Nature" importunes him "for her right." Suddenly he feels himself stripped of all ideals and in his mind "retrogrades through a scale from human being, man, Indian, and savage to primitive beast" where he struggles "in the throes of hereditary instincts, raw and wild, ungovernable — the imperious and inscrutable law of nature." (pp. 214 – 215)

Nophaie tries to escape this "law," to "run away from himself" by a supreme physical effort to climb Nothsis Ahn, but though he exercises the "eye of an eagle, the leap of a mountain sheep, the surefootness of the goat," he ends dragging his bruised and weary body into camp acknowledging that the "strange hope born there in the canyon had been burned out in the fire kindled by Marian's offer of love. Nature had deluded him. She had been a veiled, beautiful face lifted to him." (p. 219)

Nophaie has tried to find or establish an identity, a spiritual integrity, an independence of will that transcends his distress at being unable to believe in the Indian's god any longer and unwilling to believe in the white man's, as he tells Marian earlier, of being an Indian by race and a white by education, of being desperately in love with Marian, and harboring hatred and revenge against whites for their brutality and greed. Small wonder, given this ponderous load of emotional turmoil, that he should feel "nature" has deluded him. He has, Indian fashion, tried to find the answer in external surroundings, in a "nature" which seems endowed with spirit, while fighting a many-headed enemy in the form of human "nature" embodied in the lovely Marian, the ugly missionaries, and his own handsome Indian self. This sojourn fails to resolve his problems; in the spring he grows "restive" and feels "contending tides" within him.

At this point, as he feels the "hold of the silent walls" lessening, he hears a voice; it proves to be his friend Withers with news of the outbreak of war. He enlists, becomes a superhero in France, and returns. Neither war, bullets of would be assassins (an Indian and a reservation missionary), nor the influenza prove fatal.

Nophaie survives, but still not at peace with himself. He makes a second pilgrimage, this time to Naza, an Indian sacred bridge. As he watches the changing beauty of the bridge he passes from despair to a sense of freedom. He wonders if Naza has a secret, and concludes that "the spirit abiding in that magnificent bridge" is "an investiture from the soul of man." (p. 317) It is not imperishable, he realizes, but as long as it endures will stand there "under its gleaming silent walls, with its rainbow hues and purple shadows at sunset, its golden glows and rosy veils at sunrise." Somehow this experience spells peace for Nophaie; he senses an "intimation of immortality — the imminence of God!" and accepts Christianity. (p. 319)

One can draw certain conclusions from all this prowling about among "silent walls," this weaving and interweaving of landscapes. For one thing, in *The Vanishing American* at least, the variety, complexity, and ambiguity associated with "nature" go considerably beyond and sometimes contrary to critical assessments. It is a case of extrapolating from too few examples and too little attention to actual texts, all fifty-six of them.

For another, one does not — or rather, ought not — go to Grey for either profound philosophical or even consistent thought. During *The Vanishing American* external "nature" appears to the characters as imperious, inscrutable, merciless, delusive, eternal, baffling, fierce, ruthless, cruel, and glorious; it destroys and builds, has a voice but is silent, depending on the situation. Consistency was not a high priority for Grey in terms of the land; he clearly had a variety of goals and a variety of ways to achieve them. Sometimes he wanted a realistic setting as in Slone's trek in *Wildfire;* on the other hand sometimes, as Christine Bold suggests, his landscape sets "a note of insularity" and can be read partly as a strategy for distancing his fictional world from any contemporary or realist context."[34] At still other times, as with the silent-walled recesses of Nophaie's canyon hideaways, Grey aims primarily for an ambience of mystery — in part to underscore the hero's spiritual anguish, and in part simply, in another critic's words, as a "typically romantic" nostalgia "for an earlier, simpler, and morally more vital time," even though the novel's setting predated publishing by only a few years.[35]

Grey perhaps had still other goals. Carlton Jackson says that in general Grey used the desert to show men "pitted against nature" and that it was "to the barren wastelands that a man must go to transcend mere existence, to find his soul, and to grasp the idea of what Charles Darwin called 'natural selection.'" Mountains, he adds, "complemented the desert by showing that nature was larger than human life, causing the pensive man to ponder his origins and his fate." Similarly, one recalls John Cawelti's "distinctive moral and symbolic landscape with strong implications of regeneration or redemption." Well, Nophaie certainly is pensive, and does go to the wasteland to "find his soul." He even finds "the imminence of God" during his last quest to the silent walls. But even this has its ironic side; he only recovers what the early description of the young shepherd boy shows Nophaie had but lost to his white education and subsequent events, namely, that "there seemed to be life in harmony with him, a voiceless and eternal life that he felt but could not see." (p. 7)

Marian doesn't need much regeneration; she appears whole from the start — an easterner, but strong both in body and spirit — and no flirt. On her early trek to meet Nophaie she weathers the inevitable sandstorm and reacts positively to her surroundings, including the "vastness." She says to Withers, "I don't — know what I feel — and couldn't tell — if I did, I want days and months here . . . yet afterward — could I ever be happy again?" Withers responds enigmatically, "Places have more to do with happiness than people." (p. 65)

Not so. "What did he mean by that?" she later asks Nophaie. He ponders and then replies, "People are false. Human nature is imperfect. Places are true. Nature itself is evolution — an inexorable working for perfection." (p. 90)

Fortunately, Grey doesn't dabble much with this in the rest of the narrative, but in view of the outcome it too proves ironic — amusingly so. Writer of romances, Grey has this hero end where his heroes nearly always do, in or ready for the marital nest with the heroine. The "nature" that really regenerates Nophaie is that "imperfect human nature" embodied in the near-perfect Marian.

The Lovers

III

1
The Ace and King of Hearts

One of the substantial ironies that emerges from a study of Zane Grey is that commentators have accorded romance — so central to his novels — scant attention, and the erotic element — until fairly recently — almost no critical scrutiny at all. Perhaps this is in part because of his more distinctive prose descriptions of landscape, the formulaic predictability of marriage and a happy ending, and the mundane, at times sophomoric nature of the love-interest. If so, they have missed some unique trees within the larger framework of the woods. During his lifetime Grey essayed to defend himself from charges, especially concerning the unreality of his novels in general and characters in particular, by appealing to "romance." He wanted to gain an audience, he wrote in an unpublished manuscript, "through romance, adventure, and love of the wild and beautiful in nature."[1] This is no defense against weak characterization, and in fact of little help except to underscore that Grey considered himself a writer of romances. That doesn't help much either, for the significance of Grey's work in this case (as in his love plots) does not stem from his use of romance per se, but the way love interests link up in certain novels with other themes and events. What the critics have *not* explored are the ironic ways Grey pictured erotic desire as the real source of violent action, the way seduction becomes a metaphor of unrestrained economic activity, and the link — especially in one important novel —

between abduction and the early American captivity narrative.

First, the lovers. Grey "wrote many of his stories for women readers," a critic writes. "Although he is associated with masculine activities and subjects . . . over fifteen of his novels were first published in *Ladies Home Journal* and *McCall's*. This may make the matter of sexuality in Zane Grey even more surprising." Why should it? The real "surprise" here seems to be the critic's — concerning the contents of women's magazines during the years in question. He is on safer ground with his next sentence, which conjectures, "Or it may be that the readers of such magazines were actually post-Victorian in sentiment and quite ready to appreciate . . . the kind of literary eroticism that his westerns provide."[2] Evidently a lot of them were.

But any number of features in addition to the "literary eroticism" argue for Grey's appeal to women. Aside from the same heroes' action, adventure, and violence that appealed to men, women readers could admire specific heroines like Marian Warner of *The Vanishing American* or Mescal of *Heritage of the Desert,* to name but two, as well as certain character traits. It would be difficult to gauge how female readers of the decades between 1910 and 1930 would have reacted to Grey's sometimes sugary domesticity, or the way his heroines — under passionate attack by the hero — often fall limp, to say nothing of Grey's double standard which he described as his "appalling responsibility in these modern days of materialism to dare to foster idealism and love of nature, chivalry in men and chastity in women."[3]

Christine Hamilton, for example, says unlike the "violence-prone males" Grey's women "exert a restraining influence on the aggregate society of the West. Women are seen as the true harbingers of civilization: they are religious, deplore violence and are concerned with the welfare of others."[4] Curiously, Hamilton cites Jane Withersteen in support. Jane shows concern for her employees and others, begs Lassiter not to use his guns, and "maintains her religious convictions despite the perfidy of the Mormon elders" Hamilton says. But Jane in fact gives back the guns and, as for her "religious convictions," when she finally sees the light — or darkness — about Dyer and his ugly Mormon crowd, she melodramatically says to Lassiter (and ironically citing the Bible), "Your people shall be my people, and your God my God!" and abjures Mormonism for whatever Lassiter worships. They both in fact also abjure "civilization," opting for Surprise Valley. (p. 294)

Despite this inattention to ironic detail, Hamilton's generalization may hold for the most part. Insofar as women readers — and Hamilton is one — find Grey's women "harbingers of civilization," they may find here an appealing feature. Nevertheless, some qualifying examples deserve mention. The Maverick Queen, Kit Bandon (in *The Maverick Queen*), admittedly is one of a kind.

Some of Grey's other heroines are also tough cookies, not averse to a little violence. As noted earlier, Marian Warner of *The Vanishing American* thrills with an orgasm-like reaction when Nophaie kicks two of the villains into bloody, senseless hulks. Tough little Lark Burrell of *Horse Heaven Hill* shoots badman Hurd in the arm saving her lover-hero, Stan Weston. Virginia Lundeen (*The Shepherd of Guadaloupe*) fights furiously with the villain Malpass: "Then when he got her head down under his arm, pressing her helpless, choking her, she opened her mouth and like a wolf at bay she fastened her teeth in it." (p. 231) Is she forced to? So are many of the male protagonists. Martha Ann Dixon, the young woman Andrew Bonning calls Wyoming MAD in *Wyoming,* kicks a masher nearly senseless. Moreover, metaphorically speaking, the same wild fire, the same violent stormy passions rage through both heroes and heroines, as in the case of Ellen Jorth of *To the Last Man,* Hettie Ide of *Nevada,* and Lucy Bostil of *Wildfire*. Finally, Joan Randall overcomes the outlaws and sends them to their death in an ironic power struggle in *The Border Legion*.

With these qualifications in mind, one can still admire

Grey's female protagonists as, in part, civilization's harbingers. The most overt expression of the role probably belongs to Helen Rayner of *The Man of the Forest*. Milt Dale goes out to meet the villains and Helen flies in pursuit. She realizes that though Dale is "wonderful in thought and feeling," he has also become "a part of this raw, bold, and violent West." As she runs she feels in herself "a force opposing itself against this raw, primitive justice of the West." She is "one of the first influences emanating from civilized life, from law and order." This insight comes as a "flash of truth" when she sees "the West as it would be some future time, when through women and children these wild frontier days would be gone forever," but also "just as clearly she saw the present need of men like Roy Beeman and Dale and the fire-blooded Carmichael. Beasley and his kind must be killed." Helen, however, does not want "her lover, her future husband, and the probable father of her children to commit what she held to be murder." (p. 353) Helen catches up with Milt at the saloon door, they hear shots and when they enter, the violence is already over; two men lie on the floor, and Las Vegas Carmichael, her sister Bo's intended, holds a big gun and looks wild: "Carmichael drank, while his flaming eyes held the crowd; then with a savage action of terrible passion he flung the glass at the quivering form of the still living Mexican on the floor." Helen promptly faints. (pp. 353 – 355)

Even here Grey's prose creates ambiguity. On the one hand, nothing could be plainer than Helen's thought about her role as a "force" against "raw, primitive justice." Her next thought qualifies it, however: "Beasley and his kind *must be killed.*" (Italics added.) The evasive passive here undercuts her conviction. So does her swoon; as civilization's "first emanating influence," Helen proves a little too sensitive, and her standards double.

Other narrative events suggest more ambiguity. Helen is not the only female protagonist; sister Bo shares nearly equal billing. The story ends in two marriages, Bo with Las Vegas, and Helen with Milt. Helen may wish Milt spared the killing, but the wild-eyed Las Vegas compensates. And Bo is the one the outlaws abduct. As another emanating influence, this harbinger proves less faint and faint-prone than her sister. "She's a little savage. She has no fear. She'd fight like a tigress for her life," Helen says when she learns of Bo's disappearance. (p. 278) Helen is right. Bo sasses the villains, gets slapped around for her trouble and shoots three times at the lecherous Riggs. The outlaws learn they do indeed have a tiger by the tail. These features from *The Man of the Forest* again illustrate that before making surface generalizations, one needs to look closely at narrative events, context, and language to see what ironies crop up to undercut what at first glance seems to be affirmed.

Another point is that Grey's combination of love plots, abductions, and outlaw greed, plus certain tropes, narrative events, and (often slipshod) prose sometimes combine to suggest a major irony: one important way the novels comment culturally is by linking illicit economic activity — competition out of control — with erotic passion. Rape lurks beneath the surface of the stories as the unstated but implied metaphor. Grey's ace in the hole — the "ace of hearts" (from *The Border Legion*) — shows woman to be not only the focus and victim of this violent passion, but, along with male protagonists, vulnerable to its consuming power. In short, Grey intuitively locates the source of violence in an ambiguous but powerful "desire." Helen Rayner skirts the real issue; she envisions a future West purged thanks to women and children, but Grey and the reader instinctively know better; the violence stays, only the forms and names for it change.

Grey's plot again illustrates. At the beginning of *The Man of the Forest,* Milt Dale overhears Beasley plotting with Snake Anson; Anson is to kidnap Helen Rayner so Beasley can seize control of her uncle's (Al Auchinloss) ranch. Anson can rob the stage while he's at it. But an erotic joker enters in the person of Riggs, who wants Bo, and so kidnaps the wrong woman. "Our long-haired pard hyar — Mister Riggs — him with the big gun — he waltzes up with this sassy kid instead of the woman Beasley wanted." (p. 291) Given this volatile combination, trouble starts; others begin to fancy Bo. Wilson shoots Riggs, and the gang, typically for Grey, begins to self-destruct: "If they didn't get wiped out by Rangers or cowboys, why they jest naturally wiped out themselves. Thet's a law I recognize in relation to gangs like them," Jim Wilson says to Anson. He speaks of Big Bend gangs, but his "law" is already operating on their own bunch. That night Wilson sits by the campfire listening and watching the sleeping forms of the gang members: "He might have been reflecting on the strange reaction happening to every man in that group since a girl had been brought among them." He can only speculate: "the forest kept its secret, as did the melancholy wind; the outlaws were sleeping like tired beasts, with dark secrets locked in their hearts." (p. 302) Readers are in on those secrets, though.

Grey's female protagonists appeal to readers in still other ways. In two of the novels, *The Desert of Wheat* and *The Lone Star Ranger,* a woman stands as nurse and protector of a cowboy battered in body and spirit, and as a buffer between him and the violent past. Kurt Dorn, second-generation German, joins the fray in World War I, partly to exorcise his German taint. His experience at the front is nightmarish; he talks with the French Blue Devils (fighting unit) and later describes his killing of enemy Germans in surrealistic fashion. On his return, nearly dead, he relives the horror: "As she left him there came a sudden familiar happening in his brain, like a snap-back, and the contending tide of gray forms — the Huns — rushed upon him." He has internalized the violence which he experiences now as landscape (in this instance, weather):

> a ferocious and terrible storm of brain, that used to have its reaction in outward violence, now worked inside him, like a hot wind that drove his blood. During the spell he fought out his great fight — again for the thou-

> sandth time he rekilled his foes. That storm passed through him without an outward quiver. (p. 343)

In Christine Bold's words, "Lenore, his wife, combats his determinism with her religious belief, which has motherhood at its center and wheat as its symbol. As a Western version of Ceres, she can heal the ravages of time and battle."[5] Buck Duane's problem and solution resemble Kurt Dorn's, though Buck's bullet-riddled body results from a battle against bank-robbing outlaws, not Germans. Like Kurt, Buck internalizes violence, "that driving, relentless instinct for blood." The major difference is that for Buck it is "instinctive," whereas Kurt's problem is war-induced. Ray Longstreth intervenes, however, much as Lenore in *The Desert of Wheat:* the "pale, drifting, haunting faces" will return, Grey tells us, "but all his life, always between them and him, rendering them powerless, would be the faith and love and beauty of this noble woman." (p. 244)

The king of hearts, Grey's hero, also has his day in the sun. Emphasizing the adolescent appeal of the cowboy, David B. Davis says he demonstrates the physical prowess so coveted by teenagers, and, in view of approaching adulthood, "the last image of a carefree life." Moreover, his code represents a new chivalry, "a Western and democratic version of the Southern gentleman's 'honor.'"[6] With regard to Grey's male protagonists in particular, Cynthia Hamilton sees them as "oversized characters, big enough to dominate their womenfolk physically and to fill the vast landscape."[7] Perhaps. These characteristics would appeal to many. Carlton Jackson focuses on one special type, the good-yet-bad gunmen. "The Western gunman was the strongest drawn character in all the Zane Grey novels," he maintains.[8]

For example, Buck Duane (*The Lone Star Ranger*), Wade Holden (*Shadow on the Trail*), and Renn Frayne (*Knights of the Range*), all portray the feared fast gun, with a wide reputation for killings. Duane and Holden are both wanted by the law. Grey most thoroughly exploits the possibilities of the type through Duane, who anguishes because he fears his killing stems not from self-defense or a quest for justice, but from an instinctive urge. Holden, incidentally is yet another example of the economics and passion link: "Your mother loved me. . . . Jim Holden never knew," the dying Simm Bell confesses to Wade, acknowledging his paternity. (p. 26) Wade's cache of stolen money, symbol of this tainted past, troubles him until he makes an equally symbolic atonement — paying ranchers for losses suffered at the hands of rustlers with rustlers' money. Ranger Mahaffey finally shows up, but goes away apparently satisfied and leaves Wade finally at peace; the sight of Wade, his wife, and new baby evidently furnishes proof enough of Wade's reformed status, though he escapes strict justice.

But Grey knows his cards, and aces are tops. Joan Randle earns the "ace of hearts" label in *The Border Legion* by outwitting and outtalking her would-be seducer, outlaw Kells. Actually, Kells' beast-like partner, Gulden, pins the card in question to a tree, shoots out the red center with a cluster of bullets, and puts his name below, foreshadowing the novel's climax. Among the card's symbolic possibilities: intimidation (warning, threat), eroticism (phallic gun and heart), and death all figure in the exciting finish of this narrative, a power struggle which Joan wins, for she is Grey's craftiest heroine, the one most demonstrably able to control. Though her first glimpse of Kells tells her "some kind of power" emanates from him, it is no match for her own: "All that was woman in her — mounting, fighting, hating — leaped to the power she sensed in herself. If she could be deceitful, cunning, shameless in holding out to Kells a possible return of his love, she could do anything with him. She knew it." (p. 83) Events prove her right.

Others, though not so aggressive or calculating as Joan, also display an appealing ability to triumph. At the happy, playful end of *The Shepherd of Guadaloupe,* Virginia Lundeen apprehensively awaits Clifton Forrest. Though they're actually married, like a number of Grey heroes and heroines madly in love, they can't see the woods for the trees. Virginia's witty friend Ethel can though, and asserts herself: "Leave it to me. There'll be nothing to it. Poor Cliff hasn't a show on earth, or on the desert, either. War is hell, and the desert may be a lot I don't savvy, but I'm telling you the little feminine genders rule the world." (p. 271) In the land of Grey, at least, that's often true. Virginia waits in Cliff's tent, and when he finds her there, they confess their mutual love, he covers her with kisses till, typically, she is "limp and numb," and all ends well.

They have discovered the transforming power of love, the outcome for Grey protagonists, something both heroine and hero come to know. Warren Neale of *The U.P. Trail* senses it:

> Love of him had saved the girl's mind and had made her beautiful and wonderful. He had heard of the infinite transforming power of love; here in Allie Lee was its manifestation. Whether or not he deserved such a blessing was not the question. It was his, and he felt unutterably grateful and swore he would be worthy of this great gift. (p. 62)

So does Lucy Bostil of *Wildfire,* as she begins to realize what she feels toward and how she has changed Jim Slone, "a strange, intense, lonely man in whom she had brought out pride, gratitude, kindness, passion, and despair." She feels her heart swell "at the realization that she had changed him, made him kinder, made him divide his love as did her father, made him human, hopeful, longing for a future unfettered by the toils of desert allurement. She could not control her pride. She must like him very much." (p. 138)

More often the smitten one acknowledges the change. Sue Melberne knows she is "done for!" half way through *Wild Horse Mesa:*

> At last she knew. . . . Her torments had suddenly given place to a great dawning of something immeasureable. Like a burst of sun in the darkness of her heart!

> Her spirit did not rise up to crush this betraying love. It could not be crushed. It was too new, too terribly sweet, for her to want to crush. It was herself, her fulfillment; and in a moment she had become a woman. (p. 179)

These throes of love mean a new idea of herself, a transformation, just as Milt Dale in *The Man of the Forest* says they will to Helen Rayner. Ironically, Milt himself has experienced all the "natural instincts" except love. He soon completes his education and immeasurably broadens "his understanding of the principles of nature":

> "I love that girl! I love that girl!" he spoke aloud, to the distant white peaks, to the winds, to the loneliness and silence of his prison, to the great pines and to the murmuring stream, and to his faithful pets. It was his tragic confession of weakness, of amazing truth, of hopeless position, of pitiful excuse for the transformation wrought in him. (p. 206)

No wonder Helen's sister, Bo, listening to the love-struck pair, can't help laughing; Grey occasionally distances himself enough from these newly enlightened lovers to enjoy a vicarious chuckle.

The reader can chuckle too at Wade Holden of *Shadow on the Trail*. The tough, gun-slinging outlaw also finds enlightenment: "Suddenly there came a flashing light into Wade's clouded mind. It shot clear across the perplexed field of his consciousness. Like a bursting thunderbolt clarifying the murky atmosphere it burned away the little thoughts and fears." Wade ponders his past and asks a series of "whys" — Why was he illegitimately born? Why has he loved the robber Simm Bell? Why has his life been filled with violence? Why has he come to Cedar Range? "All blessings in disguise he thought in exaltation. All to fit me for this big job. All to make me a man. . . . All for that dark-eyed girl." (p. 102)

Or at Kent Wingfield when he finds Lucy Bonesteel in *Stranger from the Tonto*. Lucy slips away into the shadows and he hears the bar drop into place on her door: "Kent drew back from the wall stiff and dizzy. . . . He had never been in a trance, but this state he now palpitated under he thought might be one. His instinct, his habit of caution . . . guided him despite the fact that he had been struck to the very depths of his soul." (p. 86)

Other features besides palpitations and transformed lives characterize these stricken lovers. Like Chaucer's Cressida, they fall in love at first glance; no Pandarus furthers the cause, however, though occasionally a well-meaning friend, ranch foreman, or even parent will take a hand and try to set one or both lovers straight. Usually, the smitten ones remain incredibly dense, rejecting the obvious. Columbine's father tries to tell her of Wilson Moore's love in *The Mysterious Rider;* she's "a kid in mind and a woman in body," he says, and Wils has been lovesick and "cry-eyed" (jealous, in this case) ever since she was little. She doesn't believe it. Later, Wils tries to tell her himself: "Yes — loved you. Could you have been so innocent — so blind you never knew? I can't believe it." (pp. 19, 114) The reader can, since it proves characteristic. Kurt Dorn of *The Desert of Wheat* is as dense as Columbine. A third of the way through the novel he tells Lenore Anderson he loves her: "A year ago — that first time I saw you — I fell in love with you. . . . I fought against the — the madness. But fate was against me. . . . I saw you again. . . . And it was all over with me!" Though she responds with "small hand" and "soft, strange voice," he too blinds himself, and can only stutter, "I know there never was and never could be any hope for me." (pp. 109 – 110) Some seventy pages later Kurt has apparently retrogressed: "You mean — you consider me your friend?" (p. 183)

The same madness claims Jim Wall of *Robbers' Roost*. Helen Herrick all but invites him to propose. "Faint heart never won fair lady," she whispers. Naturally, he can't believe it. "Jim gazed down at the clearcut profile, at the shadowed eyes, hair silvered in the moonlight; then stricken and mute, he rushed away." (p. 236) Laramie of *Raiders of Spanish Peaks* can't either. He impulsively kisses Hallie Lindsay and then ponders the response:

> It did not seem logical, reasonable, possible that any girl, much less Hallie, could hit a man with all her might for kissing her and then embrace him for doing it again. But there it was. Her left arm had been clear up around his neck, and her right hand had been creeping up. He had seen it. He had felt her cool quivering fingers on his hot neck. Well, what then? (p. 258)

What then? He decides his perceptions have been "faulty." They have.

It can't be true — and yet it just might. And so Grey's heroines and heroes spend hours, and a reader pages, agonizing over their fate. Like a seismograph, Grey covers expanses of text recording the tremors which pop up, as often as not, as troubling questions. Thus Hettie Ide suffers over the titular hero of *Nevada:*

> So with unseeing eyes on the rolling, darkening desert, she admitted more and keener anguish into this strife of love and faith. How could she be faithless in hope, in trust? Had she not sworn, with her lips close to his, that she would die before she ever failed him? What if he had used his deadly gun again? (pp. 171 – 172)

Or Andrew Bonning of *Wyoming,* mad over the girl he calls MAD:

> Had she not passionately scorned him? Had she not declared that she would not marry him if he were the last man on earth? Had he not accepted this decree? Certainly he had not blamed her. Whence, then, this longing to see her, to be in the same room with her? (p. 182)

Whence indeed? Lance Sidway of *Majesty's Rancho* doesn't know either:

> "What for?" he whispered, huskily. "Why do I feel this. . . . It was — coming to her!" He was glad that he had had the courage to tell her. If she had a grain of good in her the truth would bring it out. Then why this stab in his heart, this clamor of furies in his ears this still small voice? (p. 213)

How Lance hears the still small voice through the clamor is anybody's guess, but then love seems as irrational as it does blind. Sue Melberne finds it all very confusing in *Wild Horse Mesa* and wonders: "But — how do I know this strong new self is not more truly me than the other?" she whispers to herself. "So she pondered until she seemed lost in a sea of imaginings. What good did it do to think, considering that her feelings were not dependent upon her thought or governed by it?" (pp. 162 – 163)

Agonizingly confused, these Grey lovers, and obtuse regarding their future mates, but handsome or breathtakingly pretty as the case warrants. When Georgiana May Stockwell of *Code of the West* arrives on the stage, Cal Thurman, view obstructed, first catches only "a glimpse of blond curls and the flash of a white face and a rosy cheek." Shortly, he gets the full view:

> He was halted by a vision of youth and beauty that emerged from the doorway. . . . She had big violet eyes that peered expectantly all around her. Her face was white except for a rosy color high on her cheeks. Her lips were red as carmine. She wore a tan-colored dress, stylishly cut and strangely short. It reached only to the turn of her knees. Cal's bewildered glance caught a glimpse of slender, shapely, black-stockinged legs before it flashed back to her face. (p. 33)

Cal is not only bewildered, but like the others, "done for." So is Kent Wingfield of *Stranger from the Tonto* when he finds the hideout of The Hole in the Wall gang and sees Lucy Bonesteel:

> She was young and wondrously lovely, as Elway had sworn. She had wavy hair like the gold of sunlight with dark tints in it, as Elway had so lovingly claimed. She had great dark eyes and the sweetest face Kent had ever seen in all his life. . . . Her dress appeared to be of finer quality and cut than what would have been expected of a girl living in the depths of the canyon country. She appeared beautiful with a strange charm apart from physical perfection — her lovely waving hair, her broad low brow unlined and serene, her starry brooding eyes, her oval face of golden tan, and the red lips with their sweet curve. (pp. 82, 85 – 86)

Grey has his preferences, maybe even a fetish or two. He favors violet eyes, "round" arms, and when a woman prepares to knock a man out, she wears a white dress. Aside from that, Grey provides some variety in his women in age, personality, and action. Louise, dance-hall girl in *Valley of Wild Horses,* drags Panhandle Smith on to the dance floor as he begins "to grasp the significance of these bare-armed, white-faced girls with their dark-hollowed eyes and scarlet lips." (p. 48) Actually, they nearly fit the description of Georgiana Stockwell, a "vision of youth and beauty." Be that as it may, Louise turns out to have a golden heart and becomes the bride of Pan's pard, Blinky, in one of Grey's many double romance plots. Panhandle's second meeting with Louise shows Grey attempting to expand her character:

> Pan espied the girl Louise before she had become aware of his presence. . . . He never forgot that they belonged to the same sex as his mother. So it was natural he had compassion for this unsexed dancehall, gambling-lure girl. She was pretty in a wild sort of way, dissolute, abandoned, yet not in any sense weak. A terrible havoc showed in her face for anyone with eyes to see beneath the surface. (p. 91)

Louise gets her man, but two of Grey's most memorable characters do not. Beauty Stanton of *The U.P. Trail* and Kit

Bandon of *The Maverick Queen* both fall for a cowboy protagonist who rejects them in favor of innocent youth. Both end up dead. When Warren Neale first meets Beauty Stanton he sees a woman

> superb, not more than thirty years old, with a face that must have been lovely once and held the haunting ghost of beauty still. Her hair was dead gold; her eyes were large and blue, with dark circles under them; and her features had a clear-cut classic regularity. (p. 132)

Her love for Neale is strong enough to generate over 600 words in a letter she writes while dying, stiffening fingers notwithstanding. The Maverick Queen loses too, though she is more virile and determined than the slightly over-the-hill Stanton. As Linc Bradway sees her, Kit Bandon's physical beauty is "only a small part of her charm," though her dusky eyes, soft skin, and youthful body are lovely. She also has a zest and recklessness which make her power "completely transcendent." (pp. 206 – 207)

Not completely; she loses, though not without a fight (Linc admits resisting Kit is almost more than he can manage), to her young niece, Lucy:

> A slender girl, scarcely eighteen, a pretty tanned face, paled now, blue eyes set wide apart, dark with excitement, red lips, sweet and tragic, a small bare head covered with golden curls, a lithe form typically western and capable in boy's garb, yet compellingly feminine — a girl who was clinging to him as though he were a brother. (p. 39)

As with Lucy, Grey often prefers blondes though his first success, *Heritage of the Desert,* features the dark-haired Mescal.

But love's transcendent power may have its champion in Allie Lee of *The U.P. Trail.* Joan Randle of *The Border Legion* is more adept at wielding that power, but for sheer spirit of attraction, Allie Lee is hard to beat, as Grey leaves no doubt about the potential clout of this ace of hearts:

> Not the movement of progress as typified by those men who had dreamed of the railroad, nor the spirit of the unconquerable engineers as typified by Neale, nor the wildness of wild youth like Larry King, nor the heroic labor and simplicity and sacrifice of common men, nor the inconceivable passion of these gamblers for gold, nor the mystery hidden in the mad laughter of the fallen women, strange and sad on the night wind — not any of these things nor all of them, wonderful and incalculable as they were, loomed so great as the spirit that upheld Allie Lee. (pp. 236 – 237)

Neale, obviously, is a goner like the others.

As to the handsome male counterparts, Chess Weymer of *Wild Horse Mesa* gives an understandably biased account of his brother, Chane:

> "He's tall and dark, and, say! he looks right through you. Chane's got the sweetest, gentlest disposition. But he's a fighter. It's because of his kindness that he's always getting into fights. . . . He's ridden all over and has been in many outfits. He hates cattle and loves horses. . . . He's a lonely sort of fellow — gets restless where there're lots of people. Somebody will get into trouble and then Chane takes up that trouble." (p. 59)

Chess' description makes a fairly representative Grey composite: piercing eyes, gentle disposition, disposed to helping people in trouble, a fighter when need be. Some, like Chane Weymer, are well-traveled loners (Lassiter in *Riders of the Purple Sage,* Pecos Smith of *West of the Pecos*); others seek out pards and double romances often result. And the hero usually proves the quickest gun around in a showdown. "Arizona Ames," Grey writes, "was a typical character of the period." Every range had a cowboy like him:

> He was quiet, but he could be gay. He would take a drink with his fellows, but he had never been known to get drunk. He would lend his last dollar and then borrow from a comrade to help the one who sought him. He always took the hardest, darkest, coldest watch; and most of the jobs hated by cowboys fell to him. His horsemanship and skill with a lasso, and other tricks of the trade, left no room for the ridicule and banter so common to cowboys. Then his swift and unerring use of a Colt added the last notch to the admiration of whatever outfit he rode with. (p. 99)

Give or take a detail or two and any number of Grey cowboy heroes fit this stereotype; faced with descriptions taken out of context, one would be hard put to distinguish Pecos Smith, Brazos Keene, Panhandle Smith, and Arizona Ames.

On the other hand, Grey over the years portrayed a number of other protagonist types: ex-football heroes like the ambitious Lynn Weston of *Boulder Dam;* beehunter Edd Denmeade of *Under the Tonto Rim;* injured, brooding war veterans like Keven Bell of *Rogue River Feud;* the good-bad gunmen victimized by their past like Buck Duane (*The Lone Star Ranger*); and Grey's lone male all-Indian protagonist, Nophaie, of *The Vanishing American.* Grey endows a few with some character depth or distinguishing traits, notably, Nophaie, Kells of *The Border Legion,* and to some extent, Keven Bell and Lassiter. Many, however, appear interchangeable.

Nearly all share in the agonies of love. Two of Grey's gunslinging heroes reputedly can hit a playing card placed edgeways; one can rest assured it is not the ace of hearts. Corny Cornwall, smitten lover of *The Lost Wagon Train,* illustrates; a look completely unbalances him. He watches as the girl he covets leaves in a stage with two girlfriends, and then discovers Estelle "giving him her eyes for the first time since the upheaval at Long's Road."

> What a strange, dark, wondering glance! It held a long moment. Then she waved a gloved hand and averted her face. Corny was flung aloft to the skies in ecstasy. Did not that look, that farewell wave of hand, signify forgiveness? Could they have meant more? It took many a long mile of riding for him to wear out that mad hope. (p. 181)

Sometimes, as here, Grey's prose regarding his lovers proves sentimental, melodramatic, or juvenile. On the other hand, many of his protagonists are in fact juveniles; Corny's Estelle is sixteen, as are several Grey heroines, though Corny is twenty-two. But Grey's formulaic centerpiece appeals by more than adolescent throes. A critic claims that "denial, not consummation, is the key to Grey's eroticism," and that Grey's "essential business" in his westerns is sex. Let's see if he's right.

2
Sagebrush Sex

Companion articles, William Bloodworth's "Zane Grey's Western Eroticism," and John Nesbitt's "Uncertain Sex in the Sagebrush," appeared in the *South Dakota Review* in the autumn of 1985. Nesbitt, apparently with prior access to Bloodworth's manuscript, agrees with the latter that Grey's westerns are highly erotic, the sex frequently latent or covert, and that Grey uses a pattern of "arousal" and "recontainment." The chief difference in emphasis lies in the tricky area of Grey's intent, for Nesbitt argues that Grey's fiction shows "a wavering orientation towards his subject," and "a confused and uncertain purpose in its sexual interest." Both authors offer some thought-provoking and instructive comments. Both, on the other hand, argue from a highly selective number of stories, too limited to support some of the generalizations.[10] They are almost alone in dealing with Grey's eroticism.

As Bloodworth says, Grey knew very well what he was doing with his erotic content, had "a kind of literary shrewdness," and "was obviously interested in sexual passion and found his stories of the West to be proper literary vehicles for exploring that subject."[11] Nesbitt's qualifiying point about Grey's "faltering technical control" also has merits; the flaw probably accounts for much of the "uncertainty" he finds.[12]

Be that as it may, eroticism figures prominently for Grey, and "denial, not consummation" can be said to be its key, not only in the "teasing" manner of presentation, but in the fact that there is almost no overt consummation in any of the narratives. Even in cases of marriage midway in the story — Linc Bradway and Lucy Bandon of *The Maverick Queen,* Clifton Forrest and Virginia Lundeen of The *Shepherd of Guadaloupe*, for example — the protagonists remain apart or chaste. This may be explained by the literary climate under which Grey wrote. Grey's most popular decade and a half coincides with famous court cases over *Lady Chatterly's Lover* and *Ulysses.* As the history of literary censorship shows, moral arbiters and courts have only gradually admitted a more and more explicit eroticism to acceptability. Grey, without the talent of a Lawrence or a Joyce, had enough trouble getting published — at least until his two blockbusters, *Heritage* and *Riders* — and may have followed the better part of wisdom.

There's another side to "denial." Anticipation often exceeds the actual experience, and the teasing style — arousal and postponement — may provide more erotic titillation than outright consummation. *Riders of the Purple Sage* illustrates. The Jane-Lassiter plot is heavily erotic; so is that with Bess and Venters. The narrative develops sexual interest from the opening pages, where Mormon sexual repression in general, and Tull's jealousy of Venters in particular set the scene. It continues through Jane's "hungering" when Lassiter rides up, through her preoccupation with his big black guns:

> Jane slipped her hands down to the swinging gun-sheaths, and when she had locked her fingers around the huge, cold handles of the guns, she trembled as with a chilling ripple over all her body.
>
> "May I take your guns?"
>
> "Why?" he asked, and for the first time to her his voice carried a harsh note. Jane felt his hard, strong hands close around her wrists. It was not wholly with intent that she leaned toward him, for the look of his eyes and the feel of his hands made her weak. (pp. 146–147)

Jane does not come off as "superficial and silly," as Nesbitt writes, and "a case of subconscious hot pants," though many of Grey's protagonists desire their opposite long before admitting to themselves they are in love, and often remain obtuse enough to appear foolish.[13] Obviously Jane feels desire here, and may not admit it, but she is probably not foolish. In fact, the passage points in other directions. "Blindness" and "hands" are key motifs in *Riders,* and Jane demonstrates her blindness in a number of ways, one of which is in being aware of her sexual power (consciously planning to stop Lassiter by her appeal), but unaware of its real consequences, e.g., as a source of the very violence she hopes to avert. Critics have shown a similar unawareness of this important Grey feature.

To speculate about Jane's "subconscious": is it possible her attempt to "unman" Lassiter by obtaining his guns — in view of her vulnerability to the Mormon threats of sexual oppression — could be in part also a subconscious desire to "man," or arm herself with the symbol of male power, sex, and violence as the only way to contend with the masculine-dominated Mormon community Grey portrays? In any case, the ace of hearts has power to attract, but not always to control. Bishop Dyer and Elder Tull, operating within their closed society, have the "invisible hand." Jane wisely changes her mind and lets those strong, very visible (and, one must admit, sexy) hands of Lassiter do the job, proving her, at least in this instance, less than "silly."

In *Riders,* Grey uses techniques that became his staple sources of erotic appeal: suggestive metaphor, scenes of passion and kisses, the ripped blouse and exposed breast, Lassiter's heavy black guns, and the secretive allure of Surprise Valley. There's an abduction too — of Little Fay — Grey's favorite device, though without much erotic appeal in this case except indirectly as part of the hovering Mormon threat.

Most of these recur in *To the Last Man,* one of the three novels Nesbitt draws on to show Grey's "limited awareness of what he was up to."[14] In a lengthy forward to the novel Grey defends the writing of a romance, tells of repeated trips to Arizona to hunt both game and information about the Pleasant Valley War — which involved a bloody family feud — and concludes with a statement that essentially allows him to do what he wants with his sources:

> Suffice it to say that this romance is due to my conception of the war, and I base it upon the setting I learned to know and love so well, upon the strange passions of primitive peoples and upon my instinctive reaction to the facts and rumors that I gathered.[15]

What he does, in fact, is combine an Arizona setting, a gory incident or two from accounts of the feud, and blend in Romeo and Juliet variants to complete his romance.

Jean Isbel and Ellen Jorth meet early in the narrative. Their extended time together at this meeting marks both their destiny as lovers and the beginning of Grey's erotic appeal. Jean's father has sent for the half-Indian Jean to help in the anticipated struggle against sheepmen; when Jean arrives from Oregon he encounters Ellen on the trail a few miles from his father's ranch. Ellen resembles one of the wild heroines John Cawelti says appear "on the scene like a sexy nature girl but soon reveals that beneath her sassy manner, her artfully torn chemise, and apparent promiscuity beats a heart as pure as the driven snow."[16] Finding Jean a "gentleman," she complains of her ragged garb and says somewhat bitterly that it's hard to be "nice" without decent clothes. She looks pretty nice to Jean:

> Then it was he saw her ragged homespun skirt and a few inches of brown, bare ankles, strong and round, and crude worn-out moccasins that failed to hide the shapeliness of her feet. Suddenly she drew back her stockingless ankles and ill-shod feet. When Jean lifted his gaze again he found her face half averted and a stain of red in the gold tan of her cheek. That touch of embarrassment somehow removed her from this strong, raw, wild woodland setting. (p. 9)

They talk at length, trading compliments, obviously attracted to each other, and Jean says he wants to see her again:

> He noticed then a slight swelling quiver of her throat; and he became alive to its graceful contour, and to how full and pulsating it was, how nobly it set into the curve of her shoulder. Here in the quivering throat was the weakness of her, the evidence of her sex, the womanliness that belied the mountaineer stride and the grasp of strong brown hands on a rifle. It had an effect on Jean totally inexplicable to him, both in the strange warmth that stole over him and in the utterance he could not hold back. (p. 13)

Impulsive, Jean "quite without thought" grabs her hand. Just at this time they reach the Rim, and Ellen withdraws her hand and points out highlights of the spectacular view. Jean looks in awe:

> For leagues and leagues a colossal red and yellow wall, a rampart, a mountain-faced cliff, seemed to zigzag westward. Grand and bold were the promontories reaching out over the void. They ran toward the westering sun. Sweeping and impressive were the long lines slanting away from them, sloping darkly spotted down to merge

> into the black timber. Jean had never seen such a wild and rugged manifestation of nature's depths and upheavals. He was held mute.
>
> "Wonderful!" Jean says, "even once in a while — this sight would cure any misery, if you only see. I'm glad I came. I'm glad you showed it to me first." (p. 14)

Their encounter operates in several ways for Grey's narrative strategy. For one thing, it leads to this "peak" experience, one of those stunning views from a promontory enjoyed by a number of Grey protagonists. When shared, as here, it reinforces the attraction they feel for one another. Jean, of course, responds with the deep appreciation Grey heroes show. The awe-inspiring view also reinforces the erotic appeal of the encounter. Tension between Jean and Ellen has been building, as the "swelling quiver" of her throat and his "strange warmth" indicate; Grey now transfers this growing sexual awareness to the landscape (the "displaced desire"), the "depths and upheavals" Jean views hinting at the passion already beginning to develop between the lovers. Jean's reaction — an exclamation — has a parallel in what follows. He takes her hand again and they agree to meet when he asks:

> "Shore I will." she replied, softly, and turned to him. . . . She was beautiful as he had never known beauty. Limned against that scene, she gave life — wild, sweet, young life — the poignant meaning of which haunted yet eluded him. But she belonged there. Her eyes were again searching his, as if for some lost part of herself, unrealized, never known before. Then her lips parted. (p. 15)

Jean impulsively kisses those lips whose "tremulous movement" is a magnet to him, then apologizes. She is not angry, though she calls him "sudden," and agrees to meet him "day after tomorrow" until he tells her his name, Jean Isbel. Like a "hostile enemy" she strides off through the woods, marking the first of their "upheavals."

Among the ironies of *To the Last Man* is that the unlucky star which threatens to cross Jean and Ellen is the same passion that irresistibly draws them. They ask their respective fathers about the cause of the enmity: "we both fell in love with the same girl," says Gass Isbel to Jean; "we loved the same girl — your mother," admits Lee Jorth to Ellen. (pp. 44, 82) To add to the irony, each father, hate-ridden and bent on revenge, accuses the other of rustling, and each rationalizes his hatred and hard-headedness: for Jorth, the past has "got to be wiped out in blood!" while for Gass Isbel, somehow "in a Texan hate outlives any other feelin'." (pp. 42, 45, 82, 83) Each has been guilty of criminal acts in the past. The irony further compounds in that for Jean the twin drives — love and hate — operate instinctively:

> Something was wrong somewhere. Jean absolutely forgot that within the hour he had pledged his manhood, his life to a feud which could be blotted out only in blood. If he had understood himself he would have realized that the pledge was no more thrilling and unintelligible in its possibilities than this instinct which drew him irresistibly. (p. 48)

Something has "gone wrong" for Ellen too; the same instinct is drawing her also. Like Jean she puzzles over the new love that has gotten under her skin: "And when she came to the memory of his kiss she suffered more than the sensation of throbbing scarlet cheeks. . . . Proud, passionate, strong-willed, Ellen Jorth found herself a victim of conflicting emotions." (p. 52)

These confused and conflicting feelings, hinted at in the "depths and upheavals" of nature earlier, soon erupt in an erotic scene: Ellen's father steals Jean's horse, Spades, and gives him to Ellen. Jean tracks the horse to Jorth's, encounters Ellen there with the animal and gives Spades to her. They quarrel and he humiliates her by accusing her of playing innocent while knowing her father is a horse-thief. Stung, Ellen hits back by taunting him and hinting she has been a "toy and a rag" for rustlers, and Jean, aroused, jealous, and stung in turn, first slaps her mouth, then seizes her:

> Ellen saw the blood surge in his powerful neck. She saw his dark, hard face, strange now, fearful to behold, come lower and lower, till it blurred and obstructed her gaze. She felt the swell and ripple and stretch — then the bind of his muscles, like huge coils of elastic rope. Then with savage rude force his mouth closed on hers. All Ellen's senses reeled, as if she were swooning. She was suffocating. The spasm passed, and a bursting spurt of blood revived her to acute and terrible consciousness. For the endless period of one moment he held her so that her breast seemed crushed. His kisses burned and bruised her lips. And then, shifting violently to her neck, they pressed so hard that she choked under them. It was as if a huge bat had fastened upon her throat. (p. 99)

Jean stops, says he doesn't want her that way, but Grey's prose hints he has already imagistically had her, for the account, part of it anyway, makes another passable description of orgasm. Grey surrenders to exaggeration and melodrama, and with the "huge bat" image makes a Dracula of Jean, but the eroticism of "swell and ripple and stretch," "swooning," "spasm" and "bursting spurt" likely carries the passage for many a reader.

This erotic battle functions as a mini-version of the larger war, and by paralleling the Jorth-Isbel feud continues to underscore the irony of the similarity between the blood lust of revenge and sexual passion. Ellen retaliates after Jean's assault, "beating him with her fists, tearing at his hair, scratching his face, in a blind fury." Jean makes the feud-love contest explicit by telling Ellen to take his gun: "Somebody's got to begin this Jorth-Isbel feud. It'll be dirty business. I'm sick of it already. . . . Kill me! First blood for Ellen Jorth." He's right; Ellen looks at the Isbel blood already on her hands. (pp. 99 – 100)

Soon after this prelude, the real feud explodes. With the Isbel family under siege, Jean slips out of the cabin in the dark and shoots one of the enemies lurking there. This leads to another irony, namely, that in this novel Grey's language suggests Indians have a kind of super capacity for "savage" violence. Jean's father has bragged of his "Indian son," and the enemies have come to fear him. "Mebbe thet damn half-breed Isbel is comin' some Injun on us." Jean overhears Greaves say. Jean slips up on the storekeeper/outlaw in the dark and closes his arm "like a striking snake" around Greaves' neck:

> Jean might have ended the deadly business in just one move. But when his bared arm felt the hot, bulging neck something terrible burst out of the depths of him. To kill this enemy of his father's was not enough! Physical contact had unleashed the savage soul of the Indian. (p. 127)

Jean appropriately hisses to Greaves that his hunch was right, in words that suggest revenge for Greaves' sexual slurs against Ellen: "It's the half-breed. . . . An' I'm goin' to cut you — first for Ellen Jorth — an' then for Gaston Isbel!" He does: "Then his right arm whipped the big blade. It flashed. It fell. Low down, as far as Jean could reach, it entered Greaves' body." (pp. 127 – 128) In this incident, the sex and violence interplay continues, reinforced again by the knife in the groin. But the old stereotype about Indians being super savages rings oddly in view of the Jorth gang having shot two of the Isbel clan and let hogs in to eat the bodies, a bit of savagery hard to top.

The feud and killing also continue only to shift to Grey's next erotic interlude. The horse Spades, who occasioned the lovers' earlier clash, now becomes Jean's substitute and, as with their yet earlier trek to the rim, Grey uses metaphors of nature to reflect passions, giving at least some credence to his exaggerated statement in the "Foreword" that "character and action are subordinated to setting." Ellen feels a "hidden gathering storm" in her heart. Then Uncle John Sprague tells her how Jean knifed Greaves saying, *"First for Ellen Jorth!"* When Sprague leaves, Ellen reacts:

> She sat perfectly motionless, yet had a strange sensation of being lifted by invisible and mighty power. It was like movement felt in a dream. She was being impelled upward when her body seemed immovable stone. When her blood beat down this deadlock of all her physical being and rushed on and on through her veins it gave her an irresistible impulse to fly, to sail through space, to run and run and run. (p. 165)

In this dream-trance there is no fear of flying. She runs to Spades, buries her hot face in his mane, and then mounts and plunges down the canyon trail. What follows is probably Grey's most erotically charged sequence. The gathering storm breaks with "a blue-white, piercingly bright, ragged streak of lightning," twin to her inner storm, and Ellen watches, "hands pressed to her breast" in sight "of this tempest and gulf that resembled her soul." She cries out her love for Jean in a burst of passion "like a blaze of the sun," then crawls into a pine thicket. "And here she lay face down for a while, hands clutching the needles, breast hard upon the ground, stricken and spent." (p. 167)

But not for long. Her newly acknowledged love liberates "a million inherited instincts, quivering and physical," over which Ellen has no control: "And love was a birth from the depth of her, like a rushing spring of pure water, long underground, and at last propelled to the surface by a convulsion."

> No eye save that of nature saw her in her abandonment. An ineffable and exquisite smile wreathed her lips, sad, sensuous, the supremity of unconscious happiness. . . . Through her thrilling skin poured the multiple and

nameless sensations of the living organism stirred to supreme sensitiveness. . . . The slow reaching out of her hand, to grasp at nothing visible, was similar to the lazy stretching of her limbs, to the heave of her breast, to the ripple of muscle.

She attributes her new insight to the elements:

> The dark storm cloud with its white, ragged ropes of lightning and down-streaming gray veils of rain, the purple gulf rolling like a colored sea to the dim mountains, the glorious golden light of the sun — these . . . had burst the windows of her blindness. . . . And there her body paid the tribute to the realization of life. Shock, convulsion, pain, relaxation, and then unutterable and insupportable sensing of her environment and the heart! In one way she was a wild animal alone in the woods, forced into the mating that meant reproduction of its kind. In another she was an infinitely higher being shot through with the most resistless and mysterious transport that life could give to flesh. (pp. 168 – 169)

The consummation that never happens in Grey thus happens metaphorically.

Ellen's abduction by Colter follows. He soon makes a move, telling Ellen that her dying father has given her to him. She doesn't believe him, and they play a cat-and-mouse game until Colter, demanding his way, returns with her to his cabin hideout and grabs her: "The unleashed passion of the man required violence. In one savage pull he tore off her blouse, exposing her white, rounded shoulders and heaving bosom, where instantly a wave of red burned upward." (p. 217) Wounded and armed only with his knife, Jean has meanwhile made his way to the very cabin and hidden in the loft where, voyeur-like, he watches the encounter. At this moment one of Colter's men, Springer, rides up to relate the demise of the rest of the gang. Jean gets to watch for seven pages of Springer's tale and, when Springer leaves, more cat-and-mouse between Ellen and Colter. Then Colter sees blood on Ellen's hand and realizes Jean is in the loft. As Colter starts up after Jean, Ellen grabs her rifle and kills the outlaw. The novel ends melodramatically with the lovers on their knees vowing their love and faith in each other.

There is little of the critic's "uncertain sex" here; Grey knows very well what he's doing, and *To the Last Man,* in the passages cited, remains one of Grey's most erotically suggestive works. More than most, this novel shows Grey using landscape to suggest the deep passions of the protagonists. By contrast, *Wild Horse Mesa* illustrates a quite different approach. Near the end of the narrative, hero Chane Weymer captures the wild horse, Panquitch. Sue Melberne sees her opportunity. She wants to tie down Chane and free the horse. The advantage is all hers, since Chane's brother, Chess, has told her of Chane's love. A seductive scene follows in which Sue repeatedly leans against Chane, as it were pressing her argument. She ends proposing marriage — if he frees Panquitch, she must "pay" by marrying him, she says. Chane remains unbelievably dense and a reader can only agree when Sue tells him, "If you had any sense you'd have known I — I loved you!" (p. 337) But the adolescent quality of the episode undercuts the erotic appeal. Nor does Grey make any use of landscape except a lone sentence when Chane feels "the golden amber sunlight of the canyon" move about him "like a glory of lightning." Chane frees the animal, and this "supreme handiwork of nature — a creature too beautiful, too proud, too noble, too wild for the yoke of man," rides away into the sunset alone. (p. 339) *Wild Horse Mesa* differs immeasurably from *To the Last Man* in the use of the horse, the intensity of the prose, and the role of nature, to say nothing of the irony of the latter in regard to the source of erotic passion and violence.

Grey's most sustained piece (half a novel) of erotic titillation belongs to *The Border Legion.* It also deserves attention on two other counts: one, Grey develops a full-scale captivity narrative with roots in one of our country's earliest art forms, a feature unrecognized by Grey's commentators; the second, growing out of the first, is that the novel can be read as an ironic parable of the American dream — a story of competitive individualism prevailing and rewarded by riches.

First, Grey's eroticism. Surprisingly, this intriguing novel has gone virtually untapped by critics. Early reviews of *The Border Legion* range from outright hostility ("commonplace," "illogical," and "not a good book") to praise ("not for an instant" does the narrative "lag or fall in interest"), but the criticism never gets beyond the surface. Neither does subsequent commentary. In his book-length study of Grey, Carlton Jackson briefly summarizes the plot and concludes blandly that its theme is "what lust for gold did to man."[17] More surprising, even those who write about Grey's eroticism neglect it, though it contains highly suggestive dialogue; neither William Bloodworth nor John Nesbitt mention it. Ann Ronald does better, but fails to follow up. She notes that for Joan her captor's gun "becomes an undeniable phallic symbol," but that Grey "undoubtedly did not realize the implications of what he had written," and concludes only, and tentatively, that with regard to Grey's use of sex and violence, "a strong undercurrent seems to flow against the mainstream of what the author professed."[18]

Ronald's is a near miss, and the "strong undercurrent" she observes flows most powefully in the verbal exchanges and actions of the captive, Joan Randle, and her captor, the bandit Kells. The novel opens with its heroine gazing at the "wild and looming mountain range," Grey's version of the frontier here. She has begun her errand into the wilderness. A quarrel with her suitor, Jim Cleve, occasions her quest. The night before, while she waits for him, Jim suddenly appears from the bushes, seizes her, bends her backward in a "bearish embrace," and kisses her. She gets "blindly furious" at this bit of wildness, rejects and even taunts him. He reacts, vowing to "rustle for the border" and to "get in with Kells and Gulden," two notorious outlaws. The next night Joan bitterly regrets her actions and sets out in pursuit.

The bandit Kells soon takes her captive, killing a would-be protector she has met and shooting two of his own men so he can have Joan to himself at a wilderness cabin. The plot moves on from there with much violence and savagery, and includes many of Grey's ironies.

Twin desires — for sex and gold — dominate the narrative. Grey interweaves the two. Chief tempter is the bandit leader Kells ("kills"?), whose name suggests the lethal consequences of the wilderness bargain — reversion to savagery — as does that of his more dehumanized rival, Gulden ("golden"). Kells tells Joan he will hold her for ransom and "get a barrel of gold" out of her. Joan, sex, and gold remain linked for the rest of the novel, though the real mother lode is feminine, as the climax, an orgy of gambling with the stolen gold, proves: Gulden makes a tell-tale bet — all his gold for Joan.

But Joan's repeated "thrills" prove the chief subversive in this tale of desire, suggesting that the savage life has an ambiguous character. Thrills characterize her experience throughout; they underscore the erotic and appealing nature of the psychic drama enacted — or projected — on the Idaho frontier. In the first of the book's overtly suggestive passages, Joan reacts to her captor's broad belt below his hip and the holster with a heavy gun. "That was a strange place to carry a gun, Joan thought. It looked awkward to her. When he walked it might swing round and bump against his leg. And he certainly would have to put it some other place when he rode." That night, ready to sleep, she imagines "something terrible" will happen to her. The thought has an effect: "a shudder that was a thrill ran over and over her." (pp. 14–15) Shortly after this she thinks of Jim and imagines a violent encounter between her lover and Kells when they meet, though the thought revives her terror.

> Yet she thrilled again; a ripple that was not all cold coursed through her. Something had a birth in her then, and the part of it she understood was that she welcomed

> the adventure with a throbbing heart, yet looked with awe and shame and distrust at this new, strange side of her nature. (pp. 22 – 23)

This new nature continues to thrill. One of Kells' bandits puts his hand on Joan's breast with "an instinctive animal action." She shrinks back with a cry. Kells clubs the offender senseless; she cries out, thinking he means to shoot the man. Kells pushes her back and she feels "the shock of an electric current" at his touch. (p. 25) He soon approaches her himself and she knows it will be her "supreme test." She's ready. She looks into Kells' eyes; they are "windows of a gray hell," and she gazes into "that naked abyss, at that dark, uncovered soul." And though Kells backs off — Grey wants to prolong the titillation — Joan knows there will be more ordeals, and she acknowledges "that never again would she be so near betrayal of terror and knowledge and self." (pp. 33 – 34)

Kells takes her to an isolated cabin, and this scene of her trial has "a curious fascination" for Joan. "Something — and she shuddered — was to happen to her in this lonely, silent gorge." It does, of course, but first she finds a card, the ace of hearts, pinned to the bark of a tree "by a cluster of bullet-holes, every one of which touched the red heart and one of them had obliterated it." The name "Gulden" is scrawled below. (p. 34) This touch proves ironic, foreshadowing the cutting of cards at story's end, when Gulden's ace of spades beats Kells' king of hearts, but not the ace, which in Grey's game is Joan. Around the campfire Kells again threatens: "To-night — to-night — I'll . . . one more day — and I'll be mad to do right by you — instead of wrong. . . ." She leans forward in the campfire light "with outstretched hands and quivering lips, as overcome by his halting confession of one last remnant of honor as she was by the dark hint of his passion." As he strides back and forth by the fire Joan eyes the pistol again. "The scabbard with the big gun swung against his leg. It grew to be a dark and monstrous thing in

Joan's sight . . . She must get her hands on that gun — kill him — or — !" (p. 39)

That night Kells suddenly comes near and leans over her. His face is a "dark blur," but his posture is "that of a wolf about to spring." He leans slowly lower. "Joan saw the heavy gun swing away from his leg; she saw it black and clear against the blaze; a cold, blue light glinted from its handle." (p. 42) The next morning Kells approaches and looks at her "like a cat returned to watch over a captive mouse"; she waits, "with ever a strange and cold sense of the nearness of that swinging gun." (p. 43) She will pay the ransom, he says, reiterating the sex/gold connection. This too has an ironic ring; as he later says, and the novel demonstrates, she is worth her weight in gold. Then the wolf springs. As she walks about the camp Joan hears a call which "thrilled all the weakness from her in a flash." She looks at him "to see unmasked the ruthless power, the leaping devil, the ungovernable passion" she had sensed in him. (p. 44) "Girl! . . . I'm hungry — for you!" he breathes hoarsely, and embraces her "as if his nature was savage and he had to use a savage force." (p. 45)

The eroticism continues, in fact heightens. A second point of interest in *The Border Legion,* has little to do with titillation. Namely, the novel's roots in the early American captivity narrative. This aside seems appropriate in view of Grey's double reference above to "savagery" (i.e., "savage" and "savage force"), since the transition from Mary Rowlandson's seventeenth-century narrative of her captivity by Indians to Grey's novel comes about fairly easily once one makes the initial switch of Kells, Gulden, and the "savage" border bandits for Rowlandson's red men.

For author Richard Slotkin, the captivity is the basic and uniquely American frontier myth in one of its earliest forms. Captivity accounts, he says, "completely dominate the list of frontier narratives published in America between 1680 and 1716."[19] In them, colonial writers, wittingly or unwittingly, attempted to resolve the dilemmas of the human psyche and the new American culture, especially as they involved the Indian, who became the embodiment of their desires, fears, and frustrations. In narrative pattern, language, and imagery, *The Border Legion* echoes these early fictions. For Grey's captivity, however, the "savages" are now an infamous Border Legion, and the lawless frontier wilderness of the colonists has shifted to a mountainous region near the Idaho border.

For Joan, as for Mary Rowlandson and other colonial captives, the lawless border becomes a figurative "hell," a metaphysical analogue, complete with "devils," where her secret urges, hidden under hopes and rationalizations, gradually emerge. As she and her captor ride through the "trackless" border region, Joan imagines there will be "hell" when Kells and Jim Cleve meet; she thrills at the idea. Later, at Alder Creek, hell becomes more tangible in the form of the wild and savage mining community. In between, Joan experiences her own hell — her own figurative reversion to savagery.

To return to the narrative, Kells, "as if his nature was savage and he had to use a savage force," seizes Joan. The savage drags her into the cabin and attempts to force her:

> If Joan struggled at all, it was only slightly, when she writhed and slipped, like a snake, to get her arm under his as it clasped her neck. Then she let herself go. He crushed her to him. He bent her backward — tilted her face with hard and eager hand. Like a madman, with hot working lips, he kissed her. She felt blinded — scorched. But her purpose was as swift and sure and wonderful as his passion was wild. The first reach of her groping hand found his gunbelt. Swift as light her hand slipped down. Her fingers touched the cold gun — grasped with thrill on thrill — slipped farther down, strong and sure to raise the hammer. Then with a leaping, strung intensity that matched his own she drew the gun. She lay passive under his kisses — the devouring kisses of one whose manhood had been denied the sweetness, the glory, the fire, the life of woman's lips. It

> was a moment in which she met his primitive fury of possession with a woman's primitive fury of profanation. She pressed the gun against his side and pulled the trigger. (p. 45)

On the simple narrative level, this is a vivid scene of attempted rape. From the frontier captivity view, it is a striking enactment of the captive's worst fears: "marriage" with or rape by the savages, reversion to a savage state. The language here suggests the "degenerationist's" nightmare: in a later set-to she tells Kells he has made her a "beast" (pp. 99–101); here she is "like a snake" and matches "primitive fury" with "primitive fury." Grey's description hints at the double focus of the psyche's dark urges projected onto the Indians and manifest in the imagined tortures ("blinded," "scorched") by these savages run amok ("madman") — and savored, "thrill on thrill." So does the posture, the frenzied yin-yang embrace a kind of mock marriage consummated as Joan, "with a leaping strung intensity that matched his," pulls the trigger of that big black gun.

Grey compounds the irony with an appearance-reality motif in the form of eyes which hide or reveal savage potential. It is one of a group of motifs (tropes, keywords, images) which weave an ironic pattern throughout the story.[20] Joan's body may be limp, but she goes straight for that fascinating gun, an act which reinforces her assumption of the masculine, savage role; she triumphs in this symbolic encounter "still with tight-shut eyes." An intriguing variant of the theme takes the form of the outfit of a former gang member, Dandy Dale. When Kells makes her put the outfit on, complete with mask, she looks in the mirror and sees "merely a masked stranger." She is "no longer Joan Randle." Her identity has been "absolutely lost." (p. 97) Not absolutely. She is now one of the "Border Legion," her outward appearance — that of a lawless savage — the embodiment of those ungovernable passions that have plagued her and her captive Colonial forerunners, passions which she displays with eyes closed.

Joan's savage potential, accompanied by thrills, continues to emerge. Jim shows up at Cabin Gulch with an outlaw's reputation. He has faced and wounded Gulden, the men report. Kells accepts him into the gang. They sit across a table, and the sight of the two face to face, Grey says, "thrilled Joan to her depths." (p. 105) That night she lies sleepless, "haunted by Jim's white face, amazed at the magnificent madness of him, thrilled to her soul by the meaning of his attack on Gulden." Though in bed, she still wears Dandy Dale's clothes, including his gun. She turns in "restless slumber," sometimes

> awakened by rolling on the heavy gun. . . . And at such moments she had to ponder in the darkness, to realize that she, Joan Randle, lay a captive in a bandit's camp, dressed in a dead bandit's garb, and packing his gun — even while she slept. It was such an improbable, impossible thing. Yet the cold feel of the polished gun sent a thrill of certainty through her. (p. 110)

Joan's potential (potency, power) actualizes itself particularly in terms of control and manipulation, first with Kells, then Jim, and, at novel's end, with Kells again when she sends him to initiate the suicidal destruction of the gang. Inevitably, once Jim joins the gang at Cabin Gulch, Joan meets up with him. To her dismay his eyes are "flames" and she flees with "blurred sight" to the cabin, agonizing "that she, of all women, had to be the one who made him answer, like Kells and Gulden and all those ruffians, to the instincts of a beast." An anticipated thrill here turns to grief. In her new dual identity (in Dandy Dale's outfit) as captive and captor, she becomes her own torturer in language appropriate to a savage ritual: "a brand of red-hot pitch, blacker and bitterer than death, had been struck brutally across her soul." (p. 116) But at their next meeting she takes control. Jim leaps at her "like a panther," fastens a powerful hand to the neck of her blouse, jerks her to her knees, and drags her "like a beast . . . seeking a dark place." He tells her to pray for her soul.

But she has been to this soul abyss before. She tells him she loves him while "a thrill, a tremble, a rush" goes over her, and soon quickens to "thrilling, revivifying life" when he accedes. By the end of the episode the panther has become a pussycat; subdued, Jim says, "I'll be what you want — do what you want." (pp. 144 – 149)

Slotkin says the American wilderness, on the negative side, stimulated "an obscene Faustian lust to satisfy nature by violating all bonds of obedience, religion, and morality."[21] As with Faust, the struggle for Kells and Joan proves a soul affair (echoed in the above episode with Jim). Earlier, Joan shoots Kells when he first assaults her. When he regains some of his strength, he tries again. She resists, they fight, and Joan, physically stronger at this point, prevails. He tosses her a gun (Dandy Dale's) and says, "Kill me!" She refuses and he confronts her with a Faustian twist, later repeated: "my life or your soul." (p. 99) At the end of the novel it is Joan who proposes the bargain, adding her own perverse twist: "save my life — and *your* soul!" He accepts and she sends him to his death. (pp. 270 – 271)

In the earlier proposal, Kells says in effect, kill me or I'll seduce you, "soul" an obvious euphemism for seduction. In the book's climax, Joan makes essentially the same proposal, though the language obscures the ironic point: don't kill me (save me), and I'll "seduce" you (you'll save your soul), since the latter amounts to his death warrant. Seduction is the game in either case, as the contexts illustrate (despite the surface suggestion that Kells will find spiritual salvation). In the earlier encounter Joan tells Kells he would have only the "husk of a woman . . . a cold shell" if he forced her, and that "the warmth, the sweetness, the quiver, the thrill, the response, the life — all that is the soul of a woman . . . will be murdered." To save her "soul" she offers to show him the difference: "She gave the fascinated Kells her hands, slipped into his arms, to press against his breast, and leaned against him an instant, all one quivering, surrendered body. . . ."Almost succumbing herself, she falls away "shrinking and terrified," but victorious. Kells leaves, but not before he lets slip the idolatrous nature of the encounter: "My God!" he breathes softly. (pp. 100 – 101) In the melodramatic climax too, seduction is to the fore. Joan tells Kells if she hadn't loved Jim first she would have loved him, and gives him "her embrace, her arms, her lips without the vestige of a lie." The truth is, this kiss makes Kells anything but immortal. Sealed, the Faustian bargain turns the gang in on itself; Kells rushes into the next room, stabs Gulden and the gang self-destructs in a violent melee. Joan's power — erotic — again triumphs.[22]

Joan's captivity reflects that of her colonial counterparts in a number of other ways as well. In its general pattern, the captivity begins with the protagonist in a happy state of innocence. Savages soon disrupt this, plunging the person into a trial and ordeal in which the soul is imperiled. Ultimately, the captive attains a figurative rebirth, an initiation into a new state of being. This pattern constitutes a "myth of self-transcendence," says Slotkin, in which "self-transcendence through acculturation and acculturation through acts of violence" are "the basic themes."[23] Joan's ordeal starts with "remorse and dread beginning to knock at her heart" as she gazes at the "wild and looming mountain range." Like Slotkin's Puritan counterparts, she is "on the brink of the abysmal woods" in which the savage devils move. In Joan's case, her innocence, or naivete — a prudish, over-reaction to the advances of her suitor — triggers the ensuing trial. Already feeling guilty, she enters the wilderness hoping to reclaim her lover, is taken captive by Kells, and begins her ordeal or battle for her "soul." As her subsequent interaction with Kells suggests, this contest has an ironic dimension not found in Mary Rowlandson's account.

But for Joan, as well as a colonial captive, the frontier wilderness can be seen, again in Slotkin's words, as "a vivid analogue of the condition of his own inner being — a paradigm of his mind and soul in which his sins, hidden under hopes and rationalizations, are suddenly made manifest."[24] Joan too makes this kind of self-discovery: "How silly, false, and vain had been her coquetry, her indifference!" she says, fearing that the curse she has put upon Jim Cleve will drive him into savagery and a life of crime. (p. 67) The trauma of her experience changes her: "she had become another girl — a girl wholly become a woman, and one with a driving passion to save if it cost her life." (p. 68) Ironically, she has already demonstrated her own savage potential in the primitive violence she displays with Kells and the symbolic "membership" in the gang she has with Dandy Dale's outfit and gun. Joan's recurring "thrills" throughout this experience testify that she, like earlier captives, is tempted to share in the sinful savage orgies.*The Border Legion* has a mythic ring in that its pattern is circular, a journey beginning and ending at Joan's Idaho home, a quest complete with descents into both her private "hell" and the more public one at the Alder Creek mining community where "the most primitive passions of mankind found outlet and held sway." (pp. 186 – 187) In this sense Grey's story echoes the archetypal heroic journey, where the heroine or hero travels to the underworld (in psychological terms, the unconscious), undergoes temptations, finds a magic talisman (a golden bough!), and returns. Typically, the mythic quester — here, Joan Randle — represents "the whole culture's collective consciousness and the agent of their will to survive or their aspiration to power."[25]

Within this broad mythic pattern and the concept of the enormously popular captivity narratives, Grey's chief savages (aside from Jim Cleve and Joan herself, who reveal their own potential) are Kells and Gulden. The Border Legion's lawless community is a house divided, with Gulden a constant threat to Kells' leadership. Triggered by Joan, this divisiveness leads to the Legion's undoing. In Gulden, Grey carries the reversion-to-savagery theme a step beyond Kells. His name suggests a Midas-like dehumanization, and Joan gropes for words to describe him. He is:

> an animal — a gorilla. . . . And upon his face, in the lines and cords, in the huge caverns where his eyes hid, and in the huge gash that held strong, white fangs, had been stamped by nature and by life a terrible ferocity. Here was a man or a monster in whose presence Joan felt that she would rather be dead.

Grey adds a Frankensteinian touch, twice referring to him as a machine, and has him sit "like a huge engine of destruction that needed no rest." (pp. 61 – 62) A special feature identifies him with one of the worst fears of earlier captivities, a fear that the only communion possible with savages was that of violence. "Gulden's a cannibal!" Kells says; later, Jim echoes the charge: "Gulden's a cannibal. . . . I wish I had killed him." (p. 91, 148)

But Kells, the chief, remains the most interesting, so appealing that, like Milton's Satan, he overshadows the good guy. Not surprisingly, critic Ann Ronald finds Joan's fiance, Jim, downright uninteresting, but Kells "one of Grey's best-drawn and most complex characters."[26] Necessarily so, since Joan explores her heart of hearts and acts out her psychic drama primarily with him. He is the one who remains in her memory, "indestructible." (p. 280)

Not surprising too, since the action shifts, the heightened tension of the Joan-Kells erotic confrontations subsides in the book's second half, the Alder Creek mining episode. Grey focuses here on the other "desire," greed for gold, and interest flags until the climactic slaughter. But Grey weaves the two sections together with an intriguing narrative device again reminiscent of the early captivities. Mary Rowlandson's early tale divides not into chapters, but "removes," stages suggestive of spiritual, psychic movement away from civilization and into savagery. *The Border Legion* has conventional chapters, but Joan's captive soul-journey takes place in four ironic "removes," each focusing on one of three cabins.[27]

The first is at Lost Canyon, "a little log cabin, open in front" which is "merely a shed, without fireplace or window, and the floor was a covering of balsam boughs." (p. 31, 34) An interesting irony begins to emerge here, for Grey's cabins create a symbolic variant of the "Stages of Progress" theory.[28] In this first crude shack, Kells and Joan fight with "primitive fury." She wins the erotic encounter, does not yield, and shoots Kells with his own gun.

The Border Legion subsequently assembles at Cabin Gulch, second of Grey's structural removes. Joan is given an attached, small, two-room accommodation, slightly elevated, with a swinging blanket entrance and poles so the entrance can be "shut off from intruders." Her improved quarters contain some blankets, "a blurred and cracked mirror," a table made of boxes, and a lantern. (pp. 79 – 80) Joan again triumphs, fighting "like a beast" and wearing Dandy Dale's costume. The appearance/reality theme, which permeates the novel, is prominent in this episode where Joan's deceit is compounded as, after her triumph, she finds relief on the bed in "blinding tears." (p. 101)

These cabin prisons function as bed-chambers of the secret heart. They are, literally, bedrooms — and Joan's erotic victories take place here, as they do again in the third remove to Alder Creek. Here Kells has his men build a cabin with a separate compartment for Joan. It has a "rude board door with padlock and key," a bench with blankets, and a small, square hole for a window. Joan soon has it comfortable, "a luxury compared to what she had been used to for weeks." (p. 169) Joan's triumph now takes the form of marriage, a secret night wedding with Jim Cleve through the convenient window.

At Alder Creek Kells' authority disintegrates, Jim finds a huge gold nugget, vigilantes stage a multiple hanging, and the newlyweds plot to escape from this wilderness now transferred to a frontier tent-city "hell," a place "not human," where men are "like coyotes at a carcass." (p. 179) They flee on a stage, with Jim's gold part of the shipment, only to have Gulden and a remnant of the gang rob the stage and occasion the last remove.

The "progress" of the first three stages proves ironic, Joan's cells feature increasing creature comforts and Joan counters the sexual threat represented by Kells with increasingly sophisticated — or "civilized" — means. What was primitive at Lost Canyon becomes wily titillation dressed as Dandy Dale at Cabin Gulch, and institutionalized custom (marriage) at Alder Creek, in each case the key encounter featured by some form of deceit. The "savagery" in each case continues.

The fourth stage might seem to break the progression. In a sense it does, for the remnant of the Legion returns to Cabin Gulch, finds Kells waiting, and Joan ends in her "old apartment." But a significant difference marks this final remove. For the first time, girl, gold, and gang come together. This harks back to earlier remarks of Kells that he would ransom Joan for gold, that she would herself pay the ransom, and that she is worth her weight in gold. Two sources of savagery — lust and its economic embodiment, greed — now unite and explode. "My whole cut of gold," Gulden booms, *"Against the girl!"* (p. 267) But the reader knows his winning ace of spades (over Kells' king of hearts) is no match for Joan, whose ace wins. With Kells, a projection of wilderness passions, under control, Joan can dismiss the savages. Which she does (and America did). She sends him — knife flashing and gun blazing — to eliminate the Border Legion. The "ruthless force" (Kells, et al) of the wilderness can now translate, as it does in Joan's memory, into "one last magnificent stand." (p. 281)[29]

Thus Joan Randle's wilderness quest echoes any number of colonial forerunners. She makes her journey of discovery, is, like Mary Rowlandson, metamorphosed into a "beast" (at least metaphorically), and realizes she is as capable of evil as the wilderness "devils" (displays her savage side), though she (or Grey) admits this latter point only obliquely. She has grown now "not to blame any man, honest miner or bloody bandit," Grey says, though Joan remains a bit obtuse, blaming gold instead. (280) And she emerges from her trial changed, a "woman," if chagrined at her naive past. But unlike Mary Rowlandson, for whom after her return "honey out of the rock" provides satisfaction, Joan has mined something more substantial and comes home with a horse-load of that blame-worthy gold.

It's only a step from seeing the narrative as an ironic modern captivity to viewing it as a parable of the American dream. Slotkin's extended definition of the "Myth of the Frontier" includes "those same 'laws' of capitalist competition, of supply and demand and of 'Manifest Destiny' that have been the building blocks" of our dominant ideology. In the third chapter of his work, "The Frontier Myth as a Theory of Development," he spells out the implications in detail. "If we approach this Myth with an awareness of its function as rationalizer of the process of capitalist development in America," he says, we can begin to see some of our ideology's special characteristics.[30] Exploitation of the frontier wilderness, Slotkin argues, was possible "only through a series of ordeals and labors. We had first to separate physically from the homeland and endure isolation; because the land was new and unsettled, we had to undergo regression," and because the territory was "virgin land," its resources could be "appropriated without the heavy costs of capital and labor required for productive exploitation in the Old World," and New World profits were thus "windfall profits," promising unusual returns.[31]

Viewed as an American dream parable, as a story of capitalist exploitation and success, Grey's captivity might read something like this: entrepreneur Joan Randle separates from her home, endures isolation, and undergoes regression. What for colonial captives and entrepreneurs were real Indians are now renegade whites, whose "savagery" represents the capitalist virtue of competitive individualism run amok, lawless and out of control, capitalist "sins" projected onto the wilderness and its denizens. Joan competes, wins out over her unscrupulous rival, and — with supply and demand very much at issue — comes away with the windfall profits.

Among the ironies is that the gold she and Jim carry home proves to have originated in a lucky strike, a windfall "find" first made at Alder Creek by her uncle, appropriately named Overland. Joan triumphs and fulfills the westward-moving "destiny" which has now reached the Idaho border.

There are other ironies. The "soul" competition here is carried out in economic and erotic images, gold and sex. "The West was preeminently the land of opportunity for men on the make," Slotkin says, referring to early exploitation.[32] The double entendre suggested in the phrase aptly captures the twin thrusts of *The Border Legion*. Here and elsewhere Grey combines business and sex; it is this feature of his "romance" that marks the most important of the reasons for a re-reading of Grey. And if one expands the dream to include an idyllic romance, further irony emerges, for Grey's use of the erotic here goes beyond that in some of his other works. Joan wins the competition with the aid of deceit as the pervasive appearance/reality theme and its images — "eyes," costume, blindness, "blurred sight," truth, disguise, and other variants — indicate. The novel thus suggests a duplicity and savagery lurking beneath middle-class morality and acquisitive capitalism. Troublesome dark urges of the heart must be rationalized or repressed — on the sexual side sublimated into marriage or, in their projected savage form, rejected and destroyed. Similarly, on the economic side the savage embodiments of lawless competition are destroyed, while the profits are enjoyed as a "lucky strike."

And erotic desire is at the heart of the matter. Readers may, if they like, see a paradigm of their own — or Grey's — ambivalence toward sexual morality in the thrills of Joan Randle ("randy"? "ramble"?). The novel lets one have it both ways, "wild" urges revealed and hidden at the same time, striding about as Dandy Dale with a big gun and a mask, and yet coming home chastely married and amply rewarded.

At the end, Grey provides a light-hearted touch which adds a final irony. Jim persuades Joan to wear the Dandy Dale costume and mask "just for fun" when they ride triumphantly back to their little village. They create the "sensation" he imagined. No one of course recognizes Joan until she takes off the mask. Then her Aunt Jane cries out and takes charge: "You — you wild thing! You desperado! I always told Bill you'd run wild some day! . . . March in the house and get out of that indecent rig!" (p. 279)

The Law

IV

1
"Lawlessness"

Lawlessness, a critical assumption has it, provides a building-block staple of the western. For Cynthia Hamilton, both western and hard-boiled detective novels are "subgenres" of a master American adventure formula, and there are "two crucial elements in the setting of this master formula: lawlessness and the maximum opportunity for personal enrichment."[1] For John Cawelti, "the symbolic landscape of the western formula is a field of action that centers upon the point of encounter between civilization and wilderness, East and West, settled society and lawless openness."[2]

Yes and no for Grey. Yes, in novel after novel Grey announces the absence of institutionalized law. At the beginning of *Robbers' Roost* the outlaw gangleader Hays robs a man at the Green River, Utah, ferry crossing. The man objects: "If there is law in this — country — you'll pay for this," he says. Hays laughs. "Haw! Haw! You ain't lookin' for law, air you, granpaw? . . . Wal, the only law is what you see here in my hand — an' I don't mean your money." (p. 6) In *West of the Pecos* a young boy thinks Pecos Smith must be rich to give him two pesos. If you are, he says, "pay Terrill's bill an' get him oot!" (He refers to Terrill Lambeth, Pecos' future sweetheart, dressed as a man). Pecos wants to know out of where; there's no jail. The boy tells him it's "what Brasee calls his jail, a red 'dobe back of the post." Logically enough, Pecos asks if

Brasee is a sheriff too. "Naw, sheriff nothin'. He plays at it. There ain't no law west of the Pecos, Senor." Similar statements occur, for example, in *Knights of the Range* (pp. 8, 244) and *The Hash Knife Outfit*. (p. 10)

And yet Grey does insert "law" — several forms of it — into a number of his novels. "In the settings he chooses, Grey explores several different kinds of lawlessness," Hamilton observes.[3] She is right. What needs to be added is that he sometimes explores a combination of law and lawlessness, and the result — as *Heritage of the Desert* illustrates — can prove highly ironic. In *Heritage,* one recalls, Holderness and August Naab confront each other invoking "laws" to justify their determination to possess land and water. Their arguments run from "no law" to "desert law" to U.S. government law to Mormon law to squatter's rights — everything but Indian law. Grey utilizes these variants elsewhere as well.

Grey's second popular success, *Riders of the Purple Sage,* opens on a scene in which Elder Tull specifically invokes Mormon law, and Lassiter counters with a different kind. "I've just stumbled onto a queer deal," the gunman says. "Seven Mormons all packin' guns, an' a Gentile tied with a rope, an' a woman who swears by his honesty! Queer, ain't that?" Tull snaps that it's none of Lassiter's business. To which Lassiter says:

> "Where I was raised a woman's word was law. I ain't quite outgrowed that yet."
>
> Tull fumed between amaze and anger.
>
> "Meddler, we have a law something different from a woman's whim — Mormon law! . . . Take care you don't transgress it."
>
> "To hell with your Mormon law!" (p. 10)

The status of this novel — acknowledged western classic — urges more than passing attention. The "law" can serve as entry point. Not law alone, though, for it is but one part of an intermingling of themes and images which form the ironic core of the novel. Law's ironic companions in this case are the imagery of "hands" and another powerful appearance/ reality motif especially featuring "blindness."

Tull and his "pale comrades" no sooner ride off than Jane Withersteen notices Lassiter's horse is blind; when pressed, Lassiter admits Mormons did it, thus beginning the linkage so central to the narrative. Lassiter's quest for revenge is a major thread in the book's relatively complicated plot. Years before, Mormons abducted and seduced his sister, Milly Erne. After he rides up just in time to save the cowboy, Venters, from a whipping by Tull and his band in the opening scene, Lassiter stays on with Jane, partly of course because he's attracted to her and partly because he senses he's near the end of his long search for the guilty party. In a second plot strand, Jane has inherited a ranch and other holdings from her Mormon father, but is in trouble with the lecherous Tull because she resists his pressures. He wants both her and the land. A third thread involves Bess Oldring, who turns out to be Milly Erne's daughter raised by a rustler, Oldring. Oldring himself uses rustling (with Bess along as a mysterious masked rider) as a cover for his real source of wealth — a rich gold discovery.

Venters trails Oldring, shoots the masked rider, discovers she is really Bess, and nurses her to health in the hidden Surprise Valley. Meanwhile, Mormons abduct Fay, Jane's adopted child, and Lassiter kills Bishop Dyer who, Jane tells him, was behind the abduction of Milly Erne. Lassiter then sets fire to the ranch and he and Jane flee on two of Jane's superhorses. The two love interests now cross; Venters and Bess leave the Valley, meet the fleeing Jane and Lassiter, exchange a mule for the two horses, and race to freedom. Temporarily deceived, Tull and his men again pursue Jane and Lassiter only to have Lassiter roll the ancient cave-dwellers' guardian stone that destroys the Mormons and seals off Surprise Valley, leaving the lovers in their isolated paradise.

Soon after the opening episode, the law/blindness/hand motifs come together. Lassiter leaves to sleep in the sage, and Venters talks with Jane. He says he has to leave the village because Tull is implacable. "You ought to see from his intention today that — But you can't see. Your blindness — your damned religion! . . . Well, I fear that invisible hand will turn its hidden work to your ruin." Jane is puzzled. "Invisible hand? Bern!" Venters explains: "I mean your Bishop. . . . He's the law." (p. 20) The irony latent in these early passages emerges at the novel's final famous melodramatic scene as Lassiter, Jane, and Fay emerge at the top of the divide: "He staggered to his feet — staggered to a huge, leaning rock that rested on a small pedestal. He put his hand on it — the hand that had been shot through — and Jane saw blood drip from the ragged hole. Then he fell." Lassiter explains the purpose of the balancing stone, but says he can't roll it; he has the strength, but says he's lost his nerve. At this point Jane takes over, reiterating her command to "roll the stone" (with Grey's italics, including *"Lassiter, I love you!"* and, finally, all capital letters), until Lassiter obeys this "law" — the woman's word denigrated earlier by Tull to "a whim" — and with his very visible, bleeding hands sends the stone thundering down on Tull, who falls in a parody of prayer, "on his knees with uplifted arms." (pp. 334 – 335)

In between, Grey's narrative piles up small ironies surrounding appearance/reality, hands, and law. When Jane learns her Mormon employees have not delivered messages to her from Fay's sick mother, she begins to see. "She had again caught a glimpse of dark underhand domination, running its secret lines this time into her own household. Like a spider in the blackness of night an unseen hand had begun to run these dark lines, to turn and twist them about her life." (p. 91) Later, Bishop Dyer (Dire? Die-er?) visits her. He has been Jane's teacher, the one to whom "God revealed himself in secret." He orders her to tell him why Lassiter has come. When she admits it is not only to find Milly Erne's grave but to kill the man who persuaded her to abandon home, husband, and God, Dyer pales then cries hoarsely, "That's why you made love to this Lassiter — to bind his hands!" But Jane has heard the jangle of Lassiter's step. She sees Dyer try to draw and then "clear sight" fails her. In two ways. She faints, for one, but she has just begun to have clear sight concerning Dyer, for Lassiter's step "released the weight upon her numbed eyelids. Lifting her eyes she saw — ashen, shaken, stricken — not the Bishop but the man." (p. 152)

Lassiter intentionally only wings Dyer, the bishop leaves, and Lassiter confronts Jane about the hand-binding. She admits it was true and they accuse each other of blindness. Jane says she wanted to make him care for her so she could influence him, but at first he was "stone blind." He responds. "I know you're blind. What you meant is one thing — what you did was to make me love you." "Blind" and "blindness" appear eight times on the next page. Lassiter refers to the erotic advances Jane made to take his guns and unman him. "But for a savin' innocence you'd have made yourself low an' vile — betrayin' yourself, betrayin' me — all to bind my hands an' keep me from snuffin' out Mormon life. It's your damned Mormon blindness." It's not vile, she replies, to save life; that's "God's law." He in turn says the blindness he means is what keeps her from "seein' the truth." Some Mormons are "blacker than hell," but she won't see it. "Else, why all this blind passion to save the life of that — that. . . ." As for the guns, he says, "Gunpackin' in the West since the Civil War has growed into a kind of moral law. An' out here on the border it's the difference between a man an' somethin' not a man." (pp. 156 – 157)

Several important features — including the book's central irony — emerge from this confrontation in the middle of the narrative. For one thing, Jane begins to "see," and this, as with many mysteries and detective stories, marks the course of the story — a gradual unveiling of secrets and removal of "blinders." Bishop Dyer, for example, learns Lassiter's real purpose, revenge; Jane begins to glimpse the real nature of Dyer; and Lassiter reveals his love for Jane. As the plot works on, other secrets have their out, and the full Mormon connection — including Milly Erne Oldring and Bess — comes to light. As for Dyer, the episode also foreshadows his death when, according to Judkins who relates the event to Jane, the Bishop "stared horrible at somethin'" and that "whatever he seen, it was with the look of a man who *discovers* somethin' too late." (p. 293; Grey's italics)

An overlapping feature of this mid-novel confrontation has to do with hands. Dyer's efforts to control by an "invisible hand" become ironically visible as his own meaty members. Judkins' long report to Jane later spells out the details:

> "Wal, beggin' your pardon fer blunt talk, Miss Withersteen, Dyer was on his knees an' not prayin'. You remember his big, broad hands? You've seen 'em raised in blessin' over old gray men an' little curlyheaded children like — Fay Larkin! Come to think of that, I disremember ever hearin' of his liftin' his big hands in blessin' over a woman. Wal, when I seen him last — jest a little while ago — he was on his knees, not prayin', as I remarked — an' he was pressin' his big hands over some bigger wounds." (p. 289)

Four pages later Judkins nears the end of his tale and again recalls those hands (Lassiter has shot both hands and arms before killing Dyer): "He was gaspin' an' tryin' to press his big, floppin' crippled hands over his body. . . . An' then I seen Dyer look at his big hangin' hands that wasn't big enough for the last work he set them to do." (p. 293) Earlier, Venters tells Lassiter of wounding and then falling in love with Bess. It moves Lassiter to muse about life:

> "I'm reminded of somethin' you once said to Jane about hands in her game of life. There's that unseen hand of power, an' Tull's black hand, an' my red one, an' your indifferent one, an' the girl's little brown, helpless one. An', Venters, there's another one that's all-wise an' all-wonderful. That's the hand guidin' Jane Withersteen's game of life!" (p. 227)

Presumably, Lassiter's "all-wise" refers to God, but in fact his own "red" hand proves Jane's main guide, facing Dyer (again according to Judkins' account) while "his hands looked like a hawk's claws" (p. 291), then leading her in flight until the last moment when Jane takes her destiny in her own hands and orders bloody-handed Lassiter to roll the stone.

A third feature of the Dyer, Lassiter, and Jane meeting concerns the law. In addition to the earlier Mormon law and Lassiter's "woman's word," Jane now invokes "God's law" to justify her efforts to bind Lassiter's hands and thus "save human life." Lassiter sidesteps the "universal" character of this law, as Jane puts it, in view of the need for "snuffin' out Mormon life" — those who are "blacker than hell." He offers instead "a kind of moral law" which involves manhood and operates *on the border* (author's italics). This illustrates the critic's claim that the "symbolic landscape of the western formula is a field of action that centers upon the point of encounter between civilization and wilderness . . . settled society and lawless openness," an encounter whose resolution "almost invariably requires a transcendent and heroic violence" indicating that the contending forces "reflect strongly conflicting values." This, critics imply, is a built-in feature of westerns.[4]

The conflicting values show in the conflicting "laws." They show also in the action. What values? The injunction, "Thou shalt not kill," for example, opposed to the dictum, Thou shalt, for manhood and revenge. Or? Grey has wrinkles of his own. Lassiter tells Jane he has given up his purpose. "I can't help poor Milly. An' I've outgrowed revenge." (p. 280) A few pages later he has changed his mind:

> "You'll kill him — for yourself — for your vengeful hate?
>
> "No!"
>
> "For Milly Erne's sake?"
>
> "No!"
>
> "Oh — for whose?"
>
> "For *yours!*" (p. 285)

The killing takes place in court, with Judkins' boys on trial for "hatched-up things" while Dyer acts as magistrate and judge, "layin' down the law." The virile Lassiter, manhood intact, adjourns court with his "black guns."

The value at stake here is Jane. This in turn points to the narrative's central irony. Amidst the melange of laws, secrets, and hands — visible and invisible — one nearly overlooks a small Grey trope during the mid-novel exchanges. Lassiter wonders why Jane displays such "blind passion." In context he refers to her zeal to save Dyer's life. It has a broader, more ironic application in view of the Mormon abduction and seduction of Milly Erne, compounded by Jane's revelation that it was done for her own father. Grey's plot and language suggest that the real "field of action" (to use the critic's term) is an inner landscape, the frontier of the heart, and the real operative law — the "invisible hand" in control — is passion. Appropriately enough, the chief executive is Lassiter, who tells Jane, in that important middle section of the narrative, "I'm burnin' up with hell's fire." (p. 155) As with *The Border Legion,* or *Wildfire,* a story of obsession, passion lies at the root of action, recalling Alexander Pope's well-known couplet: "On life's vast ocean diversely we sail, Reason the card [tiller], but passion is the gale."[5]

2
The Code

As his first two popular successes — *Heritage* and *Riders* — show, Grey inserted into his "lawless" frontier contending embodiments of "law": God's, Mormon, moral, desert (or nature), U.S. Government, squatter's rights, revenge (eye for an eye), and "a woman's word," producing, in these two books at least, considerable irony. In other novels, forms of institutional law also appear — trials and lawsuits, for example — though more often than not corrupt. To take but one illustration, in *Valley of Wild Horses,* Panhandle Smith learns from his mother what has happened in his absence. The family bought a promising homestead and mining claim, she says, but "along comes Jard Harriman with claims, papers, witnesses, and law back of him. He claimed to have gotten possession of the homestead from the original owner. It was all a lie. But they put us off." (p. 65)

In the face of such lawlessness, the good western community develops its own internal form of law, the "Code of the West," to deal with the problem. For writers like Owen Wister, Grey, and Bret Harte, John Cawelti says, this "unwritten and extralegal" code became "a basic factor in the hero's identity and in the specific problems he confronts in the course of the story."[6] A protagonist from the West will instinctively know and act according to the code; an easterner will soon be set straight.

In 1926, Douglas Branch offered some general comments in his *The Cowboy and His Interpreters:*

> Owen Wister traced the code of the cowboy back to middle-English Chivalry; the cowboy was a knight-at-arms, the "Anglo-Saxon tradition" come to flower again. I have linked the cowboy with the Texas tradition, the code of personal dignity, personal liberty, personal honesty, of laconic speech and quick action, that was asserted in the Republic of Texas — a frontier that, by the very dangers it offered, attracted from the old states the blood of pioneers.[7]

Branch's delineation provides only marginal help. The repetitive "personal" adds little except to stress a kind of "rugged individualism" that Branch hints is peculiarly a trait of "the blood of pioneers." But it is one that cultural commentators often claim is a general American trait. As for "laconic speech and quick action," Grey protagonists are not especially prone to either. James Arness (Matt Dillon) of "Gunsmoke" fame and John Wayne in any number of films epitomize "laconic speech," but Milt Dale of *The Man of the Forest* argues volubly with Helen Rayner that "blood is stronger than brain" in a way that would do credit to D. H. Lawrence, though some of Grey's heroes are less talkative than Dale. And as for action, Grey's protagonists are often maddeningly slow to respond. But when that "action" is a quick gun, Grey's protagonists are quicker than quick.

Branch's "Texas tradition" has some relevance for Grey, however, for Texans in his narratives can usually be counted on to embody the "code," and the Texas Rangers represent a positive embodiment of the law. Quite a few Grey good characters — beginning with Lassiter of *Riders of the Purple Sage* — have served with the Rangers in the past. *Twin Sombreros* illustrates the "Texas connection"; Brazos Keene, himself a Texan, stumbles into trouble at the outset of the novel and finds himself in the hands of a posse bent on hanging him for a murder he didn't commit. Bodkin, the posse leader, presses to "finish the job right hyar," as he puts it, but finds one of his men, a Texan named Inskip, balking. Inskip refuses Bodkin's order to ride into town and report. When Bodkin gets a noose around Brazos' head, Inskip saves him by riding close, ostensibly to see if he has some last word for "mother or sweetheart":

> "Cowboy, do you want to tell me who you air an' send some message?"
>
> "I shore do. But I don't want this skunk to heah it."
>
> "Wal, you can tell me," returned Inskip, and pulled his horse toward Brazos.
>
> "Hyar, Inskip . . . *not so close!* shrieked Bodkin.
>
> The Texan leaned toward Brazos to whisper swift and low: "Grab my guns, but don't kill onless you have to."

Brazos grabs the guns and orders Bodkin and the posse to ride into town ahead of him. Once there, he turns his guns over to the sheriff, Kiskadden, also a Texan, who says he has to lock him up to await trial. Kiskadden wonders why Brazos doesn't seem concerned. Brazos answers. "Concern? Say, I'm tickled to death. What have I got to worry about now? You're a Texan and a man. You'll see through my part in this deal." (p. 22, 27)

These same Texans respect women. If the "middle-English Chivalry" attributed to Wister by Branch implies a special attitude toward women, Grey makes that part of his own "Texas tradition." At the outset of the appropriately (in this case) named *Knights of the Range,* badman Heaver rides up to Holly Ripple's ranch at the head of a gang; they intend to steal some horses, but Heaver's actions alienate new gang member Renn Frayne, especially when Heaver threatens to maul Holly. "I don't trail with your kind," Frayne says; "When chance threw Miss Ripple in your way, out bristled the dirty dog in you. You insulted her, pawed her off her horse. . . . You would have carried her off . . . leaving your men to fight this Texan." The Texan is Cap Britt, Holly's foreman, another former Texas Ranger. Frayne adds, "You'd have made your men accomplices in a crime that Westerners never forgive." (p. 34) Heaver has violated Frayne's idea of the code.

Grey's version amplifies when Uncle Jim Traft of *The Drift Fence* gives his young nephew, Jim, specific directions as to what he should do to confront his new job on the range:

> "I'd pack the gun an' begin to learn to shoot it. I'd have a little straight talk with the boys who was to work under me an' I'd let them know I was to be boss. I'd always do my share of any an' all kinds of work. I'd show a disposition not to give any boy a job I wouldn't try to tackle myself. I wouldn't be too nice to take a drink, on occasions where it might be wise, but I'd leave drink alone. Also — an' I hardly need to tell you this — I'd leave the town slatterns alone. I'd lend my money free, but never my hoss or saddle or spurs. I'd always stand the brunt of any trouble directed against my outfit . . . an' I'd make the others respect me." (p. 53)

Young Jim proves more than able, especially at "running the gauntlet"; his cowhands play all sorts of tricks on him and he takes them on one by one with his fists.

Elsewhere, Grey centers on a relatively few features of his code. Uncle Jim Traft's advice about packing a gun finds reinforcement in *Sunset Pass* when Trueman Rock ponders a dilemma. He has fallen in love with Thiry Preston and she wants him to avoid trouble with her bully of a brother, Ash. But Ash, used to taking what he wants, has just broken a cardinal western "rule"; he's taken Trueman's horse, Egypt, without asking.

> While pondering over how best to meet this situation and still be true to Thiry, he had buckled on his gun-belt. Suddenly the fact dawned on him, and he laid hard hands on the belt and buckle. But he got no farther. There was more here to be true to than Thiry Preston; there was the code of the West. He had no right to face this vicious unknown problem, Ash Preston, without being armed. (p. 143)

Love reigns supreme in Grey, but not at the expense of the Code. Here, Trueman — wearing his guns — escapes the horns of the dilemma by good-naturedly asking Ash if he likes the horse. This approach defuses the tension. At other times, when a heroine's wish to avoid violence clashes with the hero's need to use it, the heroine acquiesces. Jane Withersteen tries to take Lassiter's guns, but just after he wounds Bishop Dyer she confesses, "If I am blind — then — I need some one — a friend — you, Lassiter — more than ever!" (p. 157) Similarly, Marian Warner of *The Vanishing American* appeals to Nophaie not to shed blood and even holds his gun but "thrills" while he kicks his two enemies senseless.

Sooner or later the gun-toting ends in a shootout; if it's man-to-man, as it most often is, the Code's most famous rule applies. Once "called out," a man's reputation rests on his response. In *The Man of the Forest,* Texan Las Vegas goes on a one-man tear, first challenging the villain, Beasley: "That was where the West spoke. Beasley would be forced to meet the enemy who had come out single-handed against him. . . . Beasley could not hire any gang to bear the brunt of this situation. His was the test by which even his own men must judge him." Las Vegas stalks up and down a suitable time in what Grey says "had an importance in that pioneer day equal to the use of a horse or the need of a plow." Beasley fails to show, so Las Vegas shoots up the saloon and rides off with a yell:

> Men running to door and windows of the store saw a streak of dust flying down the road. . . . The hour of suspense ended for them. Las Vegas had lived up to the code of the West, had dared his man out, had waited far longer than needful to prove that man a coward. Whatever the issue now, Beasley was branded forever. (pp. 361 – 363)

The western "sinner" against the Code carries his own scarlet letter. In a similar case, Brazos Keene (another Texan) calls out Raine Surface: "'Aw, go for yore gun,' snorted Brazos, contemptuously. Not about to comply, Surface argues, only to hear Brazos say, 'Yu're not even Western, Surface. Yu don't belong oot heah.'" Surface lunges away, having "sense enough to see that he was impotent in the Western creed of man to man." (p. 146)

For Grey, this sort of challenge often involves a woman. In *Western Union,* Texan Vance Shaw calls out badman Slade, who has made a "dirty crack about Ruby," a dance-hall girl (with heart of gold). The eastern narrator, Wayne Cameron, and his pard, Tom, have just taken Vance's challenge into Slade in the saloon. Outside again, Wayne sees Vance. "There's Shaw in the middle of the road. What's he doing there?" Wayne asks. Tom says, "Wal, 'cordin' to the rules of the gun game, he'll walk up an' down until Slade comes out." (p. 104) When Wade Holden of *Shadow on the Trail* rides up to the Pencarrow ranch, he witnesses a confrontation in which one of minor villain Urba's lieutenants says, "Aw,

Urb, ain't she a pippin'? Look at them eyes. An' them heavin' breasts." Wade's look spells out the Code, namely, that "the speech, the burning glance of that lewd-eyed ruffian had sealed his death warrant." Moments later Wade bores him then challenges Urba. Urba panics but has "enough manhood left to draw his gun" and also ends up dead. (pp. 110 – 112)

In one novel, Grey raises a question about this practice. What Lassiter calls a "kind of moral law" in *Riders of the Purple Sage* proves not so moral to Holly Ripple's western friend, Ann, in *Knights of the Range*. Ann explains about the Code:

> "If one man is called out by another — to fight — whether it's justifiable or not, he must go or be branded a coward?"
>
> "That's it, Holly. An' it's unfair, to my thinkin'. Because a bad man can force a good one to meet him. The moral of it doesn't seem to be considered. Every man has to defend himself with a gun, an' if he can't he just doesn't belong to the West. Thet applies to all plain Westerners. But it shore applies more to them who have killed others. It's a kind of hideous curiosity. On the part of the fighters to see who can draw quickest! On the part of the crowd to see who gets killed first!" (p. 279)

If Grey muddies the morality here, showing a seamier side of the Code, his central point stays clear: the gun remains a necessity. Unfortunately, this violence proves self-propagating, as Ann indicates and Grey notes again and again; a gunman having once killed may be challenged by all sorts of those "hideous curiosity" seekers.

Communally acknowledged, the Code nevertheless focuses on individual accomplishment. "The West stirs something in a man," Glenn tells Carley Burch in *The Call of the Canyon*. "It must be an unwritten law. You stand or fall by your own hands." (p. 95) When Andrew Bonning asks Bligh for a job in Wyoming, the rancher likes the young man's "level open glance" and "straight" talk. "Bonning," he says, "we cattlemen often hire men without names or homes or pasts. What counts here is what you are — what you can do." (p. 54)

If a man answers the challenge and otherwise lives up to the rules as suggested by Uncle Jim Traft, he will earn the "respect of his associates," which Mother Wood tells Nevada (*Nevada*) is a must. (p. 39) *Robbers' Roost* also illustrates. At the climactic shootout, Jim Wall thinks of the dead gunman, Smoky, "lion-hearted, going out to save his comrades because he felt he alone could do it. . . . That was his creed toward men." (p. 214) That same creed demands fair play. Earlier, Jim ponders what to do about foreman Hays, an outlaw he suspects plans to kidnap Helen Herrick, the ranch owner's sister. "But how could he kill his leader upon mere suspicion of sinister intent to kidnap the girl? It was a damnable predicament for a man who had always played fair, alike to honest friend and crooked ally." (p. 100) Later, Jim again deliberates; this time he thinks of killing Hays. He sees him at a distance, and "survival of the fittest" enters his mind, and yet inside Jim has "a creed born of the frontier. It was what Hank Hays had lived by before he threw everything to the winds for the beauty of a woman." Hank has gone out to bear the brunt of Heeseman's attack, expecting to die. In view of this, Jim refuses to shoot at long range. "Not even for the girl's sake would Jim force himself to such a deed, however justified by Hays' villainy." (p. 199) Interestingly, this contradicts a desert "law," the heritage learned by John Hare in *Heritage of the Desert* to "strike first and hard." But then Hare doesn't strike first either, he retaliates. "Survival of the fittest" here proves mostly window dressing; Grey tosses in the phrase, but the reader knows the hero will survive, even though he hesitates. The shootout illustrates; almost always the hero, with code-like nobility, waits until the opponent draws or at least makes a move. He sometimes ends up wounded (with Grey, most often a clean hole below the collar bone in the fleshy part of the shoulder) as he bores his rival.

At other times, the Code calls for no hesitation. In *Raiders of Spanish Peaks* Laramie watches Lonesome and three others efficiently haul on the rope that strangles outlaw Price. Afterward, the men suffer emotionally for the deed but are bolstered by the Code. "The day with its sustained suspense and final tragedy had worked its deadly havoc among the riders. . . . The creed of the range kept such men justified in their own minds; nevertheless, the dealing of death visited upon each its icy touch." Laramie recalls other "lynching bees" he's attended, ropes pulled for both horse thieves and rustlers, as he observes the hanging. "It was a common practice, inaugurated, he remembered, in order to intimidate cowpunchers going wrong. Not greatly had it succeeded." (pp. 286, 306)

In Laramie's mind, the lynching feature of the Code seems ineffective, but another feature, concerning the behavior of women, seems to work, at least in the few novels where flirting is an issue; the women come around in any case, and accede to western ways. Chief example is *Code of the West,* which, despite its title, proves disappointing as a source of insight about Grey's Code except for its indictment of the flapper-like "propensity to flirt" of Georgiana Stockwell.

> Her attractiveness and her newness made this propensity to flirt a vastly more serious matter than if she had not brought the Eastern immodesty of dress, freedom of speech, unrestraint of action, and the fatal fascination of a possible attainableness. For Miss Stockwell had to realize that this sort of thing would not do in the West. The Code of these clean, fine, young men of the Tonto would not long abide Georgiana. (p. 70)

The "fatal fascination" hints at violence or even bloodshed, a possibility underscored by Georgiana's sister Mary who lectures her about the "ruthless" men and the "risk" of breaking their code. (p. 78) But just what would these code-ridden but "ruthless" men — otherwise so chivalric — do? The "risk," apparently, is the danger of being treated like a prostitute and possibly raped, but one should not look to Grey for consistency, especially in this relatively light-hearted western variant of *The Taming of the Shrew,* with its caveman-like marriage and comic figure of Tuck Merry.

A not-so-comic example of the Code in action appears near the end of *The Light of Western Stars.* Crooked sheriff Hawe and his equally crooked deputies come to arrest Gene Stewart on Madeline Hammond's ranch. Accusations fly, including slurs on Madeline's character. The latter so outrage Stewart that he has to be restrained. At this point, old-timer cowboy Monty Price leaps from the ranch house porch and takes over, "terrible in his mood of wild justice," as Madeline views it. Monty confronts the corrupt Hawe and deputy Sneed, tells them off in a passionate speech, and then calls them out, loyal to the Code in giving them a fair chance. "Flash your guns! Throw 'em, an' be quick! Monty Price is done! There'll be daylight through you both before you fan a hammer!" he says, "But I'm givin' you a chanst to sting me. You holler law, an' my way is the ole law." The three men die in the shoot-out. (pp. 317 – 319)

3
The Outlaw

Grey's badmen subvert the law; they generally disregard, circumvent, or — as in *The Light of Western Stars* — if it is available in the person of a crooked sheriff or judge, use it. A critic puts the case:

> To understand the equivocal nature of the outlaw figure, one must look at the actions and characteristics which define the typical criminal: he attempts to achieve the power and status of the "best man" without engaging in direct individual competition; he steals property in the

> dead of night or with the aid of corrupt legal institutions; he shoots people *in the back* and he relies on the collective strength of a group of followers. In other words, he attempts to subvert the code of the West, of individualistic competition.[8]

As might be expected from Grey's fifty-six novel output, a reader finds quite a gallery of outlaw types. They range from Mormons and Mexicans to missionaries and the I.W.W. They include gangs, gunslingers, bad fathers and bad sons. In *Heritage of the Desert* Grey explored the phenomenon of Mormon settlement. With August Naab he created a powerful figure, a man with great strengths but also weakness. His son Snap, however, is a thoroughly rotten apple who joins with a gang. But in *Riders of the Purple Sage* Grey pulls out all the stops, and Bishop Dyer smacks of the villains of gothic melodrama. Grey's Mormons here are lecherous, murderous tyrants. In *Desert Gold,* his third western success, Grey took advantage of contemporary history and cast as chief villain what W. H. Hutchinson calls the *hombre del pais,* "the Mexican or anyone with swarthy skin, flashing teeth, and silver-studded costume."[9] Hero Gale's first glimpse of the "greaser" (Grey's characters repeatedly use the term), Rojas, is of "a handsome, bold, sneering face, with glittering dark eyes that flashed in sinister intentness." When Rojas and his gang show up later, the bandit appears dandily, "a gaudy, almost a dashing figure" with white sombrero, crimson scarf, and velvet jacket. (pp. 30, 151)[10] Grey elaborated this figure even further in his next novel, *The Light of Western Stars.* (see p. 129)

Grey moved on to other types. He has individual gamblers and gunslingers, but they usually play minor roles, the latter often as gang adjuncts brought in to gun down the hero. *Twin Sombreros* features an intriguing variant, a threesome, one of whom is Bess Moore who tries to seduce Brazos Keene but falls for him in the process. In a shootout, Brazos kills Orcutt and Syvertsen, then has to shoot Bess, too, when she draws. He gets the truth from the dying woman: "We were called here to put Allen out of the way. I got him to drink — coaxed him to ride out of town with me. . . . As he lay on the ground Bard shot him — in the back." (p. 154)

Gangs remain the rule for major villains — roving gangs like the titular groups of *The Border Legion* and *The Hash Knife Outfit,* or "ranch hands" of a rich cattleman masquerading as a decent citizen, like the thugs of Cheseldine, arch-criminal of *The Lone Star Ranger*. In either case, overt or covert, the gang leader is the villainous power behind the outlawry. In *The Desert of Wheat,* written at the close of World War I, Grey drew bead on the I.W.W. and foreign provacateurs and, in later works like *Majesty's Rancho* and *Boulder Dam,* probably influenced by the popular hard-boiled detective story, even introduced mobsters. In *Majesty's Rancho,* Honey Bee Uhl tries to rustle cattle with trucks, but falls victim to hero Lance Sidway's ruse to get him to escape to the hills on horseback. Grey spoofs the city mobster's inability to cope with a real westerner on western terrain.

More significant than the mere array of types, however, Grey's treatment of villains often creates considerable irony. Among the assorted badmen are bad fathers, bad sons, and bad husbands. Since in every case they involve the heroine and a love interest, they pose dilemmas for the male protagonists, mainly as rivals, as with Jack Bellounds of *The Mysterious Rider,* Ash Preston of *Sunset Pass,* and Snap Naab of *Heritage of the Desert* (sons), or John Belmont of *Black Mesa* and Wilbur Newton of *Captives of the Desert* (husbands). Grey resolves the dilemma in each case by killing off the rival. The bad fathers create different sorts of problems, especially in the effect of criminal deeds on family or heroine. Grey solves this sort of problem in *The Shepherd of Guadaloupe* by death; in the climactic scene, as Virginia Lundeen struggles with the villain, Malpass, her father rushes on scene, and in a bloody fight he and Malpass kill each other. Lundeen has admitted to Virginia that he cheated Clay Forrest, father of the hero (and now Virginia's husband), out of his land.

For Lundeen, the clash — Malpass shoots him repeatedly; he in turn breaks Malpass' arm, then his neck, and drops him from a trestle onto rocks a hundred feet below — serves as redemptive violence; he ostensibly atones for his evil deeds.

Other fathers survive, but in doing so create ambiguity around the notions of law and justice. Avil Bonesteel of *Stranger from the Tonto* leads a double and hypocritical life: as Bonesteel, head of the notorious Hole in the Wall gang, and as Cheney, a respectable Utah rancher "hell on rustlers," a gang member says. He has raised daughter Lucy in the secret hideout. Bonesteel sides with hero Kent Wingfield in the book's climax, an intragang shootout, after arranging for Kent and Lucy to escape through a hidden passage. Only slightly wounded, Bonesteel makes Kent promise to let Lucy believe he is dead. In a metaphoric sense, in his role as Bonesteel he is dead. After the lovers escape, Kent breaks his promise and explains to Lucy: "An' secondly, it was indeed the end of Bonesteel. If he were killed, well and good. If not he'd bury the name in his Hole in the Wall, an' take up that other identity — that of the respectable Cheney." To Lucy's question, "Then there is another woman?" Kent replies, "Yes, an' that is well." He adds a gratuitous bit of plea-bargaining: "Lucy, I'll say Bonesteel was great in his wicked career. God only knows what drove him to it. An' he will be greater in this newer, better life." (p. 216) As sentiment, readers may or may not find this palatable; Kent wants to put a good light on Lucy's father for her sake. But as rationale for criminal and immoral conduct it undermines the notions of justice and accountability. Bonesteel gets off with only a slight hand wound after being, according to Bill Elway in the novel's opening pages, leader of "the wildest robber gang ever known in the West." (p. 18) Ironically too, Kent suggests Bonesteel was driven to this "great" and "wicked" career, a passive notion that projects responsibility elsewhere. And in what sense "great?" And how "even greater" in his new — or renewed, since he evidently had not abandoned it — life? Grey's prose shatters logic here and renders justice problematic.[11]

The dilemma for Trueman Rock of *Sunset Pass* is twofold; he must cope with the tyrannical Ash Preston, brother of Thiry, and then find a way to save Gage Preston, Thiry's father, who along with his sons has been butchering stolen cattle. The senior Preston accounts for the strange rivalry of Ash at novel's end; Ash turns out to be the illegitimate son of an old girlfriend of Preston's given to him to raise, and thus not Thiry's brother. Trueman kills Ash in a bloody shootout, but wants to save the repentant Gage. Earlier, he makes a deal with the local cattlemen in power. He explains it to Preston:

> "You're goin' to square it all. . . . Listen. Come to town with me. I've got it all fixed. Dabb will call a meetin' of the Cattle Association council. That means him, Lincoln, and Hesbitt. To keep this out of court you will agree to pay Hesbitt for his Half Moon stock. Dabb and Lincoln have promised me they'll handle Hesbitt. It will all be done in secret. Then you and your sons who were in this deal must leave the country." (p. 312)

In addition, for $2500 of his own savings Trueman has earlier bought off an adjoining small rancher, Slagle, who has proof of Preston's illegal operation. "I love Thiry Preston and I'm goin' to save her dad because of that," Trueman tells Slagle. (p. 305) He reports this too to Preston: "I've shut Slagle's mouth. I've bought his silence. He's leavin' the range." (p. 312) The upshot is that father and three sons leave as agreed. The steer market has meanwhile jumped and, as the doctor tells the injured Trueman, the cattlemen have bought Preston out so that though it "cost Preston somethin' big to square up," he goes away "heeled." (p. 339) Reasons for their leniency, cattlemen Dabb and Lincoln say, are that Preston will make restitution, Preston's good wife and innocent children (excluding the involved sons) will be spared, and the offenders will leave the area. When Trueman thanks them and says, "Preston doesn't deserve this. Sure it's generous," Lincoln replies candidly, "We shore can afford to be generous because Preston hasn't stole from us. Then we don't want the range slandered by such a raw case." (p. 302)

Family and willingness to settle damages are the main mitigating circumstances for Preston. But do these justify the outcome, getting away free and with a sizeable bank account? Sentiment might have it so, but Grey's series of narrative events riddles the concept of justice with ambiguity and contradiction, raising the fear that the law is too often arbitrary, and slanted toward the rich and powerful. For one thing, the deal is made in secret by prejudiced parties with something to gain. Trueman makes his motive plain; he loves Thiry. Dabb and Lincoln want to suppress scandal (it's not clear why), perhaps enjoy the exercise of power within the cattlemen's group and sense of being charitable toward the family (conjectures on my part, but suggested by narrative events), and, reasonably enough, settle a troublesome case of criminal activity.

The secrecy part involves buying off a witness, Slagle, and "handling" Hesbitt, owner of the Half Moon ranch and chief victim of the rustling. As Dabb and Lincoln admit, *they* can afford to be generous; others have to be persuaded or bought off. Thus the potential lawsuit is settled out of court (the "court" hovers offstage as a possibility) in an action which suggests that influential friends, vested interests, and money can determine the meaning of justice, a conclusion reinforced when Thiry visits the recuperating Trueman at novel's end and says, "I was to learn how you had bought Slagle's silence — how you persuaded Dabb and Lincoln to *force* Hesbitt to settle out of court." (p. 349, emphasis added) In view of this subversion, engineered by the solidly named hero, Trueman Rock, Sol Winters' words to the lovers in the book's closing sentences — for anyone wanting to read beyond escape fantasy — can only be ironic. Winters looks in on the embracing couple, beams, and says, "We Westerners are a hard pioneerin' outfit. I see in you, an Allie, an' some more of our young friends, a leanin' more to finer, better things." (p. 349)

Buck Duane's dealing with Cheseldine/Longstreth, arch-criminal of *The Lone Star Ranger,* also calls in question this "finer, better" outlook. According to Ranger captain MacNelly, who hires Duane to hunt Cheseldine down, he's "the strongest, the worst outlaw of the times. He's more than rustler. It's Cheseldine and his gang who are operating on the banks." (p. 135) In the mind of Colonel Webb, a man Duane meets while on Cheseldine's trail, "Blood flowed like water over the Big Bend country, and it was Cheseldine who spilled it." (p. 149) Duane finally corners this outlaw and his henchman, Lawson. In the shootout, Duane kills Lawson, but Cheseldine seizes the dead man for a shield and wounds Duane, shooting until his gun clicks empty. Gaining control, Duane then gives his ultimatum:

> "The game's up. You're done. But think of your daughter! I'll spare your life — I'll try to get you freedom on one condition. For her sake! I've got you nailed — all the proofs. . . . Consent to demands, and I'll spare you. Maybe I can persuade MacNelly to let you go free back to your old country. It's for Ray's sake. (p. 226)

In some respects, Cheseldine's situation resembles Gage Preston's in *Sunset Pass;* as Cheseldine explains to his daughter, Ray, "I'm to divide my property — return so far as possible what I've stolen — leave Texas at once with Duane, under arrest. He says maybe he can get MacNelly, the Ranger captain, to let me go. For your sake!" (p. 227)

Mitigating circumstances? An attempt at restitution. Critic Hamilton offers the odd claim that "Duane must admire Chesaldine's [*sic*] ambition, competence, and impressive success, praiseworthy traits in the American ideology."[12] Grey's cowboys sometimes envision ranches, big ones, but nothing in *The Lone Star Ranger* supports the gratuitous claim that "Duane must admire Chesaldine." Hamilton adds, "In so far as outlaws such as Chesaldine demonstrate an ability to operate with the code of the West, their villainy is mitigated." Cheseldine, she says, "is also accused of using the law, but the weakness this implies is contra-indicated by his willingness to confront Duane man to man." Not so. The most mitigating factor is the critic's prose. For one thing, quite a few of Grey's villains are willing, even eager to confront the hero man to man, but get bored for their zeal. Second, Cheseldine's "weakness" concerning the law is actually outright perversion; as self-appointed judge of his town, he manipulates justice to his own corrupt ends, as Laramie testifies earlier. (p. 172) Third, the "Code" also includes fairness, and Cheseldine's manipulations prove him anything but fair (and does he "operate within the code" by keeping, say, commandment number two, but violating number six?). Finally, the narrative shows him to be a murderer and a hirer of murderers. Hamilton *is* right in suggesting that the story results in moral ambiguity, but her conclusion that in westerns generally "the law which is restored is not legalistic; it is the law of the survival of the fittest as determined by the rituals of individual competition" inadequately describes what happens in *The Lone Star Ranger, Sunset Pass,* and others among Grey's books.

To continue with the former, Buck Duane acts out of self-interest (his love for Ray) as he admits; but he is also an officer of the law, a secretly commissioned Texas Ranger. In this respect *The Lone Star Ranger* represents a *locus classicus* for embodiments of what passes for "law": sheriffs, judges, vigilantes, Texas Rangers, and avenging heroes. All appear in the narrative; all cast shadows on the notion of justice.

Grey further muddies the notion of law by Duane's rationalization to Ray; the passage merits full quotation:

> "Then the line between a rustler and a rancher is hard to draw in these wild border days. Rustling is stealing cattle, and I once heard a well-known rancher say that all rich cattlemen had done a little stealing. Your father drifted out here, and, like a good many others, he suc-

> ceeded. It's perhaps just as well not to split hairs, to judge him by the law and morality of a civilized country. Some way or other he drifted in with bad men. Maybe a deal that was honest somehow tied his hands. This matter of land, water, a few stray head of stock, had to be decided out of court. I'm sure in his case he never realized where he was drifting. Then one thing led to another, until he was face to face with dealing that took on crooked form. To protect himself he bound men to him. And so the gang developed. Many powerful gangs have developed that way out here. He could not control them. He became involved with them. And eventually their dealings became deliberately and boldly dishonest. That meant the inevitable spilling of blood sooner or later, and so he grew into the leader because he was the strongest. Whatever he is to be judged for, I think he could have been infinitely worse." (pp. 227 – 228)

It's hard to see how Cheseldine could have been "infinitely worse." Even after allowances for the prejudiced view of a love-struck cowboy, one has to acknowledge that Duane's argument here is full of flawed assumptions, nonsequiters, and evasions. One of the gray areas (the notion that everybody steals a little) occurs quite a number of times in Grey in relation to cattle. This is small comfort to victims, to say nothing of anyone interested in justice. As for "splitting hairs," if not to judge by "the law and morality of a civilized country," then by what? By the Code, perhaps, but Cheseldine violates that too. Duane's argument undercuts the need for any Texas Rangers. The remainder of his rationalization, with its "some way or other," "drifted," "somehow," "took on crooked form," "could not control," "became involved," "inevitable," and "grew into the leader" all serve to distance Cheseldine from any real responsibility. Logically speaking, the speech is nonsense; it adds to the ambiguity and irony surrounding the concept of law in *The Lone Star Ranger*.

There are other ironies and ambiguities in Grey's treatment of the notion of law and justice. One of the few to have even begun to examine Grey in this connection is critic Hamilton. She argues that outlaws reflect American economic processes: "gold fever occurs when the desire for gain no longer recognizes any restraint or sense of proportion." Such "aberrations" find encouragement in "the value structure of the American Dream." She cites Alder Creek, the gold city hell of *The Border Legion,* as an American melting-pot where people have gathered not for freedom, but to lust after gold.[13] These ideas accord with some of Richard Slotkin's; in short, American capitalism, operating on competitive individualism in a Darwinian dog-eat-dog free market, runs amok. People regress to a savage state. If this is so, if read on one level from this point of view Grey's outlaws portray competitive individualism gone mad, and if, as Hamilton implies, competitive individualism also drives the hero, then a picture emerges of a system which generates excesses (an Alder Creek or a Cheseldine) of violence and finds the corrective in more violence in the protagonist's fast guns.[14]

But in Grey's version the excess at least contributes to its own demise. Interestingly, Grey's corporate raiders usually self-destruct in part. His heroes dispose of quite a few notorious gunmen, but the chief villains and their gangs usually begin to disintegrate before the final confrontation of hero and outlaw leader, as *The Border Legion, The Thundering Herd, Robbers' Roost, The Hash Knife Outfit, Stranger from the Tonto,* and others indicate. Sometimes, as in *The Drift Fence,* the inner gang strife enables the hero to survive. Perhaps Grey shared with many of his contemporaries a fear of bigness — trusts, monopolies, and power centers — much as some of us today distrust conglomerates, corporate raiders, leveraged buyouts, operations we fear may be out of control.[15] Perhaps again, conversely, the failure of the gang-group suggests the positive virtues of individualism. In any case, the fact that nearly all of Grey's outlaw gangs crumble from within hints at yet another ambiguity, a self-destruct principle that operates almost as a "law."

That principle arises from passions, a feature that historian Partricia Nelson Limerick corroborates in *The Legacy of Conquest,* a study of "The Unbroken Past of the American West." Until "attachment to property and attraction to profit find their proper category as a variety of strong emotion," she writes, neither "Western past nor the Western present will make sense." Underscoring her point, she adds on the next page, that "passion for profit was and is a passion like most others."[16] For Grey, the attitudes of the outlaws toward women illustrate. Strife within the gang or partnership usually erupts over a woman. Twin lusts drive Grey's outlaws: sexual desire and/or greed (gold, money, cattle, land). The villain usually wants both the girl and the other assets, though if there's ever a question, when the stakes are on the table — as Gulden in *The Border Legion* illustrates — he'll take the girl. This close link between passion and profit, sex and capital gains, has implications for American socioeconomic mores; the unstated bottom line is rape, and it supports and offers another perspective on the titular thrust of Annette Kolodny's *The Lay of the Land.*[17]

The line in *Wildfire* cited earlier, describes the outlaw Cordts' passion for the horse Sage King as that "of a man for an unattainable woman." The link between sexual desire and material gain is seldom as crassly put, but is implicit in all the novels where a villain abducts the heroine. Grey's badmen steal women as often as horses and cattle. They're apt to treat them accordingly: "All cowboys were violent and rude at times, but this one was a man with a cruel hand as masterful and relentless as if she were a horse." Jocelyn, bad apple of *The Drift Fence,* has just seized Molly Dunn. (p. 128) The link between molestation and money occurs immediately: "I'm goin' to have you. An' you'll marry me as soon as I make the stake we — I'm figgerin' on." (p. 128) The "stake" refers to more villainy, his scheme for kidnapping, ransom, and murder; his slip — "we" — hints at his plan to betray the Cibeque gang.

Other novels offer variants. In *Desert Gold* another lay of the land threatens in the persons of Ben Chase and son, Radford. Belding tells Chase off: "You're one of the land and water hogs that has come to root in the West. You're like the timber sharks — take it all and leave none for those who follow." (p. 199) The Chases temporarily prevail. "Business is business. In business, the best man wins," Chase says."The law upheld those transactions of mine, the honesty of which you questioned. As to mining and water claims, you lost on this technical point — that you had nothing to prove you had held them for five years." (p. 250) But Radford's desire for Nell ultimately upsets their takeover triumph, the libido proving efficacious where the law fails.

The aptly named Malpass, villain of *The Shepherd of Guadaloupe,* further suggests the competitive drive run amok. Though he has long cruel Mexican spurs, shiny high-top boots, an olive tan face, and sleek black hair so that he personifies a "modern Western dandy," he scarcely shows the Spanish descent rumor attributes to him: "In his speech there was no hint of the foreigner; in fact he gave the impression of a keen and successful American between thirty and forty." Malpass has keenly and successfully swindled Virginia Lundeen's father by the scam of a "planted" mine. But Lundeen himself also carries guilt to the grave. Early in the story he admits to Virginia how he dispossessed Clifton's father of his land. When Virginia questions the deal's honesty, Lundeen says, "Wal, it was business, an' that's pretty sharp these days. Clay Forrest an' I clinched from the time we came heah from Georgia." Further talk convinces Virginia. "Father, it was crooked," she says. He replies, indicating the bestial level of competition: "Wal, it always was dog eat dog with me an' Forrest. An' I won't split hairs over it, arguin' with you." (p. 57) Not any more than Texas Ranger Buck Duane will over Cheseldine's dealings.

The climax of *The Shepherd of Guadaloupe* takes place at the phony mine. Virginia, suspecting the truth, brings a mining engineer, Jarvis, who proves the mine a fraud. While he is off pressing his investigation, Malpass arrives and mauls Virginia. Jarvis returns only to be shot by Malpass who then turns to the heroine:

> "Merciful God! . . . Would you — murder me, too?"
> "I'll do worse unless you swear you'll hide what's happened here."
> "Worse!" she echoed, and live fire seemed to touch her every raw nerve.
> "You know what I mean," he rejoined, thick with passion, as she tore his tight collar loose from a black bulging neck.
> Virginia understood him. The man stood revealed in all his monstrous baseness. (p. 229)

The "revelation" obviously is double: both his sexual and economic pretenses. Virginia's father arrives in time to save her, and business as usual is over for both him and Malpass; they kill each other. Ironically, Virginia makes a killing of her own — a huge profit in sheep futures.

But Grey nowhere so explicitly suggests the sex and business linkage as in his story of the Maverick Queen. The posthumously published "complete, unexpurgated story of *The Maverick Queen,*" boasts — for Grey — several unique features.[18] Drawing on the real-life Ella Watson, also known as Kate Averill and Kate Maxwell and frequently referred to as "Cattle Kate," Grey created his beautiful and almost irresistible Kit Bandon, "The Maverick Queen," who, like her historical counterpart, allegedly barters sexual favors for stolen cattle and is finally hanged by vigilantes.[19] Though hangings occur frequently in Grey's works, only here does a woman pay that price. Kit Bandon herself proves unique as well; none other of Grey's protagonists is so sexually and overtly aggressive. "I guess the Lord busted His mold when he made Kit Bandon," pard Mel Thatcher says to hero Linc Bradway at novel's end. (p. 294) Well, Grey did at any rate. Again, Grey features here his lone example of a range war between ranchers and cowboys.

The Maverick Queen also emerges as Grey's most detective-like narrative. The "detective," cowboy Linc Bradway, learns of the murder of his former friend Jimmy Weston, and comes to South Pass, Wyoming, with a two-fold motive: to clear his pard's name (Weston was allegedly shot for cheating at cards) and avenge the murder. In one of the novel's three main plot threads, Linc questions nearly everyone he meets — his landlady, a merchant, a stage driver, a rancher, four Mormon cowhands working for Kit, a teamster, and others — gradually gains information, and becomes convinced that Jimmy Weston's death ties in with Kit somehow. During his quest to find the guilty party, Linc, like many detectives, encounters people — including those closest to him — who withhold information. He only learns the truth and the murderer at the end when Kit tells him what really happened.

A love triangle marks the second major plot strand, as the Maverick Queen and her eighteen-year-old niece, Lucy, both fall for the hero. Early in the narrative Linc re-reads letters Jimmy Weston sent him before his death. The fifth one is especially poignant for Linc:

> "This dam black-eyed female I lost my haid over has queered me with Lucy. Honest, pard Linc, I didn't mean to be that yellow. But you know what likker does to me an' this woman made me forget all the decency I ever knew. I'll get even with her. I'll be as yellow to her as she made me be to the kid. . . ." (p. 24)

He realizes Kit's niece was Jimmy's girl and knows he must meet her to inquire about the murder. He meets the Maverick Queen first, though, by entering the "Leave It" saloon where Jimmy was allegedly shot.[20] He boldly sits in a poker game with the appealing Kit, saloon-owner-villain (and Kit's partner) Emery, rancher Lee, Emery's gunsel McKeever, and two others. Linc wins big, trades insults with Emery, and ends up wounding McKeever and showing up Emery. Kit finds the handsome Linc exciting and begins her attack to win him, but Linc soon meets Lucy and the triangle proves no contest. Linc and Lucy fall in love at first sight, and at mid-novel, after Linc follows Kit and Lucy to the town of Rock Springs where Kit plans a cattle deal, Linc spirits Lucy to a minister for a secret, five-minute wedding while Kit negotiates. Kit doesn't learn of this "treachery" until much later when she catches the newlyweds embracing in the idyllic valley Lucy has long wanted for her future home. Hell hath no fury . . . but Linc wrests a gun away from Kit and averts a tragedy.

These two plot strands — detective quest and romance — intertwine with a third, an impending showdown between ranchers and cowboys due, it turns out, to the widespread rustling of mavericks that the cowboys secretly "sell" to Kit Bandon. When Linc suspects the connections, he snoops around Kit's ranch, learns where cowboys quickly brand the mavericks they steal, and observes two of them bringing in calves at night. Meanwhile, Kit, in love with Linc and planning to sell her ranch and move away with him, has renounced her past and turns down the two cowboys. Linc disguises his voice and pretends to be a rustler himself, just to make sure, then reveals who he is.

All but Lucy gather at the novel's climax. Linc and Mel Thatcher, one of two pards he has befriended, hear that the angry cattlemen are out to get Kit and Emery. They ride out, hide, and spy as rancher Lee — rejected suitor of Kit — heads a cattlemen's masked vigilante group ready to hang the victims. Just then a rival cowboy group rides up; Linc recognizes the leader as his other partner, Vince. The cowboys lynch Emery, who has won a temporary freedom by accusing Kit. Then Lee moves to hang Kit, but Vince kills the rancher and is in turn riddled by Lee's group. Linc expects to see a return volley from the cowboys, but it doesn't come. Instead, he looks up to see Kit's body "slowly turning" under a swaying bench. In this *Hamlet*-like scene, where Grey litters the Wyoming stage with corpses, there is no redemptive hope voiced, no suggestion that the Wyoming Sweetwater country has been sweetened, only a gloomy conclusion by the watching hero. As he sees the cowboys take Vince's body away,

Linc sums up the results in his mind: "The range war was over. Vince was dead. Lee was dead. Kit Bandon was dead. Emery was dead. And Jimmy Weston was dead. They were all dead and nothing was settled." (p. 293)

As with *Heritage of the Desert* and *Riders of the Purple Sage, The Maverick Queen* shows various laws operating on a purportedy lawless frontier. On arriving, Linc looks around and quickly sees "that law and order had not yet come to South Pass." (p. 6) Later, he wonders "what would be the legal status of the case if Kit Bandon were really inducing cowboys to steal mavericks from the ranchers and sell them to her?" But then he realizes "there could not be any legal status on a new range where there was no law." (p. 112) Still later, pard Vince concurs but adds a confusing note: "on this Wyomin' border where there ain't no law or morality. . . . I jest cain't believe that even a woman, beautiful as she is, can go on forever makin' fools of men an' bein' a law onto herself." (p. 174) She can't, at least in Grey's narrative. At the end Linc sees "the law of the range once more being fulfilled." (p. 286) This "law" prevails over Kit's willfulness ("law unto herself"), though delayed by that other, internal "law," the Code of the West. Both Linc and the ranchers bump against it: "the code of most cowboys, gallant and sentimental, perhaps, but one to which they all adhered, never by word or deed to say or do anything that could be detrimental to a woman." (p. 178) Linc tries to stop the execution by appealing to the ranchers on behalf of the same womanhood: "You can't hang a woman," and adds that they'll regret the violence and that guilty or not, "hanging her is not the answer." (p. 290) He convinces two ranchers, one of whom says, uselessly, that they should "turn her over to the law," but the vigilante leader remains determined to execute.

In an attempt to make some sense of this melange of conflicting laws and lawlessness, one approach is to go beyond it to the question of motive. Linc ponders the appropriate questions: "What was this vigilante band of cattlemen really aiming to accomplish? To stop the rustling? Or was it something else? (p. 178) According to Kit it is revenge. "You knew about me from the beginning," she accuses the ranchers' leader, Lee, "but you kept it quiet because you wanted me all for yourself. And then when I refused you, you wanted your vengeance." (p. 291) In fact, revenge motivates much of the book's action: like rancher Lee, cowboy Jimmy Weston attempts to get even and is killed; "It was Emery who killed him," Kit finally confesses to Linc, "Weston was in love with me — wanted me to give it all up and go away with him. When I refused, he threatened to expose Emery and me." (p. 291) Cowboy Harkness also takes revenge. The ranchers whip him to try to extract proof against Kit; furious, he bursts into the "Leave It" and guns down ranchers Hargrove and Nesbitt, Emery's man Bannister, and wounds Emery. Linc Bradway himself, of course, has come to South Pass to avenge Jimmy Weston's murder.

The ranchers' determination to get Kit — and the cowboys' equally determined silence — may have a more covert motive in resentment over the commercialization of their manhood, that is, cattle for sexual favors. Even the cowboy's allegedly "merciful bullet" to end the hanging and the suffering of the nightdress-clad Maverick Queen could symbolically hint at the same resentment. "She's nothing but a low-down whore," Emery charges, in language which suggests the masculine double standard. (p. 288) These speculations seem plausible in view of the novel's sexual theme and the ambiguities of the plot. Had Grey been aware of the ironic possibilities of the commerce versus manhood idea, he could have underscored it by the use of "business" tropes in his prose. He does not, however, except for the "sinister, businesslike manner" in which the ranchers half surround their prisoners. Instead, he stresses the dehumanization of the vigilantes who are "faceless" (hats pulled down and blue handkerchiefs masking their faces) and move forward with "mechanical precision." (pp. 286 – 287) In any case, desire for revenge and, as with Lee and Weston, revenge for desire, issue in much of the novel's violence.

The novel's violence has another, ironic source in the land itself. This constitutes a given, a built-in fact since Cooper, for works whose setting is the "frontier," that partly mythic region where "civilization" and "savagery" have their partly mythic encounter. The two, like flint and tinder, issue in fire. Grey's treatment of the land — because he idealizes and sentimentalizes it — heightens the irony; more than most western writers he portrays the land as idyllic and hints that it is somehow "spiritual" or spirit-filled and as emotionally moving as his purplest prose can make it, while at the same time it inevitably fosters violence. While his novels profit from this irony inherent in the civilization/savagery conflict, he remains unaware of its potential for the most part so that what emerges from particular narratives are "accidental ironies" which may provide tension, but never develop into major strength.

A variant of this civilization/wilderness clash is the contrast between evolutionary progress and reversion to savagery. Some critics have overstressed the significance of Grey's use of social Darwinism, though almost no one comments on the "reversion to savagery" which occurs just as freqently in the novels. Grey wanted to appear *au courant* with popular philosophical trends and used both progress and regress motifs as a kind of dressing in many of his works. One acid test is to ask whether either theme proves structurally crucial to a given novel. Usually they do not. To take a late and atypical example, in the playful *Lost Pueblo* archeologist Philip Randolph stages a phony kidnapping of Janey Endicott and takes her to the site of his remote desert dig. When he physically attempts to force her on one of the horses he has stashed for the trip, she rebels, scratching and pulling his hair. Aroused, he "crushes his hot lips" to hers:

> Clasping her tight he rained kisses on her lips and neck. Janey felt the wet blood from his scratched face on her cheek. Her muscles grew rigid. She was like bent steel about to spring. Suddenly she sank limp. . . . Yet her

> collapse and the shaking of her relaxed body had nothing to do with reason. He had surprised her into the primitiveness of a savage. (p. 62)

Grey, who injects humor into many of his novels — cowboy jokes, teasing, and humorous incidents — is having fun here with no development of a serious savage or violence theme, though as with Marian Warner of *The Vanishing American,* the reversion to savage is a case of sexual arousal.

More typically, passing reference to the theme occurs in several novels in a more or less serious context. In *Robbers' Roost,* outlaw gangleader Hays has regressed to "savagery," but under the influence of the beautiful Helen Herrick defiantly and bravely faces rival outlaws in a shootout and is killed. Again, in the Australia-located *Wilderness Trek,* "faith" has not failed leader Stanley Dann, but it has "lost its hold on the others," who retrograde "toward the primitive." (p. 84) Grey does nothing significant with the notion here. Hero Sterl later feels himself "back to the level of the unconscious savage as represented so strikingly in the black man Friday" and discusses his mood around the campfire. Slyter laughs and says Australians refer to it as "gone bush," and that he thinks it denotes "weak mentality." Leslie gives credence to Slyter's idea by saying Sterl makes her think and she doesn't want to think, Stanley Dann predictably says such a trek would be a throwback for most without "strength in God," and Sterl himself decides he has to deal with the villain, Ormiston, and has no time to "revert to the savage!" until that's finished. (p. 103) Yet again, Keven Bell of *Rogue River Feud* sits in idyllic bliss with his sweetheart, Beryl Aard, on a mountain ridge and wavers "there on the verge, never quite attaining the savage state that his being yearned for," but this too leads nowhere. (p. 147)

Occasionally, however, Grey developed the reversion to savagery theme beyond such passing references. In *Man of the Forest,* Milt Dale and Helen Rayner argue at length during the Rayner sisters' stay at Milt's mountain hideout. On horseback, Milt, Helen, and Bo go on a wild chase after a mountain lion.

Afterward, they argue over the significance of Helen's feelings. Helen says she had strong sensations, like Bo, but "over against them was the opposition of reason, of consciousness." Milton says that's equivalent to not being true to her real nature. Helen objects. "I don't agree with you. I don't have to be an Indian to be true to myself." They argue on, Milt pressing his attack by asking if Helen has ever experienced "real things" like starvation, being lost, facing death, wanting to kill someone, or being madly in love. He concludes by saying that one of them must change, and that she — the "complex, intellectual woman" — must, not because of any superiority in him, but "because of our environment." (pp. 155 – 159) But this too is fun. It has some structural function in that it is part of the buildup of romance between Milt and Helen, but Bo falls off her seat laughing at the two of them. It's pleasantly ironic too, for some fifty pages later the "natural physical man" appears an "intellectual" himself: "And Dale, like some men of lonely wilderness lives who did not retrograde toward the savage, was a thinker." (p. 206)

Philosophical pondering, as well as wandering characterize Adam Larey in *Wanderer of the Wasteland*. Fellow wanderer Dismukes gives Larey his first lesson in retrogression: "When the desert claims men it makes most of them beasts. They sink to that fierce level in order to live. They are trained by the eternal strife that surrounds them. A man of evil nature survivin' in the desert becomes mores terrible than a beast." On the other hand, men — presumably of better nature — sometimes improve instead. "The reason must be that in the development of the desert, in case of these few men who did not retrograde, the spiritual kept pace with the physical." (p. 89) Later, they meet again, and Dismukes asks Adam about a man named McKue, a retrograde who has "gone down to the level of a beast." Adam admits having cracked every bone in the man's body with his bare hands, his "spiritual" side evidently having taken a brief respite. (p. 152) Still later in the book's messy plot, Adam again finds Dismukes; outlaws have chained his old friend to an *arrastra,* a machine for grinding ore to extract gold. Adam sizes up the situation and corners his antagonists; in the brawl which follows, Adam frees Dismukes and they mop up the villains:

> They could never get by him to secure a gun. And the fierce zest of violent strife, the ruthless law of the desert, the survival of the strongest, the blood lust, would have made him refuse any weapon save his hands. . . . Like a wolf he snapped his teeth, then locked his jaw. As he swung and battled and threw these foes backward a strange, wild joy accelerated his actions . . . as he saw, he struck out hard with savage thrill. (p. 283)

Apparently Adam, like Hamlet's representative "man," can sink to beastly depths when the occasion — or Grey — calls for it.

The point of all this, and the continuing digression, is that Grey's pseudo-philosophizing with phrases like "survival of the fittest," "law of the desert," "retrograde," "progress," and the like function mostly as filler which he hoped would appeal to his readers. Sales suggest he was probably right. But neither in the Grey canon as a whole nor in individual works like *Wanderer of the Wasteland* do these ramblings add up to a consistent philosophical position with more than a marginal relevance for the central action. If Grey intends more, if Adam Larey represents a "spiritual" triumph, his tropes betray him ("blood lust," "like a wolf"). In *Heritage of the Desert,* Hare doesn't "strike first and hard" (his "heritage"); the "nature" and "spirit" so prominent in *The Vanishing American* on close scrutiny prove elusive and inconsistent. In *Wanderer*, the Cain-and-Abel-inspired agony, suffering and alienation of Adam Larey in the desert show him less "spiritual" than lucky; he survives, retrogrades now and then, discovers the "age-long progress of man toward unattainable perfection" and "victory of humanity over mastery by primal instincts," but finds at the end he hasn't killed his brother after all.

Grey further clouds his usage of such terms and ideas by attributing the same "primal instincts" to the land and times. While his characters' motives for violence usually boil down to two forms of lust — greed for gold or profit via rustling, and sexual desire manifest in kidnapping or seduction — he also projects a mysterious source of violence onto the frontier border settings. Unless an evil genie hovers over the wilderness, this amounts to a dealing-from-the-bottom-of-the-deck way of expressing (or, more charitably, a symbolic way of embodying) the same old lusts. Thus on a frontier devoid of institutional law, "west of the Pecos" or elsewhere, settlers freed of the civilizing restraints of that law will inevitably encounter or initiate violence as if somehow prompted by the terrain itself. This is unlikely, but it endows the western land with a mystique and excitement — the promise of violence readers want and expect.

In *The Maverick Queen,* where this violence attributed to the land applies, when Linc Bradway looks over the town on arrival and can see at a glance "that law and order" have not come to South Pass, it is because he has seen similar towns "in all their frontier turbulences and color." (p. 6) Vince later expands; no longer just South Pass, it is now "in the very nature of this Wyomin' border where there ain't no law or morality, where the times is hard an' men are desprit." (p. 174) Vince's ambiguous phrase, "in the very nature of things," hints at the projected violence. That violence erupts first in the town, then on the range, and, just before the final bloodbath, in the idyllic ranch site that Lucy has dreamed of. Here Kit Bandon's "true nature" shows in an attempt to kill Linc and Lucy. But Grey has it both ways. At the same time that his Wyoming border incites violence, it has "tenderness and insistence and fire-filmed enchantment." (p. 99) When Linc lets his gaze sweep over the foothills, valleys, and mountains of the Sweetwater country, he feels love and appreciation for "this cleansing wilderness." (p. 187)

Cleansing for some, muddying for others. All get caught up in the violence, however, which claims both "good" and "bad" characters. In short, Grey takes the "savagery" of the civilization/savagery conflict, projects some of it on the land, and lets the land be healing or cleansing for a favored few. Others, "good guys" included, fare less well. Jimmy Weston, by all reports "a mighty nice boy" (as Linc's landlady says), Rancher Lee, and Kit Bandon all are killed, and each displays the same motive pattern: sexual desire, rejection, attempted revenge. At the end, Linc and Lucy will "start all over again," Linc says, "up there in our valley." In view of narrative events (and especially if Grey were more of an intentional ironist and less an accidental one), a reader might ponder the book's closing sentence where Linc and Lucy lift their eyes to their future homesite (already "tainted" by the violence of Kit's attempt to kill them); they turn "to face the dark patch against the distant hills which marked the valley that one day would be their home." (p. 295)

4
The Violence

Concerning the impact of Owen Wister's *The Virginian* on the formulaic western, John Milton says that essentially four ingredients remain: "the hero, violence, love, and the western landscape, and of these four it is violence that has been refined, not into an art but into a pattern of action and a condition of effect which the standard western cannot be without."[21] Unquestionably, the portrayal of violence is a major source of the western's appeal. This feature reveals a built-in irony. One critic puts it this way. The violent deeds which the heroes "must perform to pave the way for the arrival" of civilization "must inevitably be condemned when it does arrive." Grey perceives, however dimly, "an ironic component at the center of the process of refining a frontier society," namely, that civilization, once established, can operate by means of rationally derived laws and social mores, but it can only be established by means of vigilantism and other extralegal and antisocial behavior.[22] The critic makes the point, but at the expense of an indefensible argument, begging the question with all-inclusive "musts" and "can only be." More simply and accurately, outlaws initiate violence; the heroes (or vigilantes, etc.) often counter the problem with more violence.

Like the critic, Grey characters sometimes rationalize this violence. Thus the otherwise pacific Helen Rayner (*The Man of the Forest*) acquiesces, saying the villains "must be killed." Judge Franklidge, a Cattleman's Association member in *Nevada,* explains that gunmen "are a product of their times. The West could never have been populated without them. . . . It is the West as any Westerner knows it now. And as such we could not be pioneers, we could not progress without this violence." (p. 279) Other features of the novels reinforce the idea. Moreover, the drama plays out in a sometimes exaggerated, romanticized, and sentimentalized landscape which is itself often violent — desert sandstorms, swollen rivers, thundering herds — which, together with the similarly romanticized time (a western "frontier" era), somehow evokes violence. Buck Duane inherits his craving for violence from parents, for example, who seem to "inherit" it from the Texas frontier. John Cawelti captures the ambiguity implicit in this "frontier" when he says that "in the works of Grey and Hart, heroic deeds and character grow out of the *western landscape* of wild and unsettled nature," and that they "lead to fulfillment and happiness on the part of those protagonists who are strong and true enough to meet the challenge of lawless openness by purging the *evil forces that also flourish in this environment.*"[23] (emphasis added)

Critics, again rationalizing, have stressed and re-stressed that for Grey, social Darwinism provides a justification for the violence. Cynthia Hamilton says that "as popularized in the United States," social Darwinism "provided a justification for the brutality of competitive individualism." She cites Andrew Carnegie's view that we can accept "great inequality of environment; the concentration of business, industrial and commercial, in the hand of a few; and the law of competition between these, as being not only beneficial, but essential to the future progress of the race." For the western genre generally, "projecting the brutality of current social conditions backwards onto a frontier setting demonstrated the universality of social Darwinism," and as for Grey, she says that the triumph of the hero of Owen Wister's *The Virginian* "may be interpreted in social Darwinist terms, but Wister did not advocate this philosophy directly. That advocacy was left to Zane Grey." Five pages later, after discussions of *Wanderer of the Wasteland* and *Heritage of the Desert,* Hamilton retreats to safer ground; Grey's "direct advocacy" of social Darwinism has become a "championship . . . decidedly ambivalent" (and, disconcertingly, one page earlier she maintains "Women provide the rationale for men's violence").[24]

Carlton Jackson, in a section labeled "Darwinian Influences," argues that *The Man of the Forest* "showed more clearly than most of his books how mountainous settings inspired thoughts of evolution," and that passages in the book indicated "that man was but a part of a grand, inscrutable design." Put into other terms, these statements "amounted to thoughts of 'natural selection,' or 'survival of the fittest.'" While small-town middle classes suspected Darwinists of error or atheism, "when Zane Grey said the same things in less formal language the middle classes regarded him as a man of great common sense and insight." In this way, Jackson adds, "Grey unwittingly became an acceptable interpreter of Darwinism to a great mass of America's citizens."[25]

It's difficult to disprove such claims about the "great mass" of middle class folk, but in any case Jackson provides little evidence in the examples he chooses. To take but one, in *Under the Tonto Rim* Lucy Watson sees as "a law of life" that savages have "progressed mentally and spiritually." Noting this, Jackson says, "At the end of the book, however, Lucy Watson, social worker, married Edd Denmeade, hunter of wild bees and a resident of the Tonto." Has Lucy thus erred? Is this good-hearted social worker (not a flapper) to the "backwoods" Tonto folk herself really a throwback? Has her sponsoring "civilized" society retrogressed? Jackson doesn't say, of course; he follows his "At the end of the book" statement with a non-sequitur: "Grey was a close student of Darwin, so evolutionary beliefs in his novels were to be expected."[26]

Gary Topping does better. Though "perhaps Grey's most original contribution to the view of the West found in his novels was his Darwinism," Darwin's works "seem to have offered simply a convenient rationale for the Western phenomena he observed, a rationale that could be expressed in the common intellectual currency of the time." The latter half of this, to apply current jargon, is right on, but when Topping cites his prime example, *The Man of the Forest,* he fails to catch the qualifying twinkle in Grey's pen. He cites part of the Helen Rayner/Milt Dale dialogue where Dale says, "An' Nature has only one mission — toward greater strength, virility, efficiency — absolute perfection, which is unattainable." Helen wonders, "What of the mental and spiritual development of man and woman?" Dale says, bluntly, "Both are direct obstacles to the design of Nature." Topping notes that Dale "becomes the victim of some of Helen's rebuttals and even of his own Darwinism," but does not mention the oddity of Dale's argument — worth at least a chuckle — about a natural evolutionary "mission" somehow divorced from or hindered by anything "mental," especially in view of the ironic demonstration and acknowledgement some pages later that Milt himself is a thinking man given to philosophizing. Nor does Topping note that Helen's sister Bo falls off the log laughing at the arguments of the two lovers.[27]

Russell Nye's characterization of Grey as "shrewd" again seems apt, for critics sometimes take Grey both too seriously and not seriously enough: too seriously in his "Darwinism" and some of his public pronouncements and diary entries, not seriously enough concerning his use of the romance and seduction plots and the ironies that emerge through them and other features of his novels.

Grey may have appropriated dog-eat-dog and survival of the fittest — "Darwinian" tropes — as convenient, but he scarcely needed a rationale for violence, as the earlier remarks of Milton and Cawelti suggest. He had plenty of precedent in Cooper or as far back as one cares to trace adventure fiction in general. That violence plays a major role in his novels, however, is hardly debatable, though even here critics differ as to the extent. For example, Topping says that "compared to many of his successors, Grey seemed to relish violence very little," and that much of the carnage in his novels takes place off stage.[28] Cawelti, on the other hand, speaks of the "all-out range wars and violent clashes of rival groups that Grey and Hart delighted in," and "the orgies of violence in such novels as *To the Last Man, Riders of the Purple Sage,* and *The U.P. Trail.*" Grey's "avengers of the innocent and destroyers of evil" carry out their acts of violence "with a kind of transcendent religious passion that might be seen as a sort of manic blood lust were it not in such a good and holy cause."[29]

Topping does not name any of the "many successors" who he says discovered "the romantic potential in uninhibited violence," but, as with sex, twentieth-century writing generally shows a trend toward such "uninhibited" portraits. Grey in any case supplies considerable: some of it is "offstage"; a lot of it is not. Topping's offstage example of the massacre of a wagon train in *The U.P. Trail* comes from one of the novels Cawelti points to as having "orgies of violence." There are others. In addition to Cawelti's examples, and Nophaie's kicking the villains senseless in *The Vanishing American,* consider the following:

> "Shore you must be swift! . . . *Dodge this heah bullet!*"
> The gun spouted flame and boomed. One of Riggs'

starting, popping eyes — the right one — went out, like a lamp. The other rolled horribly, then set in blank dead fixedness. Riggs swayed in slow motion until a lost balance felled him heavily, an inert mass. (*The Man of the Forest,* p. 308)

When he straightened up it was to meet the red flame, the blue spurt of Manerube's gun. He uttered a gasp and fell limply, as if his legs had been chopped from under. . . . At that instant, perhaps a fraction of a second before, Chane heard a tiny spat. He knew what it was. A lead bullet striking flesh!

Chane's gaze shot over Manerube's outstretched hand to his face. It was the same, but fixed . . . . over Manerube's glazed blank eyes, in his forehead, appeared a little round hole, first blue, then red. He swayed and fell, full length, face down. (*Wild Horse Mesa,* pp. 353 – 354)

Belton, with distorted visage, attempted to draw right in front of Bruce's menacing gun, which on the instant belched fire and smoke. Belton's sombrero sailed off his head and he plunged flat on his back. . . .

With gun extended he faced the hotel front. Except for the prostrate men, the space was deserted. Belton was writhing in what appeared the throes of death. . . . Bruce turned at the first corner and looked back. He could still see Belton, black-garbed and full-bodied, flopping about like a slaughtered chicken. (*The Fugitive Trail,* pp. 58 – 59)

Edd seemed released from a tremendous strain. He staggered back toward Lucy. For a single soul-riving instant she watched, all faculties but sight shocked into suspension. Then Middleton swayed aside from Edd, both his hands pressed to his breast. He sank to his knees. Lucy's distended eyes saw blood gush out over his hands. (*Under the Tonto Rim,* p. 238)

These are not offstage and not very inhibited. And they are only a few; Grey has any number of lynched twitching bodies as in *Raiders of Spanish Peaks,* bloody knock-down fights, as in *The Dude Ranger,* or *The Drift Fence* where Slinger Dunn "roosters" Jim Traft with his spurs, and slaughters such as the climax of *The Border Legion* for which Calwelti's "orgies" proves apt. Grey was not squeamish in picturing violence.

But violence occurs in other forms than these bloody confrontations. Language is one, though readers at the end of the twentieth century may be so inured to tough talk or put off by Grey's dated expressions that "I'll bore you" — a Grey favorite — seems quaint, not violent. More significant for an understanding of Grey, however, are the numerous abductions with their implicit threat of rape. In a brief comment on *Robbers' Roost,* Carlton Jackson says the novel "was about outlaws who captured a beautiful woman, sister of a rich English rancher, ostensibly for ransom money; but a close reading of the earlier manuscripts revealed another purpose," and that Grey wrote to Dolly, "It never occurred to me that the motive was really rape. But I'm glad to get a chance to correct the blunder."[30] Grey's "blunder" notwithstanding, many of his novels, from *Heritage of the Desert* on, carry veiled or overt threats of sexual violence. In *Heritage,* Snap Naab kidnaps Mescal but runs into trouble with gang boss Holderness. Snap tries to enter the cabin where they have Mescal, saying that he's taking her to White Sage, when Holderness stops him, saying, "Bah! You say that only for the excuse to get into the cabin with her. You tried it last night and I blocked you." Snap prepares to draw only to discover the rustler chief has "a trump card to play" (he has emptied Snap's guns):

> "Naab, you don't get the girl."
> "Maybe you'll get her?" hissed Snap.
> "I always intended to."
> Surely never before had passion driven Snap's hand to such speed. His Colt gleamed in the camp-fire light. Click! Click! Click! The hammer fell upon empty chambers.

> "!H — l!" he shrieked.
>
> Holderness laughed sarcastically.
>
> "That's where you're going!" he cried. "Here's to Naab's trick with a gun — Bah!" And he shot his foreman through the heart. (pp. 272 – 273)

The shot, appropriately "through the heart," suggests the erotic motive here, its illicit nature underscored in that Snap has just bound Mescal's hands.

The violence of the sexual threat against female protagonists does not occur "offstage" — as in a massacre related to have taken place — but is implicit in the situation: kidnapping, coercion, or other intimidation, like the near-maniacal pursuit of Mercedes Castaneda by the villain Rojas in *Desert Gold,* though sometimes the violence takes the more overt form of physical struggle, as in *The Border Legion* or *The Shepherd of Guadaloupe.* At other times, as with Mescal, the victim remains relatively helpless, a captive taken by force.

And yet Grey's heroines are never really helpless, for they embody the erotic power which vanquishes hero and villain alike. Hands tied and locked in as she is, Mescal in a very real sense "triggers" the self-destructive violence between Snap Naab and Holderness and the beginning of the gang's disintegration in *Heritage of the Desert;* invariably, in this way, the abducted heroine initiates the undoing of the gang from within, though the hero and his pards come in and mop up. In *The Border Legion,* Joan Randall gets the job done by herself, for she's the ace of hearts par excellence. She is also worth her weight in gold, for Grey continues to link sex and money, illegal competition and erotic drive. As entertainment, all this linked eroticism and violence provides what many readers obviously want and expect. But insofar as the novels comment on American culture, they continue to suggest that competition run wild has much in common with rape. *Robbers' Roost* is a case in point. Evidently Grey's early manuscript — containing his "blunder" — suggested too plainly that the real illicit gain the kidnappers of Helen Herrick had in mind was Helen, not ransom.

But the connection remained, even if more subtly couched in the narrative language, from the Mormons' lecherous desire to possess both Jane and her estate in *Riders of the Purple Sage* to the sexual economy suggested in the white slavery of *The U.P. Trail, Thunder Mountain,* and *Boulder Dam.* The twin lusts show up in this way: out of control as "love," the erotic drive — often imaged in landscape metaphors of "storm" and "flood" — renders hero and heroine agonized, thunderstruck, and swooning; out of control as illicit competition, desire — imaged especially in abductions and rustling — renders the outlaws ambiguously linked with both girl and goods. In short, a sizeable number of Grey's narratives suggest that the real rationale for violence is desire, not Darwin, good when chastely united in a true love match, bad when obsessively linked with seduction and stolen cattle, but the prime mover in either case.

Aside from its entertainment value, then, Grey's use of violence from one point of view can suggest the competitive spirit run wild, and then turned against itself in the form of the hero's actions. Richard Slotkin's *Regeneration through Violence* offers yet another, more psychologically oriented approach. Central to this approach, as noted earlier, is the "myth of the frontier." Slotkin explains: "the conception of America as a wide-open land of unlimited opportunity for the strong, ambitious, self-reliant individual to thrust his way to the top" has consequences:

> The first colonists saw in America an opportunity to regenerate their fortunes, their spirits, and the power of their church and nation; but the means to that regeneration ultimately became the means of violence, and the myth of regeneration through violence became the structuring metaphor of the American experience.[31]

Slotkin argues a complex evolution of the myth, but finds it typically embodied in the "myth of the hunter" in "an intimate conflict between male avatars of the wilderness and civilization for possession of the white female captive." This conflict suggests, on one level, a projection of psychological forces.[32] The violence shows in chopped trees, bleached buffalo hides, and decimated Indians, as well as the killing between "avatars."

Critics have mostly ignored Slotkin's insights in connection with Grey. Slotkin's two works carry his discussion of the frontier myth to 1890, and do not deal with twentieth-century westerns as such, but it is again only a step from the "hunter myth" to Grey's heroes. Grey, in fact, features several hunter types: Edd Denmeade, bee-hunter of *Under the Tonto Rim;* buffalo hunters like Clint "Buff" Belmet of *Fighting Caravans;* Milt Dale the hunter of *The Man of the Forest;* the wild-horse hunters of *Forlorn River, Wild Horse Mesa,* and *Horse Heaven Hill;* and other shirt-tail descendants of Natty Bumppo and Daniel Boone. Moreover, Grey's hunters are, in character and deed, virtually indistinguishable from his other hero types.

Thus one might, drawing on Slotkin's explications, see a Grey hero and his enemies as "male avatars of wilderness and civilization" respectively, vying for the female captive, as Grey so frequently has her. As psychological projections, the villain — say a Bishop Dyer — represents the perversion of the "laws" Slotkin mentions. Slotkin's second book, *The Fatal Environment*, outlines "'laws' of capitalist competition, of supply and demand, of Social Darwinian 'survival of the fittest' as a rationale for social order, and of 'Manifest Destiny' that have been the building blocks of our dominant historiographical tradition and political ideology."[33] Thus in Dyer one can see "competition" undermined through coercion, "supply and demand" distorted by rustling, "fittest" twisted into most successful at intimidation. The female, say Helen Rayner, embodies civilization and stable domestic life and the "other half" of the hero's individual nature or anima (Slotkin's term). As psychological drama, the plot has the hero destroy his own dark urges, projected onto the "outlaw," and unite with the heroine who, though she may balk temporarily at the violent means, eventually supports the ends, agreeing as does Helen, that they "must be killed."

The action takes place in a western wilderness. Though the real frontier is gone, the author — Grey in this case — creates one. Edwin Fussell contends that the "frontier" for a number of America's literary greats — Melville, Whitman, Thoreau — was really a mindset, not a place.[34] For Grey too the "frontier," though he endeavors to give it verisimilitude, describing panoramas he has himself seen, listing the Mogollon Rim and other real landmarks, is part mindset. In his stories of this mythic frontier, if one takes a Slotkin-slanted view, one can envision parables of aggressive American capitalism run amok (ultimately, the heart's desires), then self-corrected in the form of the avenging hero who unites with his "civilizing" half in an ironic affirmation of the underlying values involved, including the violence.

What if one were to endorse this rather troubling format and even glorify it with a high-sounding rationale like "Manifest Destiny?" Slotkin suggests two perspectives: "Under the aspect of mythology and historical distance, the acts and motives of the wood-chopper, the whale and bear hunter, the Indian fighter, and the deerslayer have an air of simplicity and purity that makes them seem finally heroic expressions of . . . the human spirit." See them more realistically, and a different view emerges, "the Indian debased, impoverished and killed in return for his gifts; the land and its people, its 'dark' people especially, economically exploited and wasted; the warfare between man and nature, between race and race, exalted as a kind of heroic ideal."[35] In light of Slotkin's view, a lot of westerns, not only some of Grey's, could be read as veiled rationales for and critiques of capitalist exploitation in general, but particularly embodied in the winning of the West.

What if the protagonist in a novel involving Slotkin's general scenario should become aware that the urge to violence came from within and anguished over that troubling awareness at the same time as he set about to purge the land of the exploiters? His story might be expected to prove ironic, and his status — "outlawman" — ambiguous. Torn by contradiction, he might even be tempted to self-destruct. Such, at any rate, is a possible approach to Grey's *The Lone Star Ranger*.

As of this writing, the legal community engages in self-analysis under the rubric of "The Critical Legal Studies Movement." The effort forms part of a larger critical concern with the relationship between law and literature.[36] One thrust of this critical effort is the attempt by legal apologists to establish some sort of interpretative authority that will refute the charge, variously stated, of arbitrariness, of interpretative chaos rooted in personal whim, of a view of law as a "situation where one person gives another an order backed by threats" and thus "obliges him to comply."[37] Ironically, the legal fathers of the new Republic could point to a source of interpretative authority in those "general principles of universal law" which appeared to govern. Ironically too there was linkage, since lost to the demands of specialization, between literature and the law, for the best way to understand the "general principles" rested in no small part on a knowledge of literature.[38]

The western surely cries for attention to the realm of the law, though it has received little.[39] Where but in the "lawless" West does the law appear so arbitrary? Where but in the realm of the sixgun does the law's coercive potential appear so menacing? And where does the very meaning of the concept "law" come under such scrutiny as in the "oater" where its many faces include a vaguely and variously defined "Code" of behavior, corrupt or impotent lawmen, whiskey-inspired vigilantes, and blazing Colt .45's? "The only law is what you see here in my hand," one may recall Hank Hays saying at the beginning of *Robbers' Roost*. Interestingly, the metaphor of a gun at the head has emerged prominently in the early dialogue of critical legal studies antagonists.[40] Unlike the academics, Grey's exploration of the possibilities inherent in law and lawlessness rises out of the needs of his romance and adventure plots. It is nonetheless intriguing and relevant to the ongoing dialogue.

For an anonymous reader writing in *The Atlantic Monthly, The Lone Star Ranger* was a "book for the tired businessman."[41] Perhaps so, but the tired critic can take to it too; it comprises Grey's most extensive brush with the law. Grey fashioned two shorter works into the novel, labeling them Books I and II. In Book I, Buckley (Buck) Duane, son of a notorious gunman, kills several outlaw gang members while he is himself an "outlaw," a fugitive as a result of a shootout where he kills a bully in his home town. In Book II he kills several more gunmen, but as an "inlaw," a commissioned member of the Texas Rangers on a secret mission. Clearly the bad guys deserve killing; the irony, one of many in the book, arises from Duane's dubious relationship to the law when he performs this good work.

Grey prefaces *The Lone Star Ranger* with a dedication "To Captain John Hughes and his Texas Rangers." In it he states that his novel "deals with the old law — the old border days." This does not say what the "old law" is, but does raise the issue of its relationship to place and time. The novel takes place in southwest Texas, and "border" is a specific reference to the Rio Grande, the U.S.-Mexico boundary. But "border" in this sense has less to do with the action than border in the more general sense of "frontier," and Duane's adventures take him farther and farther west to the "lawless" realm presided over by the arch-rustler, Cheseldine. Here another irony arises. Cheseldine's town, Fairdale (anything but "fair"), has institutional law, but in the form of Cheseldine who, known there as Longstreth, is mayor and holds court daily as judge — a court which Duane instinctively knows is "a sham, a farce." (p. 163) As chief embodiment of the law, Cheseldine/Longstreth does what he wants. His rustlers have robbed a man named Laramie of his cattle; the mayor/judge then sues the victim for money owed. As Laramie puts it simply to Duane, "It come to a lawsuit — and I was ruined." (p. 172) Later, Cheseldine has Laramie shot.

Duane's earlier escape into and then out of the river brakes, arguably the novel's most exciting episode, creates further ambiguity concerning the law and justice. Duane, at this point still an "outlaw," ventures out from his campsite one night and chances upon a somber group of men by a clump of cottonwoods. One glance tells him the situation — "two dark, limp, strangely grotesque figures hanging from branches." This vigilante scene "was common enough in southwest Texas," Grey says, and common enough in westerns generally, one can add. It holds special peril for Duane, however. While one of the men orders him to "ride down an' account" for himself, another says not to take chances but "plug him." One of them does, and Duane, left forearm wounded, flees for his life. (p. 98) Here not mere vigilante law prevails, but reason run amok. Their decision to shoot first and ask questions later erases the distinction between "outlaw" and "criminal" Duane elsewhere tries to make, declaring him guilty and precluding any chance to prove otherwise. Ironically too, following his escape and subsequent trip to the Ranger camp, Captain MacNelly says hundreds in southwest Texas would swear Duane never committed a crime.

MacNelly and his Rangers constitute a new form of institutional law opposed to the "old" corrupt, coercive forms (presumably Grey's meaning in the preface). "The Rangers mean law and order for Texas," Duane's uncle says at the beginning of the novel. At the end of the narrative they seem to prevail, joining Duane to wipe out the remnant of Cheseldine's gang in a shootout when the outlaws arrive to rob a bank. But it is Duane who first tracks down and captures Cheseldine, kills some of his band, and arranges the final trap for the bankrobbers.

By his heroic actions, moreover, Duane has saved the Rangers from extinction, according to Captain MacNelly, for not everyone agrees with Duane's uncle. Some, in high places, favor disbanding the Rangers. When MacNelly persuades Duane to enlist, he admits that "there's a good deal of friction in the Department of State in regard to whether or not the ranger service is any good." (p. 133) Duane later meets a Colonel Webb (a good guy) who champions the Rangers. "A fine body of men, sir, and the salvation of Texas," he tells Duane, and erupts in disgust when Duane notes that "Governor Stone doesn't entertain that opinion." Understandably, MacNelly gloats when Duane tells him of his plan to capture the rest of Cheseldine's gang at the attempted bank holdup. After the smoke clears, MacNelly sends Duane a message: "You have saved the ranger service to the Lone Star State." (pp. 148, 242) So the "new law" rests after all on the broad shoulders and lightning gun of Buck Duane.

The irony here compounds when one considers the conditions under which Duane signs up. After repeated invitations from MacNelly, Duane visits the Ranger camp at night. MacNelly offers a proposition: "If I place a pardon in your hand — make you a free, honest citizen once more, clear your name of infamy, make your mother, your sister proud of you — will you swear yourself to a service, *any* service I demand of you?" Duane eagerly agrees. "I've a deep game. I'm playing it square," MacNelly says. But those square edges buckle here and there. The Ranger captain has a signed pardon from the governor which he says is "conditional" upon Duane enlisting in the Rangers. It has no date, and after explaining something of the task he has in mind — to break up Cheseldine's gang — MacNelly adds that "perhaps we can make it appear that all or most of your outlawry had really been good service to the state." It has, of course, but this obscures the issue, for MacNelly admits that he has found "hundreds of men in southwest Texas" who swear to Duane's innocence. "The farther south I get the clearer this becomes." He wants to hear it from Duane, though, and does. "Have you ever done anything criminal?" he asks. "That way my hands are clean," Duane says. (pp. 130 – 136)

Why then must Duane "pay" in this way? Presumably because he left the scene after shooting the bully who had threatened to kill him in the novel's opening pages, though witnesses there could testify to the victim's threats. Elated by Duane's claim to innocence, MacNelly says, "all the same, in spite of this, you are a Texas outlaw accountable to the state. You're perfectly aware that *under existing circumstances,* if you fell into the *hands of the law,* you'd probably hang, at least go to jail for a long term." (p. 132, emphasis added) Whose "hands" are these? What are these "existing circumstances?" Hasn't Duane in fact walked into the hands of the law, albeit by invitation? MacNelly's assessment suggests another embodiment of the "law," one less understanding, which competes with the Rangers, and operates independently. And yet the governor presumably exercises a "lawful" right in granting a pardon; he represents a still higher law which comes with his political office. Couldn't he intervene, in effect tie the "hands" of that other "law" should Duane fall into its clutches? Why then must it be only if Duane pays by hunting down Cheseldine?

The answer — one answer, rather — is that Grey's plot demands it. Cynthia Hamilton speaks of the "double-edged nature of law in the Western."[42] She notes that "much of the action and violence of the Western are ostensibly directed toward the restoration of law," but that in fact "the law which is restored is not legalistic; it is the law of the survival of the fittest as determined by the rituals of individual competition."[43] This Darwinian-slanted explanation has some relevance for some westerns, but proves ultimately simplistic, and cannot begin to account for the events of a work like *The Lone Star Ranger.*[44] The more one probes into the novel, the grayer the concept of law becomes, details first multiplying, then blurring, its edges.

That tired businessman may understandably choose to ignore nagging details and get on with the action, but the critic ought not, fatigue notwithstanding. Buck Duane emerges in a position similar to that hypothetical victim of the critical legal studies movement — with a legal gun at his head, its coercive authority resting on the hand of the governor who signs the pardon and the "hands" of that vague other law MacNelly refers to, but actually smoking in the hand of the Ranger captain.

Grey has still more to say about the man who saves the Texas Rangers. *The Lone Star Ranger* begins with the twenty-three-year-old Buck Duane facing a dilemma. He learns that a bully and murderer, Cal Dain, wants to kill him, so that he must fight or run. Duane already has his father's eye and slick hand with a gun. He has something more, as the book's opening sentence announces — "an inherited fighting instinct, a driving intensity to kill." He hunts up Cal Dain, out-draws and shoots him, and heads for wild country where, his uncle tells him, he'll have to be an outlaw for a time. In the book's first reference to the dubious nature of justice, Duane's uncle says, "If we had money an' influence we'd risk a trial." (p. 10)

Duane makes his way to the border hideout of Bland, a noted outlaw. There an old-timer named Euchre befriends him, introduces him to Bland's flirtatious wife and a young woman named Jennie who is prisoner in the Bland house, and they plot to rescue Jennie and take her away. In the attempt, Euchre dies and Duane is wounded but escapes with Jennie. He reaches a friend's house where he stays while his wound heals, then he and Jennie head away from the Rio Grande only to have an unknown band of men abduct Jennie. After a sojourn in the wilderness by himself, Duane takes to the trail, stumbles on the vigilante hanging, and has to flee when the vigilantes suspect he is "another one." The rest of Book I describes efforts to avoid capture. He finally escapes by crossing the river in the fog, then makes his way to the Ranger camp to see Captain MacNelly who has repeatedly sent word to meet him there at night. In Book I, in addition to shooting Dain, Duane kills two outlaws, Bland and Alloway, a man named Sellers, shatters the arm of another with two quick shots, and at some point (we learn later) shoots the notorious outlaw Wes Hardin.

In Book II, Duane, now a Ranger, heads west to unmask and capture the mysterious rustler, Cheseldine, who turns out to be Colonel Longstreth, mayor of Fairdale, running his outlaw empire secretly. On the way to Fairdale Duane meets Longstreth travelling with his daughter, Ray, and her cousin, Ruth Herbert. At Fairdale, Duane soon discovers the situation, announces that he is a Texas Ranger, and begins to organize ranchers for a stand against Longstreth. Inevitably, Duane and Ray fall in love. At one point Duane rides out and finds the rustler's secret mountain retreat. He learns of the gang's plan to rob a bank in the town of Bradford and sends word to MacNelly to be waiting there with his men. Duane then returns to Fairdale and with no particular plan in mind goes to the mayor's house and eavesdrops on Longstreth and a comrade, Lawson, who are arguing. Lawson wants to force Ray into marriage. Duane steps out to challenge the men and shoots Lawson. Using Lawson's body as a shield, Longstreth wounds Duane, but runs out of shells. Duane says he'll spare him for Ray's sake if he'll surrender. He does, and with Ray and Ruth, accompanies Duane to Bradford where they arrive just in time for Duane to take part in a shootout at the bank when the rest of the outlaws arrive. Duane, seriously wounded, survives, and at book's end plans to return with Ray to her Louisiana home.

Critics, from early reviewers on, have noted Duane's near-fatal inheritance from his father, but have not explored its relationship to the notion of law.[45] Carlton Jackson, for example, says the novel is "pessimistic, hinting broadly that Buck Duane . . . really did not have a choice in the matter; that some chromosome factor dictated that he be a gunman."[46] Grey does make "heredity" important in his narrative; he pursues the theme throughout, from the opening sentence to Duane's dogged determination to face gunman Poggin at the end, when his "abnormal and stupendous instinct, now deep as the very foundation of his life" demands "its wild and fatal issue." (p. 237) Duane fights against this powerful urge, as after he knocks a gun from the hand of an outlaw, Bill Black, who is about to shoot a "halfwitted Indian" walking innocently by:

> Inside Duane's body there was strife. This third facing of a desperate man had thrown him off his balance. . . . The better side of his nature seemed to urge him to die rather than to go on fighting or opposing ignorant, unfortunate, savage men. But the perversity of him was so great that it dwarfed reason, conscience. He could not resist it. He felt something dying in him. (pp. 60–61)

Later, he acknowledges "how dangerous" he really is, and "how little stood between the sane and better self and a self utterly wild and terrible." Only intelligence can save him, he decides, "a thoughtful understanding of his danger and a hold upon some ideal." (p. 84) That ideal assumes the form of remembering that he has promised to rescue Jennie after the Bill Black incident and saves him from despair. This foreshadows the final "solution" when Ray Longstreth tells Duane at novel's end, "Always, I shall be between you and that — that terrible thing." (p. 243)

But heredity proves only half the problem. Its imperatives — "dwarfed reason," "utterly wild and terrible," "raged fiercely . . . and could not be checked" — raise questions about the source of violence, the responsibility of perpetrators, and, necessarily, the nature and responsibility of the law designed to deal with them. (p. 204) Environment complicates the matter, as it does, for example, in the Wyoming border of *The Maverick Queen*. Duane's uncle sums up the role of both heredity and environment early in the story. Duane has just killed Cal Bain. In distress, he asks, "My God! Uncle, what have I done?" It is not Duane's fault, his uncle says:

> "You're not to blame. This is Texas. You're your father's son. These are wild times. The law as the rangers are laying it down now can't change life all in a minute.

> Even your mother . . . has had her share in making you what you are at this moment. For she was one of the pioneers — the fightin' pioneers of this state. Those years of wild times, before you was born, developed in her instinct to fight, to save her life, her children, an' that instinct has cropped out in you. It will be many years before it dies out of the boys born in Texas." (p. 10)

Duane's heritage comes not only from his gun-slinging father and "fightin'" mother; it "develops" in "wild times" on the Texas frontier. The land again becomes, in some mysterious way, a source of violence, "a vast wild territory — a refuge for outlaws" as well as for Duane. (p. 92) And here, the "little difference between an outlaw and a criminal doesn't count for much," Duane tells Jennie when she passionately says he is no criminal. (p. 79) "What a bloody place Texas was!" Duane thinks; "Men who robbed and men who were robbed both wanted murder. It was in the spirit of the country." (p. 84) This "spirit" affects its inhabitants, as with Duane's parents, and, subsequently, Duane, until someone — the "Law," for example — has to deal with them. Duane's first glance at Cheseldine's co-conspirator, Floyd Lawson, shows a case in point: he appears a young man who "had drifted out to the frontier, where rough and wild life had wrought sternly." (p. 60)

Implicit in this stress on the powerful effects of place, of the frontier or border, is a fear common to the earliest literature of the Republic, namely, that of reversion to savagery. Endorsed by French philosophers and retailed by Jefferson, Crevecoeur and others, the once-popular "Stages of Progress" theory discussed in connection with *The Border Legion* landed on its head, or, more accurately, on its side. As one moved westward, one passed from the civilized and industrial zone through stages to a barbaric hunter-savage society where, in Crevecoeur's words, a new mode of life "brings along with it a new set of manners, which I cannot easily describe. These new manners being grafted on the old stock, produce a strange sort of lawless profligacy, the impressions of which are indelible." The worst of such people are those who have degenerated altogether into the hunting state.[47]

The theme is implicit, and at times explicit, in *The Lone Star Ranger.* As Duane hunts for Cheseldine he notices "the farther west one traveled along the river the sparser the respectable settlements, the more numerous the hard characters, and in consequence the greater the element of lawlessness." (p. 147) Later, when he spies on Cheseldine and Lawson, he notices how the latter has changed. "Lawson, like the great majority of evil and unrestrained men on the border had reached a point where influence was futile. Reason had degenerated." (p. 188) Animal imagery suggests a similar change. Bosmer, an outlaw who challenges Duane, comes at him "with a snarl like an angry dog"; Duane's image of the dread Poggin is of "a jaguar with his rippling muscles." (pp. 29, 237)

Similarly, Duane himself roams the border as a "lone wolf," Grey's favorite metaphor for his hero in this novel. Soon after fleeing his hometown Duane makes a new friend, a fellow "outlaw" who says to Duane, "You'll never mix in. You'll be a lone wolf. I seen that right off. Wal, if a man can stand the loneliness, an' if he's quick on the draw, maybe lone-wolfin' is best." (p. 23) Later, Duane sits in despair thinking of Jennie, and then of his mother and the old homestead. "I am Duane, the Lone Wolf! . . . What hellish thing drives me? Why can't I end it all? What is left? Only that damned unquenchable spirit of the gunfighter to live." (pp. 90 – 91) When he flees from the vigilantes to the river brakes he suffers not so much from his untended wound as the "old hell" within:

> He was now enacting the tragedy of all crippled, starved, hunted wolves at bay in their dens. Only his tragedy was infinitely more terrible because he had mind enough to see his plight, his resemblance to a lonely

> wolf, bloody-fanged, dripping, snarling, fire-eyed in a last instinctive defiance. (p. 114)

Still later, seeking Cheseldine, he camps out rather than stay in town so the outlaws will see in him "the lone-wolf fugitive." (p. 144) Inner gang strife shows when outlaw Knell taunts Poggin by crying out, "BUCK DUANE! Yes . . . The Nueces gunman! That two-shot, ace-of-spades lone wolf!" (p. 220)

These quotes suggest Duane's acquired skills and his anguish over his outsider status, as well as his savage inheritance. But Grey doesn't stop here; he associates the metaphor with all outlaws. Duane sits thinking of that "unfortunate horde" of outcasts, hopeless criminals, avengers, wronged wanderers, and an occasional man "not yet lost" to good. "But all of them were akin in one sense — their outlawry; and that starry night they lay with their dark faces up, some in packs like wolves, others alone like the gray wolf who knew no mate." (p. 92) Metaphorically speaking, when you've seen one outlaw you've seen 'em all.

Two other features still further complicate the novel's fuzziness concerning the "law" and related notions. One, discussed earlier, is Duane's decision "not to split hairs" but to rationalize arch-criminal Cheseldine's "drifting out" west and "drifting in" to crime, a bit of soft-headedness displayed because of his love for Ray. The other is Duane's own trek through the novel's pages as a one-man task force who, Rambo-like, "judges" the likes of Poland, Alloway, Sellers, Hardin, Knell, and Poggin. By what law? In Book I he takes the "law" into his own hands, cleaning out the nests of thieves along the frontier, a task he continues to do "legally" as a Ranger in Book II. The difference? A pardon, offered conditionally, by the governor of a territory that instills its "spirit" of violence into the Duanes and others who "drift out" and then "drift in" to trouble, some (Bland, Hardin) "succeeding" like Cheseldine at their criminal ventures until blown away by Duane.

The cumulative effect of the contradictory details, animal images, ironic events, and other blurrings is to question the meaning of the concepts of "law" and "justice" and render them ambiguous. By extension, related concepts like "outlaw," "criminal," "guilt," and even "civilization" and "savagery" also become ambiguous and at times nearly meaningless, as in Duane's scrape with the vigilantes. Here, "justice" has no meaning; innocence and guilt are beside the point. At other times some kind of "law" operates, but influenced by political considerations, as with the Ranger captain; corrupted to personal use, as with Cheseldine/Longstreth; or swayed by romance as when Duane bargains with the rustler king. More often than not "law" is a sixgun, and the interpretative authority passion. In *The Lone Star Ranger* this passion in turn has twin roots in heredity and environment.

All this fuzziness troubles Duane too, and plagued by doubt and inner turmoil he tries to maintain distinctions. Pardoned, and working for the Rangers, he finds an "imperious desire" to run the chief outlaws to their dooms. However, he has "never called them outlaws — but rustlers, thieves, robbers, murderers, criminals." Something inside makes the distinction dubious:

> He sensed the growth of a relentless driving passion, and sometimes he feared that, more than the newly acquired zeal and pride in this ranger service, it was the old, terrible inherited killing instinct lifting its hydra-head in new guise. But of that he could not be sure. He dreaded the thought. He could only wait. (p. 145)

In the novel's climactic episode, in fact, even Ray Longstreth's passionate kisses and plea bargaining fail to overcome this old instinct, and Duane insists on shooting it out with Poggin. For Duane, then, the ultimate "law" operates on an inner authority, and one can say of him, as Stanley Fish concludes concerning the "structure of pressures, of purposes, urgencies, interests already in place" which invariably affect any "chain" legal interpretation: "the gun at your head is your head."[48]

By now that tired businessman, happily heeding Duane's advice "not to split hairs," presumably sleeps. The critic still can't, however, because the problem of violence lurks beneath the book's ambiguous portrait of law and justice. In this connection, two writers dealing with violence raise issues relevant to Grey's story. In *Violence and the Sacred* Rene Girard explores the way societies attempt to contain violence. Girard sees three categories developing in the course of the history of the western world:

> (1) preventive measures in which sacrificial rites divert the spirit of revenge into other channels; (2) the harnessing or hobbling of vengeance by means of compensatory measures, trials by combat, etc., whose curative effects remain precarious; (3) the establishment of a judicial system — the most efficient of all curative measures.[49]

The wild West of the western has something in common with the primitive societies engaged in the first, but its technology — Colt .45s, Winchesters, et al — lends itself to action in category two, where combatants often meet in the shootout of individual competition. *The Lone Star Ranger* opens on an act of gratuitous violence. Cal Bain wants to kill Duane. When Duane asks "What for?" his uncle replies, "Lord knows there ain't any reason. But what's that to do with most of the shootin' these days?" Just as with primitive societies, for Duane's southwest Texas this mindless violence seems a form of contagion. "He's got a fever that's rampant in Texas," the uncle says. "He wants gunplay."

Unchecked, the contagion dooms a society. In this light, one reading of *The Lone Star Ranger* can see the record of an attempt by the society to purge itself of the virulent "fever" through the agency of Buck Duane, first as a "lone wolf" among wolves, then as an agent of political and legal authority. These trials by combat, following a ritual pattern

("Code") are meant to contain violence; they are, in Gerard's words, steps "in the direction of a legal system."[50] But, as Girard reiterates, all such measures involve and invoke violence. "While acknowledging the differences, both functional and mythical, between vengeance, sacrifice, and legal punishment, it is important to recognize their fundamental identity." Thus, "precisely because these three institutions are essentially the same they tend to adopt the same types of violent response in times of crisis."[51]

Once unleashed, the violence begets more violence, and one might logically expect a buildup to some sort of climactic Armageddon. Grey's description of the final shootout at the Bradford bank suggests just that sort of infernal climax. "Hell's Fire!" Poggin cries when he sees Duane framed in the bank's entrance. Then the guns explode. "A tearing agony encompassed his breast. He pulled — pulled — at random. Thunder of booming shots all about him! Red flashes, jets of smoke, shrill yells! He was sinking. The end; yes, the end!" (p. 239) Here Duane becomes almost robot-like, semiconscious, pulling the trigger repeatedly and "at random," the calm alertness of his earlier confrontations lost to the reigning chaos.

"The end" doesn't come for Duane; he survives, of course, and heads for Louisiana with Ray. The melee marks the end of his gunman career, however, and the end of Cheseldine's gang. It will not likely end the violence of southwest Texas border society. Grey seems to sense that the "curative effects" will remain as "precarious" as Girard suggests. At any rate, in the preface he tells Captain Hughes he wants to tackle the territory again: "Soon, perchance, I shall have the pleasure of writing of the border of today, which in Joe Sitter's laconic speech, 'Shore is most as bad an' wild as ever!'"

Finally, Richard Slotkin again proves relevant, providing a kind of ironic footnote to the novel's course of violent events. Our heroes, he says, gain mythic stature through violent conquest: "Benjamin Church decked in the scalps and royalties of the slain Philip; Leatherstocking accepting a mythic name from his slain Indian enemy; Davy Crockett grinning by a mountain of 105 bear-hides."[52] For Buck Duane, the "trophies" are lead, an impressive collection of slugs testifying to his exploits and "hero" status. After the final shootout he takes his bullet-riddled body home to the adulation of his uncle: "Five in that last scrap! By gum! And you had six before? . . . Five and six. That makes eleven. By gum! A man's a man to carry all that lead." (p. 242) In the uncle's eyes these lead trophies signify mythic status, but call forth the last of the novel's ironies; now an old man, Duane's uncle, Grey tells the reader, has become senile.

Grey tries to resolve some of the ambiguities of his novel with the figure of a strong woman; violence, at least for Buck Duane, will end because Ray Longstreth will throw her "faith and love and beauty" between Duane and his past. (p. 243) But the reader, with Slotkin and Girard at hand, may feel less sanguine about "legends" which are "an index to our character and conception of our role in the universe" (Slotkin), or a world where absolute values may be lost, "legitimacy as a principle no longer exists," and "only the introduction of some transcendental quality that will persuade men of the fundamental difference between sacrifice and revenge, between a judicial system and vengeance, can succeed in by-passing violence" (Girard). Of these ominous comments, the latter hovers very near the heart of the critical legal studies movement. Both bear on the troubling details of *The Lone Star Ranger*.

The Dream

V

1
The Frontier Idyll: Paradise Lost

Grey's novels comment on the nebulous concept of an "American Dream" in different ways. One of them is in images of Eden or an earthly paradise. Writers early on attributed Edenic qualities to the American West, first as part of the arcadian New World generally, then, as with Daniel Boone's idyllic forest, in terms of a "frontier."[1] Attitudes toward the "Garden of the World," as Henry Nash Smith calls the growing edge, changed as experience and facts accumulated, but the ideal lived on as a mythic West, a beckoning new home and opportunity in the minds of many who itched for a second chance.[2] John Milton, describing the evolution of the western, comments on this theme of restlessness:

> There is the escape from a confining past, and therefore the freedom of a new land not yet bound up in social and political restrictions; there is the quest for Eden, the last stage in the world-wide "course of empire"; and there is mobility, both social and physical — the democratic freedom of individual enterprise, and the large open spaces of a relatively unpopulated continent inviting the takers and the exploiters.[3]

Such visions of freedom and opportunity challenged many to face westward; others could do it vicariously by picking up a good western. If one of Grey's, the reader might find vivid descriptions of the land, including mini-Edens such as the Garden of Eschtah and Surprise Valley of Grey's first two commercial successes, *Heritage of the Desert* and *Riders of the Purple Sage* respectively.

Critics continue to stress the idyllic element in Grey's work. For Ann Ronald, "Grey's West, seeming almost a Garden of Eden, becomes a proving ground for man. Here he loses his innocence and gains knowledge."[4] According to John Cawelti, "the Wild West was a place where people rediscovered and reaffirmed the most important values of life, a quality that would be central to the western romances of Wister and Zane Grey.[5] Ronald focuses on a more general or Biblical initiation experience (loses innocence or gains knowledge), but Cawelti's West has become a more specifically American Eden, a place to recapture values associated with sets of ideals often called the "American Dream." Cawelti makes these specific as "an affirmation of such traditional American values as monogamous love, the settled family, the basic separation of masculine and feminine roles, and the centrality of religion to life," and again as "the reestablishment of the basic norms of nineteenth-century small-town society: religious piety, monogamy, feminine chastity, temperance, and the family circle."[6] Again, Cynthia Hamilton says Grey's plots allow the heroes "to achieve personal happiness as well as social and financial success," which are "stock American values, stock American dreams," and that "by placing such heroes and plot patterns in the wild and woolly West Grey emphasizes the continuity of key American values."[7] Of course some of these values, as Grey repeatedly underscores, have already been corrupted or lost in the East.

The dream soon gets corrupted in the West too. In 1930 Grey quit Arizona; the West he had fallen in love with was gone. The triggering event was a denied request of Grey's to hunt bear out of season, but in his public announcement — a letter to the Flagstaff newspaper — he said that commercial interests were taking over, and spoiling, Arizona's forests and desert resources.[8] Thereafter he would deal only with the "real" Arizona — the one he had come to some twenty years before, and only as part of the mythic West of his novels.

Disappointed, yes. But he must have known the original Eden had to go. Or so even his early novels suggest. August Naab doesn't have to leave his idyllic Garden of Eschtah, but he sees it bear bitter fruit, as the graveyard full of sons, the snake-like river, and the rebellion of son Snap testify. Evil forces attack his paradisiacal oasis from within and without; at the end, though he gives it willingly, twenty-five percent of his Mormon estate goes to the gentile John Hare, who accepts the land but not the faith. In *Riders of the Purple Sage,* Jane Withersteen quits one Eden for another, the wealthy Mormon ranch estate inherited from her tainted father for the isolated Surprise Valley: paradise regained, but only via a rejection of "civilized" society which, embodied in the Mormon villains, proves intolerable.

Moreover, these villains represent that recidivist danger Grey so often mentions. Cynthia Hamilton asks and answers a question:

> What kind of savage, then, is it that the West brings out in men? It is the magnification of those values enshrined in the American dream and basic to a capitalistic economy which makes a man savage. When these civilized instincts are given free reign in the lawlessness of the West, they clearly demonstrate the need for the restraints of civilization.[9]

Among the problems here is that "American dream" enshrines "those values" which, in the next sentence, become "these civilized instincts." (Are "instincts" and "values" the same? What "values" are we talking about?) Adding to the confusion is that elsewhere in her discussions Hamilton speaks of Grey's "small-town values," "Christian humanism," "social Darwinism," "competitive individualism," "simple virtues of the past," "personal happiness," and "social and financial success."

The confusing array of terms aside, Hamilton grapples with a central problem when she points to a "rift within American values themselves," and elaborates by saying, "In so far as Christian humanism promotes the virtues of mercy, charity, fellowship and humility, it is diametrically opposed to the aggression of social Darwinism."[10] In fact, depending on the critic, that slippery term "American Dream" encompasses a number of character traits (endurance, honesty, courage), philosophical packages of attitudes (Social Darwinism, Christian Humanism), socially approved customs (Cawelti's temperance, monogamous love, etc.), and, for Hamilton, the basic "competitive individualism" (which may *be* an instinct masquerading as a "value)." Some of these values prove contradictory.

The point is that the same Edenic frontier West, source of, in Milton's words, "the democratic freedom of the individual enterprise," and the place which can encourage the regeneration of prized values, is also an ironic realm which for critic Hamilton "brings out" savage behavior through "magnification" of those same values. This dual role of the "idyllic" land — restorer of values and instigator of excess — when internalized in a character, produces a Buck Duane, for whom the "frontier" is a kind of third parent whose contribution to the hero is the urge to kill.

Not surprisingly then, given this ironic built-in feature of the land, Grey's novels might be expected to question in some way notions of the West as "Eden." But he is committed to the central love story, a happy ending with one or two marriages, and, usually, a prosperous ranch or the prospect of one. The questioning, then, must come in some relatively subtle or ironic form, as it does in fact in *Heritage of the Desert* and *Riders of the Purple Sage*. And, needless to say, in *The Lone Star Ranger;* at the end of the novel Duane and Ray Longstreth leave the West, and Buck's mementos of the idyllic land are an agonized psyche and a body harboring eleven lead slugs.

Other examples also illustrate Grey's questioning. In *To the Last Man,* the lovers prevail but at an enormous cost. Jean Isbel makes his way to Grass Valley at the call of his father. On his way he awakens one morning to the appealing gobble of wild turkeys; soon he stands with Ellen Jorth gazing at a wild vista he calls "Wonderful!" a sight "that would cure any misery." (p. 14) Surely an "idyllic" start. The plot of the ensuing feud is borrowed in part from the historic Pleasant Valley War, itself an oxymoronic version of paradise lost. At the end, Ellen with blood on her hands (she has just shot Colter at close range) and Jean wounded, the lovers pledge their love, ending a feud which has nearly wiped out both families. But their passion expended in both love and war, its "savage" intensity, and the taint of blood suggest, obliquely, that their future happiness may not be immune to the disease.

Again, for Stephen Latch of *The Lost Wagon Train* an idyllic plan goes awry. He gives up his evil ways — slaughtering wagon trains — and buys a valley, "wonderfully rich in grass, water, climate" and abounding in game and timber, from Indian chief Satana. But at novel's end, though Corny and Latch's daughter Estie marry happily, Latch remains "haunted," with a "sleepless and eternal remorse," and bereft of his wife, Cynthia. (p. 292) Yet again, Logan Huett of *30,000 on the Hoof* finds himself looking at what other settlers have missed, "the most wonderful range in Arizona":

> Apache had once used this beautiful site for a hunting camp. The bench on the east side had waited for ages for the homesteader to throw up his log cabin there. It was a level bit of ground, above the swift bend of the stream, and marked by a few splendid pine trees. A magnificent spring gushed from the foot of the slope. Deer and elk trails led up through a wide break in the rock wall. (p. 13)

But Sycamore Canyon, as Huett names his ranch, offers a succession of trials that would break any but the most enduring. At the end of the narrative Logan, minus two sons lost to the War and having been cheated of a fortune, will start over with the one remaining half-Apache son he does not know isn't his own. *The Maverick Queen,* in addition to its seamy sex and business theme, ends with the immediate range war over, but "nothing settled." And Kent Wingfield enters the paradisiacal stronghold of The Hole in the Wall gang in *Stranger from the Tonto* and finds "the most perfect sylvan hidden nook imaginable, steeped in solitude brooded over by the grand wall and murmuring waterfalls, fragrant and sweet, lonely as the spot where the first man evolved upon the earth." (p. 89) Eve (Lucy) soon shows up, but at the climax of the story Eden erupts in violence and the lovers abandon it, escaping to a new life.

But Grey's record is mixed. In a number of other novels the protagonists either remain on ranches or anticipate new ones under circumstances that qualify as idyllic. Panhandle Smith, at the end of *Valley of Wild Horses,* calls to his father and his new bride, Lucy: "See that first big notch in the wall? Thick with bright green? There's water. And see the open canyon with the cedars scattered? What a place for a ranch. It has been waiting for us all these years. . . . That's where we'll homestead." Blinky matches his pard: "See the red circle wall, with the brook shinin' down like a ribbon. . . . That's the homestead for me." The party rolls on toward the virgin land, "the rich grass where no wheel track showed." (p. 220) And there's no doubt about the homestead of Milt Dale and Helen Rayner:

> "Homestead! What's that?" murmured Helen dreamily. The word sounded sweet.
>
> "The government will give land to men to locate an' build," replied Dale. "We'll run up a cabin."
>
> "And come here often. . . . Paradise Park!" whispered Helen. (p. 383)

Still, Grey suggests the fragile nature of the frontier idyll in other ways besides the loss of Eden, often with an accompanying emphasis on the human penchant for "savagery." His heroes continue to marry more or less happily, but some of them are veterans carrying the scars of World War I. Upset like many others at the devastation and what he considered the folly of events, Grey put some of his bitterest invective in the mouths of these protagonists. Keven Bell (*Rogue River Feud*), Glen Kilbourne (*The Call of the Canyon*), Clay Forrest (*The Shepherd of Guadalupe*), Nophaie (*The Vanishing American*), and Kurt Dorn (*The Desert of Wheat*) all fight the war to end all wars and return home (or head west) only to find the violence of the civilized East has its mini-counterpart on the western frontier in their own personal battles. "Cannon blew up. I stopped the breechblock with my face," Keven tells his father of a training camp accident just after returning home. "And I don't sleep well. In the army I learned a lot of rotten things. But you get so you don't care. They wanted you not to care — to revert to savagery." (pp. 5 – 6) When his old pal, Garry, puts himself down as a "no-good, rum-guzzlin' riverman," Keven responds, "Ruin? Ha! I'd like to know what I am now. The army sounds great. But it's a hideous lie." (p. 14) And Minton, a good merchant, tells Keven, "Chuck that uniform, Kev, and forget the war. It was a dose of hell for all of us." Keven takes Minton's advice and burns the uniform. "No more of that patriotic bunk for me," he mutters as he watches it burn. (pp. 15, 23) Keven heals, thanks to rest, work, and the love of his old sweetheart, Beryl Aard, but finds the "savagery" the army wanted has followed him home in the person of Atwell, a cowardly former major who spreads lies about Keven. Atwell now "about runs Gold Beach" Garry tells Keven. As superintendent of the biggest cannery on the coast, Atwell also deals in illegally caught salmon. For Keven, the Rogue River country itself proves restorative, but "civilization," in the form of institutional law, shows a house divided; a bad sheriff in one county hounds Keven, while a good sheriff in the next befriends him, and Keven finds himself an "outlaw" in this novel where greed makes Pacific Northwest salmon and cedars endangered species.

Like Keven Bell, Clifton Forrest comes home from war injured. By the time Virginia Lundeen gets him home in her car, he's done in: "Virginia, with sudden distress added to her agitation, was not quick-witted enough to keep the young man from falling. He sank at her feet; his hat slipped out of a nerveless hand. For a moment his white face struck her dumb." (p. 30) He too heals, thanks to Virginia and hard work on the "flinty desert," but must fight his own battle with Malpass, who uses the same regenerative land — in the form of a fake mine — and shady financial manipulations to cheat Cliff's father out of his ranch. Cliff eventually gets both Virginia and ranch, but at the cost of her father, killed by the villain.

But Grey's fullest treatment of the World War I trauma comes in *The Desert of Wheat,* where Kurt Dorn's experience in France occupies about one-fourth of the novel, which concludes with the half-dead hero's return and debate with Lenore Anderson who marries Kurt and nurses him. Though the book made "The One Hundred 'Best Sellers' of the Last Quarter Century" in *Publishers Weekly* two years after publication, early reviews were mixed, and one downright scathing. W. B. McCormick, writing in the *New York Sun Books and the Book World,* said *The Desert of Wheat* depicted "class hatred and mankind at it's worst," and decried its "tasteless assault . . . on American women in their relations with our soldiers."[11] Such perceived failings aside, as commentary on "paradise lost" the focus is again on savagery. Keven Bell's claim, "They wanted you . . . to revert to savagery," proves true for Kurt Dorn. "I shudder at what war will make me," Kurt writes. "Actual contact with earth, exploding guns, fighting comrades, striking foes, will make brutes of us all." (p. 253)

At the front, Dorn regards a visit with the famous French fighting group, the Blue Devils, as a high point in his life.

"He was full of gladness, of exultation, in contemplation of the wonderful gift the hours had brought him. More than any men of history or present, he honored these soldiers the Germans feared." Dorn tells himself, "there was a divinity in those soldiers." Seemingly again unaware of the irony American history and literature have attached to the notion of "savage," Grey adds, "Like an Indian, Dorn respected brawn, courage, fortitude, silence, aloofness." (p. 280) The reversion to savagery continues. Seeing a German plane shot down, he has mixed feelings, including exhilaration. "Dorn pitied the destroyed airman, hated himself, and had all the fury of savage joy that had been in his comrades." Soon he has "blown out the brains" of his first German. A short time later, in the thick of hand-to-hand fighting, he has become the savage brute he spoke of:

> His immense and terrible joy bridged the ages between the past and this moment when he leaped light and swift, like a huge cat, upon them. They fired and they hit, but Dorn sprang on, tigerishly, with his loud and nameless laugh. . . . With sweep and lunge he killed one and split a second's skull before the first had fallen. A third he lifted and gored, like a bull, in one single stroke. The fourth and last of that group . . . had scarcely struck the ground when that steel transfixed his bulging throat. (p. 299)

Grey reverses the narrative strategy used in *The Shepherd of Guadaloupe* and *Rogue River Feud* where the heroes return from war at the beginning of the story. In *The Desert of Wheat* Dorn fights his own mini-war first against I.W.W. agitators and foreign agents, then goes to war in Europe. His battle with the agent, Glidden, prefigures events in France. When Glidden is caught sabotaging the harvest, Dorn beats him to a pulp: "Glidden's coat and blouse were half torn off; blood covered him. He was beaten and bent back. His tongue hung out, bloody, fluttering with strangled cries. A ghastly face, appalling in its fear of death." Observing the violence, Lenore has an experience akin to that of Marian Warner in *The Vanishing American* as she watches Nophaie batter his enemies:

> Lenore, seeing clearly for the first time, suffered a strange, hot paroxysm of emotion never before experienced by her. It left her weak. It seemed to stultify the cry that had been trying to escape her. She wanted to scream that Dorn must not kill the man. Yet there was a ferocity in her that froze the cry. (p. 201)

This hint of her own savage sexual potential is another foreshadowing. One night, after Kurt returns home, Lenore overhears her father talking with cowboys about the war. His account of Kurt's war deeds ("He lifted an' slung those two Germans, one after another, quick as that! — like you'd toss a couple of wheat sheafs with your pitchfork, an' he sent them rollin', with blood squirtin' all over.") evokes a sympathetic reaction from Lenore:

> Who was this person whose image stood reflected in the mirror? Lenore's recognition of herself almost stunned her. What had happened? She saw that her hair fell wildly over her bare shoulders; her face shone white, with red spots in her cheeks; her eyes seemed balls of fire; her lips had a passionate, savage curl; her breast, bare and heaving, showed a throbbing, tumultuous heart. And as she realized how she looked, it struck her that she felt an inexplicable passion. She felt intense as steel, hot as fire, quivering with the pulsation of rapid blood, a victim to irrepressible thrills that rushed over her from the very soles of her feet to the roots of her hair. Something glorious, terrible, and furious possessed her. (p. 316)

This sexually savage (or savagely sexual) reaction, Lenore admits to herself, has "retrograded" her, for the moment, to the female of the species, "more savage and dangerous than the male. No use to lie! She had gloried in his prowess. He was her man, gone out with club, to beat down the brutes that would steal her from him." (pp. 316 – 317) Despite this new knowledge, or perhaps because of it, Lenore knows she must "see beyond the physical," she tells Kurt, who has returned minus an arm and, like Buck Duane, full of lead and having internalized violence. And like Duane's Ray Longstreth she must stand between Kurt and his nightmares with their compulsive repetition of killing, the "savage orgy of remurdering the Huns." (p. 326)

The wheatfields of eastern Washington become the "Garden of the World" in this novel; they form the book's final image too, but not before Kurt responds to Lenore. He has experienced the shock of recognition (as has Lenore in her own way): "The truth is that life is a fight. Civilization is only skin-deep. Underneath man is still a savage. He is a savage still because he wants the same he had to have when he lived in primitive state." (p. 235) It hasn't changed. "Today it's called competition in business." (p. 335) Having felt it herself, Lenore can hardly deny it. Instead, she argues for "something in woman — the instinct of creation — the mother — that . . . is the hope of the world." Lenore takes the golden wheat as her symbol and as a modern Ceres argues for the world's "slow growth and perfection."[12] We'll never reach it, she says, "but is not the growth a beautiful and divine thing?" (p. 336)

But evil has already entered this Washington garden in the form of violent agents and, by the extension of war, the world, and the reader has encountered Lenore's "divinity" before — in the Blue Devil killers Kurt so admired in France. Kurt loses an arm, Anderson a son (Lenore's brother), and the earthly garden its virginity. Grey, with pious rhetoric and committed to the lovers' happiness, locates Eden in the only place he can — a vague and uncertain future — "the fertile fields of a golden age to come," but his tropes tell where Kurt finds the real paradise: "in the sense of her compelling presence, in the tender touch of her hands, in the whisper of woman's love." (p. 344) Grey's novels, through irony and metaphor and despite the expected and drippy endings, continue on one level to question the value of competitive individualism and, along with it, the American Dream of conquering the land in order to create the abundant life.

2 Native Americans

The frontier "Eden" was never such for Indians once the white man arrived, and anything but "an elevating moral force," as one commentator views it. Strangely, Grey's major critics, with the exception of Carlton Jackson and Candace Kant, pay scant attention to Grey's Native Americans, though they figure substantially in many of his novels. Several are protagonists: Nophaie of *The Vanishing American* is a full-blooded Indian; Mescal of *Heritage of the Desert,* Beryl Aard of *Rogue River Feud,* and Jean Isbel of *To the Last Man* are half-bloods. Others, like Yaqui of *Desert Gold,* Nas Ta Bega of *The Rainbow Trail,* and Magdalene of *Captives of the Desert* play major roles.[13]

As with his treatment of the land, the law, and terms like "nature" and "savage," Grey shows considerable variety — and irony — in handling these Native Americans. His Indians range from stick-like Sioux warriors who repeatedly attack the train in *The U.P. Trail* to the psychologically complex Nophaie, caught between two cultures. Some of them are traitorous enemies like the Papago herder of *Desert Gold,* some loyal friends like Toddy Nokin of *Wild Horse Mesa,* and some victims like Gekin Yashi of *The Vanishing American.* Grey views them sympathetically. "All the way from *Betty Zane,* written in 1903, to *The Lost Wagon Train,* published in 1936, Grey defended the rights of the American Indian," Carlton Jackson writes.[14] Thus, in *The Thundering Herd* Comanches and Kiowas have good reason for their hostility:

You are stealing their food," Milly Fayre tells Tom Doan. "Their meat — out of their mouths. Not because you're hungry, but to get rich. Oh, Tom, it's wrong!" (p. 160) She refuses to marry him until he gives up buffalo hunting.

But Grey doesn't capitalize on, or even seem to recognize, the irony often implicit. "Would you steal money from the Indians?" Milly asks Tom. With "uplift of head" Tom shows his surprise. "Why, certainly not!" he declares. So Tom, who is above stealing their money, quits stealing their buffalo and takes their land instead. At novel's end he marries Milly and goes back to his American dream: "of a ranch — a home, cattle, horses, tilling the soil." (p. 400) August Naab has been dreaming for years as *Heritage of the Desert* opens; the Edenic Garden of Eschtah is no longer Eschtah's but "my" Navajo Oasis, he says, and argues his claim with an assortment of "laws" against the more candid view of another landgrabber, Holderness, who calls it what it is, "business." (p. 27)

Indians appear somewhat differently and a different brand of irony emerges in *Desert Gold*. Grey draws on the hostility of the Mexican government toward the Yaqui Indians whom Grey's character Yaqui represents. Savagery runs through the novel as a leitmotif. Grey uses the term in three senses: "primitive," fiercely violent, and Indian. Hero Dick Gale becomes a border ranger and gets his training in his toil on "a desert that was harsh and hostile by nature, and perilous by the invasion of savage men." (p. 90) He soon meets some. While scouting, he sees two Indians, a Papago and a Yaqui, ride toward an old campsite already occupied by three Mexicans. As he watches from hiding, he sees one of the Mexicans shoot the two Indians and then trample the Yaqui, all three Mexicans showing a "savagely jocose" manner: "He turned the black to ride again over the other Indian. That brought into Gale's mind what he had heard of a Mexican's hate for a Yaqui. It recalled the barbarism of these savage peons, and the war of extermination being waged upon the Yaquis." (p. 95)

Gale saves the Yaqui and gets him back to the Belding

ranch where he can be nursed back to health. Yaqui becomes a loyal friend, and in a major part of the narrative leads Gale, his friends Thorne, Jim Lash, Ladd, and the Mexican beauty Mercedes (married to Thorne) into the wilderness to escape the bandit, Rojas. After a long trek with Rojas in pursuit, they arrive at a "zone of craters" and finally at one huge and awful crater, a "red chasm" that to Gale resembles "an inferno." If not Dantesque, the scene is at least suggestive, and Grey, not overly given to symbolism, suggests some here willy-nilly. Yaqui shows them a shallow cave, spreads blankets, puts a canteen and a sack of food inside, and leads Mercedes in. The plan is to hide her there while the men take cover along the rim to attack Rojas when he arrives. There is little doubt about the heart of Grey's matter here either. Earlier, Gale looks at Mercedes with the realization: "She represented something in life that men of all races for thousands of years had loved to see and own, to revere and debase, to fight and die for." (p. 165)

Savage violence erupts in this crater of hell around the focal point of Mercedes' cave, heart of hearts and source of competitive desire. Gale repeatedly senses the situation as unreal, a tactic which Grey uses to underscore the dream-like, nature of the event. "It was a weird, ghastly mouth of hell," the hero feels. "Gale stood fascinated, unable to tell how much he saw was real, how much the exaggeration of overwrought emotions." He has to fight against retrogression. "It was a moment — an hour for a savage. . . . Since Gale was not a savage he fought that call of the red gods which sent him back down the long ages toward his primitive day." (pp. 187 – 188) At the battle's climax Rojas — "this savage" — finds the cave, and with rape his intent, attacks Mercedes:

> Rojas had not killed Mercedes. He was overpowering her. His actions seemed slow, wearing, purposeful. Hers were violent. Like a trapped she-wolf, Mercedes was fighting. She tore, struggled, flung herself.
>
> Rojas's intention was terribly plain. (p. 190)

At this critical moment Yaqui drops down to the cave ledge. "He was the savage now," Grey says. Yaqui backs Rojas to the cliff's edge, then knifes the bandit and sends him to the bottom of the chasm. This violent episode, with its symbolic center, reiterates a lesson Gale has learned earlier when "the difference between himself and Yaqui, which he had vaguely felt as that between savages and civilized men, faded out of his mind forever." (p. 175) Clearly, everyone has "savage" potential, and Grey, typically, links erotic desire with its source as he does with that desire's appetitive twin, commercial greed.

After an agonizing stay in the cratered wilderness, Gale and his party make their way back to Belding's only to encounter a much less dream-like bit of savagery in the form of the Chases' (father and son) "business" takeover of Forlorn River land. Again the solution involves violence. The Chases have threatened Nell and made life a "nightmare" in an attempt to get Nell for son Radford. They have dynamited Belding's spring to force him off his land. "Grasping and conscienceless agents of a new force of development of the West," the Chases are determined to ruin Belding and get his daughter. (p. 241) When Gale hears of the threats he goes after Radford and finds him in the Chase "club" room. While Gale beats Radford into "a limp, torn, hulking, bloody figure," Ladd cripples two Mexicans who attempt to draw on Gale. At the novel's end, Yaqui makes a last (ironic) payment of gratitude and leads Gale to gold in the hills above the valley. A bonus is the source of Forlorn River which Gale realizes will enable him to have economic control over the entire valley, including the Chases. The American dream comes true for Dick Gale; Yaqui, dispossessed, but evidently caring more for spiritual comforts, rides off into the sunset, his debt paid.

Indians figure prominently in *The U.P. Trail,* but only as stage props. They appear at the beginning as "bloody savages" who massacre a wagon train and repeatedly attack the railroad workers throughout. At the end of the book Grey attaches a coda acknowledging that the train signals the Indians' demise. A band of Sioux and their chief pause on a promontory and watch "this beast that puffed smoke and spat fire and shrieked like a devil of an alien tribe." The old chief recognizes "a superior race, but not a nobler one," and stands "somber as death" in his "acceptance of the inevitable bitterness." (p. 313)

Grey's character Slingerland, a trapper dressed in buckskin and reminiscent of Daniel Boone or Natty Bumppo, is sympathetic to the red man's plight and speaks for trappers and Indians alike. "I know Injuns thet beat white men holler for all thet's noble," he says early in the story. (p. 45) He becomes a surrogate father for Allie Lee until she's abducted while he's away tending a trap line. When he returns and finds her gone, he sees it as "the result of civilization marching westward," and asks himself, "What right had the government to steal land from the Indians, to break treaties, to run a steam track across the plains and mountains?" (p. 95)

His rhetorical question goes unanswered except in terms of the novel's events and scattered commentary on the notion of "progress." Warren Neale, the hero, is himself "a dreamer," but realizes that however grand in conception the transcontinental railroad may be, "its political and mercenary features could not be beautiful to him." (p. 82) Sabotage, attempts of corrupt engineers to bribe Neale, reference to the Credit Mobilier scandal, and the role of Allie Lee's father, a railroad bigwig, all emphasize the seamy side of the railroad's advance. The train itself becomes the symbol for a dehumanizing rush for profit. Beauty Stanton, caught up in it, is "a cog in the wheel, a grain of dust in the whirlwind, a morsel of flesh and blood for the hungry maw of a wild and passing monster of progress." (p. 247)

Slingerland, himself a vanishing species, hates this "great, shining steel band of progress connecting East and West," knowing that "what one group of greedy men had accomplished others would imitate." Slingerland in fact shares the same viewpoint as the Indian, "that far-seeing eye cleared by distance and silence, and the force of the great, lonely hills. Progress was great, but nature undespoiled was greater." He envisages the future, a "marvelous prosperity from timber, mines, farms, and in the distant end — a gutted West." Given this foresight, he has but little choice; he heads into the hills to find an Edenic garden, and does, in "the very heart of the great wild range." This is still virgin land: "No foot, not even an Indian's had ever desecrated this green valley." Here he can live out his remaining years as another Adam, sans Eve, a realm which Grey's lush prose carries into fantasy, useless passions like "discontent and longing, and then hate" unable to survive amid the rosy dawns, and so on. (pp. 311 – 312)

Despite Slingerland's role and the comments on "progress," sympathy for the Indian in *The U.P. Trail* gets muted, for the busyness of Grey's plot; the business — crooked — of engineers, financiers, and the chief villain, Allie's stepfather, Durade; and paeans of praise glorifying the American working man (embodied in Casey and his exploits) focus the reader elsewhere. Durade's illegal actions, typically for Grey, link sex and economic exploitation; he abducts Allie, then plans to use her for a shill in his crooked gambling den, with the threat of prostitution or rape hovering in the wings. The tumult of the railroad's temporary "hell-cities" and the rest of the narrative terminate with the line's completion at Promontory Point. Even Neale watches with shining eyes and sees the scene as "great, beautiful, final." Among the crowd Grey includes the Vice President, California's governor, railroad dignitaries, Mormons, soldiers, and laborers — Irish, Negro, Chinese, and Mexican. Though there were some at the historic original, no Indians appear.

Grey's most direct commentary on Indian-white problems comes in two relatively early works, *The Rainbow Trail* and, especially, *The Vanishing American,* where he harshly criticizes missionaries, government agents, and others who seduce Indian women, sell illegal whiskey, and otherwise exploit the Native Americans. In *The Rainbow Trail's* opening, the protagonist, Shefford, encounters a white man struggling with a young Indian woman. The man's face is "corded and dark with passion," and Shefford knocks him flat. The woman turns out to be Glen Naspa, sister of Nas Ta Bega, a Navajo who has spent fourteen years in white schools. "They took fourteen years of my life," he tells Shefford shortly afterward, "They wanted to make me a missionary among my own people. But the white man's ways and his life and his God are not the Indian's. They never can be." (p. 41)

Grateful for Shefford's intervention on Glen Naspa's behalf, Nas Ta Bega befriends him, tutors him in the Navajo's sacred relationship to nature, and aids him in the rescue of Fay Larkin, held captive by a Mormon who desires to make her a sealed wife. Someone knifes the Mormon villain, Waggoner, in time to prevent him from forcing Fay, who is found in a faint and presumed to be the murderess. Near the narrative's end, Nas Ta Bega admits that he killed this man "who believed he had conversed with God on earth, who believed he had a divine right to rule women," thus more than repaying his debt. (p. 177) Fay escapes, but Glen Naspa is not so lucky. Midway in the story Shefford confronts the Indian woman's assailant — the missionary Willets — and chokes the truth out of him. He has seduced Glen Naspa and lured her from her home. (pp. 130 – 132) When Shefford hears she has returned, he finds she has died in childbirth. For Nas Ta Bega, his sister's death symbolizes "the vanishing of his race from the earth." (p. 268) Shefford paces outside the Navajo hogan "with an aching heart for Nas Ta Bega," and "something of the white man's burden of crime toward the Indian weighing upon his soul." (p. 167)

Shefford wonders if Nas Ta Bega will kill Willets, and Grey has the Indian reply that he is above revenge. He then gives Shefford a lengthy lecture on the history of Indian-white relations, recounting how first the Spanish padres came — for gold — then pioneers, then prospectors "mad like the padres," then missionaries. Had the latter demonstrated "humanity," they would have helped the Indian "in his ignorance of sickness and work, and left him his god." Unfortunately, they came "to trouble the Indian about his god" and thus "worked at the roots of his nature." Nas Ta Bega concludes by acknowledging that the Navajo way is passing and says that "leaving religion, greed, and war out of the question, contact with the white man would alone have ruined the Indian." (p. 170)

Grey doesn't do much with the term "savage" in *The Rainbow Trail*, but one notable passage suggests an ironic link with the term in all its nuances. The passage also argues against critic Cynthia Hamilton's contention that Grey's formulaic marriage "requires the heroine to surrender her conscience in the name of practicality."[15] *The Rainbow Trail* provides a different perspective. When Shefford and Fay talk about the mysterious Mormon's threat, Fay asks Shefford if he will keep her away from the villain. "If you love me you will do it," she says. Shefford, "almost beside himself," wonders how. *"You can kill him!"* she says (Grey's italics). "It was there, deep and full in her voice, the strength of the elemental forces that had surrounded her, primitive passion and hate and love, *as they were in woman in the beginning*." (p. 164, emphasis added) This is "male ego prop" of a different kind than Hamilton envisions. Ex-minister Shefford's passions understandably flame at the thought of being asked to — and wanting to — murder. He swears to save her and take her away, and they part; Shefford watches her take the stepping stones "with her old free grace" and stride down the path "swift and lithe as an Indian." (p. 165) Clearly, Fay Larkin has the "savage" potential discovered by Lenore Anderson and some of Grey's other heroines.

While the fate of Glen Naspa focuses on the Indian as victim, her brother, Nas Ta Bega, illustrates another, more positive side, for Grey sees in the Navajo a kind of spiritual guide intimately associated with nature. In *Desert Gold,* Dick Gale realizes "a man must know a savage as Gale knew Yaqui" before he could authoritatively assess the significance of desert experience. He observes two "stages" in this Native American, one marked by "tenaciousness of life, stoicism, endurance, strength," the other by a colossal "honor, loyalty, love." (p. 238) Nas Ta Bega exhibits similar qualities, though he is less mysterious than Gale's Yaqui. He is "a sage and a poet — the very spirit of this desert," trader Withers tells Shefford. (p. 62) Near the end of the book Shefford sums up what he has learned from his Indian mentor: "Life was eternal. Man's immortality lay in himself. . . . Brotherhood — that mystic and grand 'Bi Nai!' of the Navajo — that was religion." (p. 226) Thanks to this Indian "brother" Shefford has come a long way from the mean-spirited congregation he once tried to serve.

John Cawelti repeatedly stresses the "religious" element in Grey. The heroes' "acts of violence are carried out with a kind of transcendent religious passion that might be seen as a sort of manic bloodlust were it not in such a good and holy cause," he says, and the western landscape is "symbolic of the transcendent religious and moral forces of wilderness." The "ultimate result of the confrontation with wild nature and violent men" affirms American values which include "the centrality of religion to life."[16] This overstates the case and overlooks the ironies that so often crop up. Granted, some of Grey's landscape suggests "transcendent religious and moral forces," much of it does not. Early in *The Rainbow Trail,* Shefford climbs a slope preparatory to camping. He sees "lofty crags and cathedral spires" (a candidate for "religious/moral") and a wonderful canyon with "huge beetling red walls." (p. 18) This is followed by a full paragraph of lush prose describing the sunset. But a menacing stranger interrupts this idyllic scene, draws a gun, and Shefford senses disaster; the stranger is about to desecrate this "cathedral" with Shefford's blood. "He had a brain and a soul," Shefford thinks in near panic, "and between them he might have worked out his salvation. But what were they to this ruthless night-wanderer, this raw and horrible wildness of the desert?" (p. 20) What indeed? Nas Ta Bega arrives just in time to scare the stranger away, and takes Shefford for a missionary. "Navajo no savvy Jesus Christ," he says bluntly.

(p. 22) Moreover, the same nature that, embodied in the cliffs, appears like "cathedral spires" seems quite something else in the form of the Colorado River near novel's end: "It moaned, whined, mocked, and laughed. It had the soul of a devil. It was a river that had cut its way to the bowels of the earth, and its nature was destructive." (p. 238)

The hero's "kind of transcendent religious passion" and "holy" cause are the critic's terms, not Grey's, and Cawelti cites no passages in support of them, nor of the "religious-erotic" treatment of hero and heroine, nor of the "centrality of religion" to life. Some of the trouble here perhaps stems from the connotations of religion. In any case, religion, at least in some of its American forms, does not fare well in Grey, as his use of Mormons and missionaries attests. Shefford, a former minister, has been "driven" from his calling by a "narrow congregation" that "repudiated his ideas of religion and immortality and God." Grey's clergymen are available for quicky weddings — as in *The Arizona Clan* or the five-minute nuptials of *The Maverick Queen* — but have virtually no other function. Again, at the end of *Boulder Dam* both "a Catholic priest and a Presbyterian minister" visit hero Lynn Weston in the hospital simultaneously, but he dismisses them saying he has no great need of their services at present. (p. 184)

What Grey does stress is "spirit" as the keyword to a vague nature mysticism. "There was a spirit in the canyon," Shefford senses near the end of the story:

> and whether or not it was what the Navajo embodied in the great Nonnezoshe, or the life of the present, or the death of the ages, or the nature so magnificently manifested in those silent, dreaming, waiting walls — the truth for Shefford was that this spirit was God. (p. 226)

This seems akin to the "sacrality" Max Westbrook speaks about, a reasonably appropriate term both for Grey's response to external nature and the contribution offered by the Indian.[17] Grey's fullest exploration of both comes in *The*

Vanishing American, which contains several Indian prayers and repeated efforts by hero Nophaie to find spiritual peace in the white man's world. "The great breathing spirit of nature all around him was as true to him as any spirit the Indians might have worshipped. It was there — the mysterious power — the eternal thing — the infinite," he thinks at one point. (p. 115)

But "nature" in *The Vanishing American* is ambiguous. So is the breathing "spirit" that inhabits it. Later, when Nophaie makes one of his trips to his sacred desert retreat, he reaches the snowline of Nothsis Ahn and gazes at "the naked earth" below: "Over all the immensity of ghastly desert brooded a spirit of desolation and death and decay. The sun blazed down a terrible truthfulness of light." (p. 218) For Nophaie, at this moment at least, the breathing spirit breathes death. Moreover, the desolate scene proves prophetic; in the remaining part of the novel, the corrupt whites cause Indian deaths, influenza claims more, and Nophaie kills Germans in the war. In one of the book's many ironies, Nophaie, the most spiritually conscious character, tries to save the lives of the three white villains when other Indians are about to burn them out. One of them is the lecherous missionary, Morgan, who, "foaming at the mouth," yells out, *"Kill that Indian atheist!"* Another, Glendon, nearly does, shooting Nophaie in the chest. (p. 329) Grey's use of "spirit" in the desolate scene on sacred ground proves less "religious" than a piece of ominous and ironic foreshadowing. Nowhere does Grey make religion "central."

All in all, Grey shows considerable sympathy for Native Americans and some understanding of the Indian's cultural bind caught between two conflicting world views. He endows them with a sacral stance, as with Nas Ta Bega and Nophaie, or, as in *Captives of the Desert,* embodies it in the Hopi snake and other dances. But though he remains aware of the original injustice of the seizure of Indian lands (by having characters comment on it), he avoids confronting this issue directly and the result is the irony in the possessive remarks of August Naab in *Heritage of the Desert*. Insofar as the narratives approach any solution for Indian grievances, there is none really, only resignation, as in *The U.P. Trail;* intermarriage, as in *Heritage of the Desert, To the Last Man,* and *Rogue River Feud;* or a little of both, as in *The Vanishing American*. For contributing a sense of the sacredness of nature to the package of elements that makes up Grey's westerns, Indians get little narrative return except abuse, the friendship and admiration of a few protagonists, and the prospect, at best, of being absorbed into the American stream (or American's dream).

3
Roundup

On the surface at least, Grey offers a kind of dream experience with his western entertainment package. Some of this package features elements common to many westerns; like a number of other writers he provides wish fulfillments in terms of violence, erotic titillation and idyllic marriage, an escapist fantasy in a setting which offers romantic distance, adventure — some of it melodrama full of chase and pursuit, masked identities, and secret retreats — and shoot-outs, both man-to-man and large-scale eruptions.

As Grey commentators often remark, much of this has an adolescent appeal. For Cynthia Hamilton, Grey writes as Leslie Fiedler's "Good-Bad Boy," romanticizing the role of the artist and recasting his own experiences in terms of the western frontier.[18] This is that "timeless cowboy era," as David B. Davis puts it, where a reader finds a "reflection of the sense of approaching adulthood."[19] In this connection, Grey himself made a revealing comment in a letter to Dolly. On April 30, 1938, he wrote asking a question. "Where do I find these romances?" He answered it himself. "Somewhere, sometime, they happened," he said, and added that his reward and faith in himself came "from the many letters I get from simple readers — old women, and young girls and boys, to all with hearts full of romance, all true to the children in them."[20] While readers come in all stripes and colors, Grey's choices here for the appeal of his works are striking.

In such an imaginative era — an era which Cawelti says becomes "the locus of an adolescent dream society without the complex institutions and restrictions on impulsive freedom associated with the East" — a reader can live out fantasies of power, courage, virility, and success.[21] Richard Slotkin puts it somewhat differently. Speaking of the "relative absence of social restraints" in the New World generally, he says, "In Europe all men were under authority; in America all men dreamed they had the power to become authority." Thus a strong man, "by mastering the law of the wilderness-jungle" could "impose his personal dream of self-aggrandizement on reality."[22] To the extent a Grey reader's fantasies covet such power or "authority," she or he can indulge in forbidden violence and have that violence justified in a good cause. *Riders of the Purple Sage* and others illustrate this dream fulfillment.

Part of the fantasy package, but a highlight for Grey, is the pair of handsome lovers and their quest for romance. Grey's protagonists, Cawelti says, have a "mixture of maturity and innocence, of experience and purity, of shyness and latent violence."[23] They range from mature, notorious gunmen, like Renn Frayne of *Knights of the Range,* to determined youths like Buff Belmet of *The Thundering Herd,* but all are deadly if forced to fight, tender when faced with love. Similarly, heroines range from the exotic Mescal of *Heritage of the Desert* to the confident Marian Warner of *The Vanishing American* to the sexy Ann Vandergrift of *Boulder Dam*. Davis' "ten-gallon" specimen may be "the hero of the pre-adolescent," but for Grey the "revolt against femininity" doesn't apply.[24] Brazos Keene may ride away from Las Animas at dawn in *Twin Sombreros,* but he's awfully glad when June

Neece catches up to claim him. And he's anxious to see the tell-tale birthmark on her "laig," the only way to tell the Neece twins apart. Grey's erotic appeal may have been lost for a time on the critics, and have paled a bit with time, but many, like critic William Bloodworth, evidently read Grey for "the sex," even if not fully realizing what, on returning some twenty-five years later, seemed so evident. Good, safe sex too — lecherous villains aside — for the hero and heroine chastely marry and corral all those metaphorically stormy passions and bare breasts.

But the land may be the feature most remembered from the Grey package. Vast and majestic, it offers both challenge and opportunity, a chance not only for romance, but a new start. At least Grey's mythic West does. According to Robert G. Athearn, even through the 1920s reports made it seem so for easterners:

> Space, the West's great and lasting resource, gave man room to breathe, provided him with freedom of movement and fertile ground for the growth of personal dignity, which was so rapidly being lost in the crowded concrete jungles of big eastern cities. There, men had surrendered their identities, but out in this still-untamed land, such words as *stranger* or *pardner* had that special meaning, one denoting an unfenced society or the scarcity of humans, and it acted as a flavor or a scent whose fragrance hinted at older times when the West was new and wholesome.[25]

As a haunting possibility, such an opportunity for a fresh start — both psychic and physical — is no small item. It evokes some of the appeal of *Robinson Crusoe* and *The Swiss Family Robinson*, both Grey favorites. In *Wild Horse Mesa* Sue Melberne, with the help of Jake, fashions a simple tent dwelling in a manner reminiscent of the heroes of those classics. Sue and Jake make a mattress of boughs along one side of the tent, spread a tarp over it, then cover the remaining floor space with more boughs:

> Upon this springy carpet she spread the few Indian blankets she had. Jake fashioned a crude little rack to hold whatever she chose to hang upon it. Her duffle she placed in a corner. Then upon the chest, which could serve as a table, she placed her little mirror and the other toilet articles she possessed, her sewing kit, and a bag of sundry materials. Whereupon she surveyed the interior of her canvas home with a great deal of satisfaction, and sat down to consider which of her other numerous tasks she would begin first. (p. 66)

Grey's "little," repeated, gives the passage a juvenile tone, but the experience conjures up images of Crusoe-Robinson efforts to make a primitive home out of the wilderness. Similarly, most of Grey's novels describe a plentiful supply of wild game which appeals to a pioneering sense of self-sufficiency. In *The Hash Knife Outfit,* Jim Traft lives at his uncle's ranch, but "starts from scratch" by building a cabin in the wild and beautiful Yellow Jacket area where "wild turkeys and deer scarcely made an effort to move into the green brush." (p. 104) *30,000 on the Hoof's* entire story recounts such a new start and, given Logan Huett's bad luck, re-starts.

In these idyllic fresh-start settings Grey's heroes and heroines find true love; usually they find financial reward too. "Grey's heroes do not make the transition to capitalists," Hamilton says.[26] But that depends on how one defines "capitalists" and "make the transition." In any case, the protagonists often end up on a ranch with potential for fifty thousand head of cattle, a situation "capitalistic" enough for most. Grey lashes out repeatedly at greed, but likes his heroes to be well-fixed, deservedly so, of course. Having demonstrated their skills, they sometimes marry the wealth, as does Gene Stewart (*The Light of Western Stars*), Milt Dale (*The Man of the Forest*), Jim Wall (*Robbers Roost*), and others, or find gold, as in *The Border Legion* and *Desert Gold,* or are offered the job of chief engineer, a top-of-the-trade position as in *The U.P. Trail* and *Boulder Dam.*

For the reader, this land of the fresh start and the rewards that go with it probably seems part mythic, part real. Grey tries to give the ring of authenticity to his works particularly in terms of setting — naming and describing real places — and sometimes, less successfully, by referring to historical persons like Billy the Kid and events like the Pleasant Valley War. The romantic adventure plots, however, inevitably introduce fantasy. Cawelti captures the gist of the matter succinctly when he says that many of Grey's qualities "were exemplary of that ability to color history with romance and to clothe fantasy with verisimilitude that are of the essence of the successful formulaic creator's skills."[27]

Grey was upset with critics who said his works were not "authentic," and yet they never could be, as Cawelti aptly intimates. In the "Foreword" of *To the Last Man,* the two sides, "fantasy" and "verisimilitude," emerge; Grey tells us how hard he sought for the facts of the Pleasant Valley War, yet earlier in the same preface defends the dream-like character of romance in language that suggests a fictive portrayal of what he takes to be psychologically authentic: "And I have yet to know anyone who has not some secret dream, some hope, however dim, some storied wall to look at in the dusk, some painted window leading to the soul." (n.p.) He ends up essentially doing what he pleases, writing according to his "conception" of events.

W. H. Hutchinson's terms "outside-in" and "inside-out" add a different perspective to the same point. James Folsom's summary of Hutchinson is useful: "Westerns written from the 'outside-in' are judged to be a type of escape literature whose hallmark is irresponsibility to the world of fact. Westerns written from the 'inside-out,' in contrast, honor the world of fact and are faithful to it."[28] Grey might have thought of himself as writing from the "inside-out." Having visited nearly every place he describes, he tries to "honor the world of fact." In *Arizona Ames,* for example, Grey talks of the outlaw gangs that infest the region:

> Up in the wild notch where the Gros Ventre River crossed from the head of the Wind River Range, or where the Snake River cut through the Teton Range, the Wind River gang had their rendezvous. Down in Utah, in the canyon fastnesses of the Green River, hid the outlaws of Robbers Roost and the Hole in the Wall. These desperadoes sometimes rode far north along the winding Green River, across the Union Pacific Railroad, to the rich ranch lands of the Wind River Valley. These gangs engaged in conflict with one another more often than with the cowboy posses. (p. 79)

The geography rings with authenticity.

Yet some critics still argue the "real" versus "unreal" case. "One hint after another reminds the reader," Christine Bold maintains, "that events in Grey's works have little to do with the larger world of reality." In support, she cites remarks of characters, descriptions of landscape, and Grey's use of traditional forms as "a strategy for distancing his fictional world from any contemporary or realist context."[29] Carlton Jackson, on the other hand, says Grey's works are "in a very real sense" historical novels "because he gave, on the whole, accurate reconstructions of the periods he wrote about," and produced "a fairly authentic picture of the Old West."[30] Jackson's "Old West" is itself mythic, but that aside, Grey does give a reader some inside knowledge of people, places, and things, but then in a number of ways "distances"—to use Bold's term—his stories from anything like a slice of real life, hoping, presumably, that his combination will encourage that willing suspension of disbelief.

Yet another feature of the dream package a Grey western offers is the affirmation of values. The question is, which values? Again critics disagree. Some are hardly in dispute; Grey's narratives affirm a chaste romantic love ending in marriage, the triumph of "good guys" over "bad," a set of traits—loyalty, courage, fair play—under the rubric of a "Code," and the appeal (beauty, challenge, awesomeness) of the western land itself. But these are general, and fairly obvious. The problem arises particularly with critical attempts to assess the ways in which a Grey novel — or the entire canon — might be said to comment on American politico-economic practice.

Thus for one critic Grey's heroes "represent an entire system of values that contradicts, point by point, the values of modern capitalist society."[31] By contrast, another, speaking in general of "the values and assumptions built into the American adventure formula," says that these values "are also central to the ideological tradition of the United States; to that body of ideas which form the basis for its political, economic and social system."[32] The first critic elaborates neither an "entire system" nor "point by point," but shifts instead to Grey's sometime concern with "flappers" and "effeminate Eastern dudes" who represent "the decadence and failure of bourgeois cultural aspirations that can only be cured by a return to a more natural moral system."[33] The second is on far more solid, and important, ground, and spells out Grey's narrative implications for capitalism. In this view, the Grey western reaffirms the importance of individual competition in an era of Big Business, showing that the loner hero has the skill and courage to prevail and succeed even over the combine.

But "Big Business" here implies not capitalism per se, but capitalism out of control. As competitive individualists, Grey's heroes in fact embody capitalism at its best: they have the managerial and practical skills (running a ranch, managing men, engineering a dam); they are aggressive (persistent and often seeking out the enemy for a showdown); they triumph and succeed fairly (drawing quicker but letting the opponent try first) — though, ironically, not always within the "law"; and they "profit" financially (ranch, gold). In short, they refute not capitalism, but capitalism gone haywire in the form of villains who exploit weakness and vulnerability by unfair means.

Finally, the reader who wants to probe more deeply to

determine what else Grey's works might imply about America and its values will find a number of ironies, some small, some large, which of course render Grey distinctive beyond his other contributions to the western.

One irony concerns the Indians. "There are many American Dreams and nightmares," David Madden says, sensibly.[34] For Indians the various American dreams were never anything but nightmares; from early on, the availability of land, the dynamics of capitalist competition, and, in many cases, an abundance of good old-fashioned greed, dictated the dispossession of the Native American. American literature — to say nothing of Kentucky and other ordinances offering rewards for Indian scalps — contains a storehouse of ironic commentary on this dispossession, some of it direct, some of it oblique.

To cite one of the earliest examples, Charles Brockden Brown, the first American novelist to try to make a living at it, tackled the problem in one of America's earliest fictions, *Edgar Huntly* (1799).[35] In it, the titular hero's sympathy for Clithero Edny causes him to follow the sleepwalking man into the Pennsylvania frontier wilderness. He finds him in a cave with a seemingly impassable "gulf" between them. Later, in a dream-trance himself, Huntly returns to the cave only to fall into the bottom of a pit. When he regains consciousness, "immersed in palpable obscurity," he gropes about; the first object he encounters is an Indian tomahawk. "This incident afforded me no hint from which I might conjecture my state," he says. The reader need not remain in such darkness. Hunger and fear reduce Huntly to an instinctual, "savage" state; he contemplates suicide with the tomahawk, then uses it to kill a panther (which he calls a "savage"), gorges himself on the warm flesh, and eventually fights his way back to civilization, slaughtering five Indians along the way. In words which sum up much of the book's irony, Huntly concludes that "no one knows the powers that are latent in his constitution. Called forth by imminent dangers, our efforts frequently exceed our most sanguine belief." (p.

159) As with any number of Grey protagonists, Huntly discovers his own savage potential (the wilderness cave his "heart of hearts"), but in a way which throws ominous shadows on the Indians' future.

James Fenimore Cooper, to whom the western owes so much, and who himself had so much to say about "savagism," missed the point. In the preface to *The Spy* (1821) he patronizingly expressed his apprehension about palates that could relish the cave scene in *Edgar Huntly,* "because it contains an American, a savage, a wild cat, and a tomahawk, in a conjunction that never did, nor ever will occur."[36] But Brown's symbolic conjunction of course did occur; by the 1860s Huntly's tomahawk had become a Civil War musket, the wildcat a guerilla marauder, and Americans demonstrated again their potential for savage violence and parricide. The decimation of the Indian continued apace. On the red man's scale of values, white men qualified as "outlaws" and "savages."

Grey's *Captives of the Desert* illustrates. The abused Indian woman, Magdalene, puts her thoughts bluntly:

> "I do not think there is a God, John Curry, and if there is, what can He have to do with our little lives?" she pursued. "I have been thinking of it all morning. Why, if there is a God, did He make races, one to conquer the other, one to be superior to the other, one to break the hearts of the other?" (p. 99)

Curry, the hero, admits the "poignant truth" of her thoughts. The novel in fact offers another first-rate example of Grey's use of irony, irony which in this case involves the story's only significant Indian, Magdalene.

First, the book's title proves ambiguous. "When it gets you, it never lets go," Mrs. Shelley warns narrator Katherine concerning the desert making her a "captive" in the good sense. (p. 117) But Katherine's friend, Mary Newton, is captive in two senses, one good, one bad. Married to the villain, Wilbur Newton, and in love with John Curry, Mary describes her plight in a desert simile: "I've been like a plant born in a dark canyon that once in the year of its life happened to feel the sun. After that the plant would struggle more than ever toward the light, wouldn't it?" (p. 110) She alludes to her love for Curry.

Curry returns her love and feels himself trapped in the same "canyon." Late in the novel he applies the simile to life in general and includes both himself and Magdalene, to whom he speaks. "Going through life is something like riding a deep canyon where the light seldom shines," he says, and trying to encourage the Indian woman adds, "Don't you want to struggle on a little longer, Magdalene? I'm boxed in at present myself, in a canyon as dark as hell, but I'm feeling around for the way out." (p. 197) Magdalene, Mary, and Curry share the metaphorical captivity, though in different ways. Curry's is relatively simple — frustrated love. Mary's is complicated in that though her love too is frustrated, she struggles inwardly concerning ideas of loyalty toward her no-good husband (though she doesn't know the worst of his crimes and infidelity). Magdalene's — if frustration can be measured in these terms — is deeper yet; her desert captivity seems death-laden, and turns out to be, though not for her. "By birth and tradition I am part of the desert," she says. "Perhaps that is why you send us back to the desert when you are through changing us." Like Nophaie of *The Vanishing American,* her white education alienates her from her people. "I feel as if the great walls of rock under which my people love to ride would fall and crush me if I went close." (p. 101)

This all adds up to a "captivity" narrative of a different sort. Newton has seduced Magdalene and she tells Curry she is pregnant with his child. Magdalene represents the virgin desert land and its natives, Newton an example of its worst exploiters. As with most of Grey's outlaw villains, he lusts after both gold and girl, running a bootleg liquor operation to the Indians. The commercial nature of his exploitation is clear: "He can't marry me. So I got paid. Fifty dollars instead of marriage," Magdalene tells Curry. (p. 199) Ironically,

Magdalene becomes the "light" which lets Curry and Mary out of the desert "canyon" by killing Newton. The villain, on the run, tries to rape Magdalene and in the struggle she shoots him. In her words of the awful event, "I tried to scream and I could not scream. I tried to pull away. His arms came around me tight and his face so close, and he pushed me back on the bed. Your gun was there." (p. 230)

Thus the novel's chief Indian/desert representative ends one part of her own captivity — that involving Newton — and completely frees Mary and Curry from theirs so they can marry. At the same time, whites, minus their worst representative, continue to take over the desert land, a process nearly complete at the time of the novel's setting. The early scene of Indian dancing at the village of Oraibi illustrates. However sacral, and however sympathetically Grey treats the Snake Dance, it has already become a "point-of-interest" on a scenic desert tour. Good Mrs. Shelley's words, "it won't let you go," become, in retrospect, doubly ironic; with whites, it is also the other way around. Mrs. Shelley might well have directed her "warning" — slightly reworded — to the Indians.

A second of Grey's significant ironies concerns the law. As with the Indian, sexploitation is at the root. *The Lone Star Ranger* offers Grey's most searching study of the complexity of the concept of "law." The term "outlaw" — given a context of conflicting "laws" — dissolves into ambiguity. Grey — or his narrative — calls into question the meaning of law and illustrates both its arbitrary application and corruption. Noah Webster, sometimes marvelously expansive in his 1828 *An American Dictionary of the English Language*, gives twenty-six definitions for "law." One of them (number 3) is that eighteenth-century favorite, the "Law of nature," which is "a rule of conduct arising out of the natural relations of human beings established by the Creator, and existing prior to any positive precept." Confident in his source, Webster adds, "Thus it is a *law of nature*, that one man should not injure another, and murder and fraud would be crimes, independent of any prohibition from a supreme power." Number 16 suggests another kind, "That which governs or has a tendency to rule; that which has the power of controlling."[37]

Number 16 is really a variant of the westerner's "law of the sixgun," or passion armed. Webster's illustration, in fact, makes the passionate point. He quotes St. Paul: "But I see another law in my members warring against the law of my mind, and bringing me into captivity to the law of sin which is in my members. Rom. 7." The ambiguity of number 3's "natural relations" aside (since it only further confuses the issue; can there really be unnatural relations between people?), Webster acknowledges with his supporting Biblical authority that passion often prevails over reason, thus rendering "law" even more ambiguous.

As it does in *Raiders of Spanish Peaks*, the role of erotic passion, the last of the Grey ironies to underscore, joins with the exploration of law. The novel is not as rich as *The Lone Star Ranger* concerning things legal and illegal, but shows Grey pondering them nonetheless. Vigilante hangings frame the narrative, occurring at the beginning and again at the end of the action. Hero Laramie, camping out, awakens to the noise of a lynch party talking. Laramie intervenes and saves the intended victim, young Lonesome Mulhall. Corrupt rancher Price has caught Lonesome "brandin' calves" that weren't his. Lonesome admits it but argues that every rider has stolen a head of stock at sometime, including Price. Price says, "If I done so, nobody ever ketched me," and laughs. (p. 3) About to be strung up, Lonesome bursts out with the real reason for Price's enmity: "I knowed it. Yu're hangin' me cause she has no use fer yu." Price throws the rope over a branch. "I've seen more'n one of yore brand dangle from this cottonwood," he says "with a coarse grim humor that failed to hide passion." (p. 4) Lonesome later explains to Laramie that Price had been "loony" over Annie Lakin and according to the cowboys "had a chance" until Lonesome showed up. Erotic desire and resulting jealousy, not rustling, lie behind the attempted hanging.

Lonesome and Laramie become pards and happen on Tracks Williams, a former pard of Lonesome's. Tracks has been jailed in a raid to round up newcomers to the town, though he committed no crime (a minor bit of extra-legal activity). Laramie and Lonesome rescue him, breaking open the jail and freeing eight others as well. Tracks joins to form a troika. Ironically, "passion" ended the partnership of Lonesome and Tracks earlier. Lonesome tells Laramie that he fell in love with a young redheaded woman about to be married to a stockman, and Lonesome called the stockman, Cheesbrough, "a big cheese," and was beaten up "somethin' awful." Tracks saw his pard's condition, called Cheesbrough out, shot him and had to flee. Thus passion on the part of the "good guys" — but similar to Price's — results in a killing.

Erotic passion figures heavily in the novel's major action too. The three pards hire on with an easterner, Lindsay, who conveniently has three daughters. Lindsay has purchased Spanish Peaks ranch from a man named Allen. A double-dipper, Allen cheats Lindsay on the original sale and then buys and resells cattle that a rustler named Arlidge steals from Lindsay. In the book's climactic event, Price, Chess Gaines, and some others of Arlidge's outlaw gang abduct Lenta, the Lindsay sister Lonesome falls for. At the climax, Gaines says, "So help me Gawd, I'm goin' to have you," leaps on Lenta "like a tiger," and is "crushing her tight in a mingled anger and passion" when she bites him. Laramie has been hiding in the loft of the cabin and has his gun on Gaines, but Lonesome shows up in the doorway and shoots, spattering the chimney with the outlaw's brains (Gaines, incidentally, having no chance to draw).

Subsequently, Laramie, et al, force the truth out of a black cowboy, Johnson, by threatening to lynch him. They then hang Price. Laramie and Lonesome watch the strangling man and the novel thus comes to an ironic full circle. Laramie sees the "wild justice" of lynching, part of the western Code, as both ugly and futile. Moreover, both Laramie and Price — hero and villain — have been part of many such lynchings.

But a major irony is that Laramie thinks "the advent of women" will alter the situation, when in fact a frontier woman (Annie Lakin) is behind the first attempted lynching, another behind Tracks' shooting of Cheesbrough, and a third (Lenta) behind Lonesome's shooting of Chess Gaines and lynching of Price. Not only is the law here ambiguous and ineffectual, but erotic passion — issuing in jealousy and desire for revenge — proves the major motive for those who "administer" it.

This irony that escapes Laramie is double-barbed, pointing both at the concept of law and the theme of the killing power of erotic desire. And once again Grey's tropes, characters, and narrative events suggest the intermingling of economics and sex, not so overtly as with *The Maverick Queen,* but, in *Raiders of Spanish Peaks,* covertly — rustling as the "cover" in this case for the heart of the matter. And that "heart" is again a savage potential transcending "good" and "bad": both rustler Chess Gaines and hero Laramie Wilson try to manhandle the women they desire (Lenta and Hallie respectively), passion getting the better of them. Both women fight back, each drawing blood. Gaines calls Lenta a "she-cat"; Hallie finds herself "a savage, a tigress." (pp. 276, 293) What has the West done to her? Hallie asks herself. Brought out the "primitive," just as it has for Laramie, Tracks, Lonesome, Price, Chess Gaines, and Lenta. Passion is the "wildfire" that burns in good and bad alike. To his credit, Grey seems instinctively to have rested much of his work on this earthy base.

When it translates into exploitation (economic/sexual) as it so often does in Grey, the result is an oblique but telling commentary on any system's potential for violence and abuse — U.S. capitalism included. Since Grey locates the problem within the heart, he tells us something about ourselves, not only as Americans, but as human beings. As John Milton says on the first page of his study of the western novel, "The western seems to explain to us something about ourselves and our dreams, on both a personal and a national level."[38] This surely applies to Zane Grey.

Appendix

Summaries of Grey's Fifty-six Westerns

Note to the Reader: This list starts with *Heritage of the Desert* and follows the book publication order conveniently printed in Kenneth W. Scott's reference guide, *Zane Grey: Born to the West*. Endnotes indicate the particular editions and printings of Grey novels which are cited throughout the text. Each entry includes a "key" word or phrase intended merely as a suggestion to help the reader.

Heritage of the Desert (1910), which triggered Grey's rise to fame and financial independence, features the love affair of easterner John Hare and the half-Indian beauty, Mescal.[1] The reader's heritage from this irony-laden novel is considerable: Grey places his lovers within what was for many an exotic and controversial religious — Mormon — context. He adds murder, disguise, deceit, abduction, chase, and rescue — all the appealing elements of adventure — chooses a Utah-Arizona border setting characterized by fertility, grandeur and challenge, and gives that an ironic twist by a "Garden" analogy where evil inevitably arises. He includes the powerful figure of August Naab and a solitary rescue quest with his first magnificent super-horse, Silvermane. The villains rustle, seize water-rights, and abduct Mescal. Indians play a prominent and ironic role in connection with "law" and "possession." Key: hands.

Grey followed the deservedly popular *Heritage* with another blockbuster, ***Riders of the Purple Sage*** (1912).[2] Its complicated plot features two pairs of lovers, the young Venters and Bess Oldring (Erne) and the older Lassiter and Jane Withersteen, a Mormon beauty — all westerners. Mystery and secrets loom large in the novel and involve Lassiter's quest to avenge the abduction and ruin of his sister by Mormon villains — worst being a Bishop Dyer — factors which delayed the acceptance of the novel for publication for fear it would offend too many readers. This time Grey uses three super-horses — Night, Black Star, and Wrangle — in daring pursuits and escapes, the last being that of the four lovers. The Mormon villains steal cattle, kidnap and murder in their attempts to break Jane's spirit, but she and Lassiter escape to Surprise Valley, discovered earlier by Venters. In the book's famous conclusion, Jane tells Lassiter to "Roll the stone!" that cave dwellers had ages before left to guard their hidden valley. In ***Riders,*** Grey continues the lavish description of nature which was to become a special Grey mark. The book's erotic appeal stems from the actions and dialogue of the four lovers and the hovering threat of seduction through forced marriage to a Mormon. Key: blindness.

Grey moved his setting south and the time to the present in ***Desert Gold*** (1913), which has the Mexican revolution as background, and the chief villain a Mexican military bandit, Rojas.[3] The romantic plot is again a double: Dick Gale and Nell (Burton) Belden, George Thorne and the exotic Mercedes Castaneda. Rojas' obsessive lust for, abduction of, and later chase after Mercedes provide erotic titillation and the book's real climax and shootout at the desert "Crater of Hell," though additional evil emerges late in the book in a father and son combination (Ben and Radford Chase) who attempt by "plain business" to steal Belden's ranch. This secondary plot ties in the "prologue," a frame element which holds the secret of Nell's real father. Hero Gale is a tough easterner (football star under Stagg) who early takes on Rojas and his lieutenants. He saves an Indian, Yaqui, who subsequently leads the escape from Rojas to the desert and, later, guides Gale to a deposit of gold. Horses, especially Blanco Sol, again figure prominently. Irony arises in connection with "savagery" and passion. Grey expands his description of external nature. Key: Yaqui.

For Madeline Hammond of ***The Light of Western Stars*** (1914), the symbolic stars hint of fulfillment, something she lacked in New York.[4] Her lover is cowboy Gene Stewart, last of the "old hard-ridin' kind." Villains include another Mexican, Don Carlos, his gang of vaqueros, and crooked sheriff Hawes. Don Carlos' designs on Madeline and Gene's attraction for her provide erotic appeal. Madeline reclaims Gene from drink and despair. Her horse, Majesty, and Don Carlos' black furnish super-horses and a chase and rescue episode. The Mexican Revolution hovers on the edge of the action until the final rescue scene when the automobile — a first for Grey — enables Madeline to arrive in time to save Gene from execution. Key: stars.

The Lone Star Ranger (1915) features Buck Duane, first of Grey's "outlaw" gunman heroes.[5] The book has a two-part structure; in the first half Duane, on the run because of a self-defense killing, cleans out nests of desperadoes along the Texas-Mexico border; in the second, now an "in-law" (secretly a Texas Ranger), he goes after arch-criminal Cheseldine, who turns out to be the rich rancher and judge, Longstreth. Duane and Ray, Cheseldine's daughter, fall in love. Shootouts abound. Action includes kidnapping, rustling, murder, and a final bank robbery shootout where Duane is nearly killed. Duane's arduous escape from vigilantes in the river brakes highlights the novel and illustrates one feature of the novel's irony-riddled portrayal of "justice." Key: The Law.

With a "wound in his soul" but not in his fists, protagonist Shefford knocks down a lecherous missionary who is molesting an Indian girl in the opening pages of ***The Rainbow Trail*** (1915).[6] Having failed in the East as a minister due to a "narrow" congregation, Shefford finds new purpose under the influence of the desert and the Indian, Nas Ta Bega. Rescue of Mary (really Fay Larkin of *Riders of the Purple Sage*) from a Mormon town of "sealed wives" provides the central action. Indians — and the cruelty of whites — figure prominently. Erotic appeal stems from villain Waggoner's midnight visits in an attempt to seduce Mary/Fay. Highlights include Shefford's infiltration of the sealed wife community to win Fay's love, Fay's trial for alleged bigamy, and the lovers' escape. Key: Nas Ta Bega.

A sustained captivity narrative and Grey's most erotically suggestive work, ***The Border Legion*** (1916) features Joan Randle's confrontations with her captor, Kells, leader of a notorious Idaho border gang of thieves.[7] The circular plot finds Joan kidnapped in the opening pages; at the end she returns home with her lover Jim Cleve, also a westerner, who has joined Kells' gang after being rejected by Joan. Filled with ironies, this intriguing tale flags in the second half when the gang goes to plunder the mining town "hell" of Alder Creek, but ends with a bang as the gang self-destructs in a wild shootout, and the lovers return home with all the gold. Highlights include the characters Kells and his beast-like cohort, Gulden, and a rich appearance/reality theme, but Joan is the "ace of hearts" who tops all, shivering with manipulative power as she lies in bed wearing the dead outlaw Dandy Dale's clothes and rolls on the heavy gun with a "thrill of certainty." Key: thrill.

Insignificant in *The Border Legion*, horses are center stage in ***Wildfire*** (1917), Grey's next book.[8] The western lovers are Lucy Bostil and Jim Slone, a wild horse hunter, who makes the longest single trek in Grey's trek-laden novels in search of the splendid red stallion. Major action involves three events: Slone's capture of Wildfire, Lucy riding Wildfire to victory over Sage King in a big race, and the already familiar abduction of the heroine. Villains are the horse-rustler Cordts, the Creeches (father and half-crazed son, Joel), and in part, Lucy's father. Bostil has wronged Creech; in retribution he kidnaps Lucy. Cordts wants her too. In the climax, Wildfire races to his death to save Lucy, completing a narrative heavy with irony concerning "wildfire" — horse, fire, and passion. Key: wildfire.

The U.P. Trail (1918) raised Grey to number one on the bestseller list.[9] Two interweaving threads fashion the bulk of the plot: the building of the Union Pacific Railroad and the attempts of Warren Neale, New Englander, to reclaim his sweetheart, Allie (Lee) Durade, whose real father is a corrupt railroad magnate, Allison Lee. An Irish worker, Casey, embodies the human spirit that carries out a project like the Union Pacific. Obstacles include hostile Indians who threaten and attack the project throughout. Melodrama abounds in this wild West of "no law but gold and guns." Allie survives a Sioux massacre and meets Warren only to be kidnapped by four men, then by Indians, then twice by her stepfather, Durade, who wants her for a gambling shill and his own use. Beauty Stanton, a hostess-with-a-heart-of-gold in one of the railroad "hell towns," dies trying to help Allie escape. Beauty is memorable, as is Grey's praise of the working man and that "scientific army of toilers" who forge the U.P. trail. Grey closes his novel with an elegy to the vanishing Indian. Key: Beauty Stanton.

Grey shifted to the Pacific Northwest, setting ***Desert of Wheat*** (1919) in Washington state during World War I.[10] Major obstacle for the western lovers, Kurt Dorn and Lenore Anderson, is the effort of the I.W.W. and foreign agents to destroy the wheat crops of their respective ranches. The infiltrating agents, not the I.W.W., prove the real villains. One, Ruenke, alias Nash, kidnaps Lenore, but ends hammered to a pulp by Kurt. Glidden, the other provocateur, suffers the same and is then lynched by farmer vigilantes. The war hovers over the narrative: Kurt's German father, stubborn, sympathizes with Germany and plots against Lenore's father; Lenore's brother dies in the war; Kurt enlists and regresses to the "savagery" necessary, returning home a half-dead hero, minus an arm. Highlights include a shootout between armed farmers and I.W.W. and foreign agents, a mass harvest scene, and Kurt's nightmare experience in the trenches of France. Key: harvest.

Milt Dale is the "man" in ***The Man of the Forest*** (1920) which features another double romance: Milt and Helen Rayner, the cowboy Las Vegas and Helen's spunky sister Bo.[11] In the major action, Milt and some Mormon pards spirit Helen and Bo from the train station to Milt's idyllic mountain retreat to foil a plot for their abduction which Milt has chanced to overhear. Despite the success of this move, the villains, Beasley and Snake Anson, later kidnap Bo after the sisters have gone from Milt's hideout to their uncle's ranch. Bo's feigning and Milt's pursuit put fear in the kidnappers, and the gang begins to self-destruct. The sisters' sojourn in "Paradise Park" (as Bo calls it) with Milt, Milt's tame cougar, Tom, and philosophical arguments about human nature between Milt and Helen highlight the narrative. Key: Paradise Park.

As with John Hare of *Heritage of the Desert,* Wilson Moore of ***The Mysterious Rider*** (1921) must win his lover from the clutch of a rancher's renegade son.[12] Bill Bellounds, pioneer rancher, raises the foundling, Columbine, and intends to see her married to his no-good son, Jack. The "mysterious rider" of the title is Hell-Bent Wade, who turns out to be Collie's real father. He hires on as a handyman and dog handler with Bellounds; he eventually atones for his abandonment of Collie and resolves Wilson's dilemma. He tracks Jack Bellounds, links him with rustlers, acts as go-between for Collie and Wilson, and he and Jack finally kill each other. Highpoints include nature descriptions during Wade's solitary treks, and a crippling fight between Jack and Wilson. Key: Hell-Bent Wade.

Part Indian Jean Isbel and Ellen Jorth are the western lovers burdened with feuding parents in this Romeo and Juliet variant, ***To the Last Man*** (1922).[13] The historical Pleasant Valley War serves as background, but the real issues are rustling and desire. The Jorth-Isbel feud starts over a woman, and during the central action the rustlers abduct Ellen. In addition to the horse, Spades, and the high feud action heavy with violence — a siege at the Isbel ranch and other confrontations — special features include strong erotic appeal, especially in descriptions linking nature with Ellen's "mysterious transports" of passion. Key: bloodlust.

Grey returned to the desert setting for ***Wanderer of the Wasteland*** (1923).[14] A Cain/Abel clash sets the plot and Adam Larey wandering. Thinking he has killed his brother, Guerd, Adam flees and spends fourteen years roaming the deserts as Wansfell the Wanderer in agonized self-struggle and metaphysical pondering over his guilt. Aided by Indians he learns desert survival and desert ways, then sojourns in Death Valley to comfort a fellow-sufferer, Magdalene Virey, whose husband has brought her there to avenge the wrong she has done him. After both Vireys die, Adam roams again, befriends and cares for young Genie Linwood till she finds an appropriate mate, then returns "full circle" to the scene of his crime, first to find Ruth Virey, Magdalene's daughter, and then to learn his brother still lives. Robbers and a corrupt sheriff demonstrate lawlessness in this most trek-laden of Grey's novels. ***Wanderer*** features extended descriptions of nature, the prospector Dismukes (who becomes Adam's long-time friend), a melodramatic avalanche in Death Valley, and repeated references to "retrogression." Key: waste.

First of Grey's westerns to feature two eastern lovers, ***The Call of the Canyon*** (1924) focuses action on the troubled love affair of Glenn Kilbourne and Carley Burch.[15] First Glenn, gassed and shell-shocked in World War I, hears the "call," then Carley, who follows him west. Many of the book's events function as initiatory rites for Carley, including character-shaping treks in the wild and the threat of seduction from an embodiment of the "raw, crude violence of the West" appropriately named Haze Ruff. Features include Carley's agonized introspections and lush passages suggesting nature's transforming power. Key: call.

In ***The Thundering Herd*** (1925), a tale full of buffalo hunting and Indian fighting, two pioneer orphans, Tom Doan and Milly Fayre, fight obstacles to their love.[16] Aside from Comanches and Kiowas enraged by the incursions of white hunters, major threat to the romance is Milly's lecherous stepfather, Jett, and his small group of hide thieves. He abducts Milly from a trading post, but the gang self-destructs and Milly escapes to begin a long trek to safety. Special features include details of buffalo hunting, skinning, and pegging-out of hides; attack by Tom Doan and fifty other hunters who track down and then battle a tribe of Comanches; and Milly's trek where, chased by Indians, she escapes swallowed up in a buffalo stampede and afterward presses Tom to give up hunting buffalo. Key: killing field.

In love, easterner Marian Warner and Indian Nophaie of ***The Vanishing American*** (1925) face two obstacles to their love: corrupt missionaries, and the spiritual torment of Nophaie, a man with a moccasin in two worlds (educated at Carlile, now back among his people).[17] Nophaie repeatedly visits isolated and sacred Indian desert retreats in search of inner peace. Like Kurt Dorn (*The Desert of Wheat*), Nophaie enlists in World War I and proves a terror to the enemy in France. He returns to find Gekin Yashi, an Indian girl he has earlier rescued from lecherous missionaries, dead of the plague along with her half-white baby. Nophaie finally accepts "absorption" by Marion and her love, and watches remnants of his tribe disappear into a "dying sunset." Highlights: wilderness treks, erotically charged passages of Marian's emotional transports (as when she watches Nophaie bloody the villains), and Grey's first serious probe of an Indian cultural dilemma. Key: nature.

A bee hunting trek — rough, hilly, and extended — suggests the course of romance for Lucy Watson and Edd Denmeade in ***Under the Tonto Rim*** (1926).[18] Main action centers on social worker Lucy's efforts to bring culture and better homemaking methods to the backwoods people of the Tonto Rim. Lucy's sister Clara joins midway. Clara has eloped with a no-good cowboy who refuses to marry her and leaves her with child, and she sends Lucy an S.O.S. The result is another double romance, Lucy with Edd, and Clara with Edd's brother Joe. The novel highlights the bee hunting trek (Edd and Lucy) and a climactic fight when Edd beats up backwoods rival Bud Sprall and kills a stranger who turns out to be Clara's faithless early companion. Key: learning.

Forlorn River (1927) holds another double romance — westerners Ben Ide and Ina Blaine, Jim "Nevada" Lacy and Ben's sister Hettie — and concludes as Nevada squares an old debt to Ben by shooting two villains then rides off at novel's end.[19] The somewhat disconnected action centers on Ben's wild horse hunting with his pards, Nevada and the skilled Indian, Modoc, and the attempts of the rancher/rustler Setter to steal both Ina and the Blaine ranch. Two captures stand out, one the Modoc-led trap of a huge band of horses at an ice cave waterhole, the other Ben's roping of the magnificent California Red on an iced-over lake aided by rustlers he has caught but lets go in exchange for their help. Key: Nevada.

Nevada (1928) picks up near the end of *Forlorn River*.[20] An unjustly-made lone wolf "outlaw" like Buck Duane (*The Lone Star Ranger*), Nevada learns the Ides have moved to Arizona and need help. In the main action he infiltrates a rustler gang and foils a plot to steal what's left of Ben Ide's cattle. In yet another double romance, Hettie's brother, Marv, wins the love of Rose Hatt, while Nevada and Hettie finally unite. Highlights include the Ides' long trek to Arizona, vintage Grey prose with sunsets and sunrises, crooked lawmen, and descriptions of Hettie's emotional "topography." Key: sunset.

"You are Panquitch and I am Wild Horse Mesa," says Sue Melberne at the end of ***Wild Horse Mesa*** (1928), a book with another double romance of westerners: Sue and Chane Weymer, Ora Loughbridge and Chane's younger brother Chess.[21] Central action involves the Melberne and Loughbridge families' plans to capture wild horses as a prelude to homesteading in Utah. Chief villain is handsome horse thief Ben Manerube, a masher cruel to horses. Chane stops him from carrying away Sosie, a Piute (*sic*) Indian girl. Features include a long trek by Chane, two superhorses (Brutus and wild Panquitch), a discourse on methods of wild horse capture, Chane's Piute (*sic*) friend Toddy Nokin and his braves, erotic appeal as Sue persuades Chane to set Panquitch free, and a final shootout as inner strife again contributes to a gang's breakup. Key: Panquitch.

Thirteen-year-old Clint (later "Buff") Belmet gives two sunfish to ten-year-old May Bell to open the long-delayed romance of ***Fighting Caravans*** (1929).[22] Buff becomes a pioneer freighter and the action, beginning in 1856, involves Indian fighting, long treks, and several lynchings of renegade whites before Buff, repeatedly criss-crossing the West, can catch up with May. Chief villain Murdock, a gambler and murderer, hounds May until Buff tracks him down. Highlights include Indian attacks, wrongs done the Indians, Maxwell Ranch scenes, and Buff's shootout with Murdock and his gang. Key: initiation.

Nearly broken in body and spirit, New Mexican Clifton Forrest returns home from war to find a reversal of fortunes in ***The Shepherd of Guadaloupe*** (1930).[23] A former nester, Lundeen, now owns the Forrest ranch; Clay's parents occupy the nester's old cottage. The villain, Malpass, has cheated and now controls Lundeen and wants Lundeen's daughter, Virginia. In central action, Cliff and Virginia outwit and expose Malpass. They marry secretly — due to Virginia's charity, Cliff thinks — and separate, Cliff to the desert to shepherd and regain his strength, Virginia to pursue her suspicions about Malpass' phony mine. Both find desert inspiration. Special features: a whip fight in which Cliff beats Malpass senseless, Virginia's friends Helen and the hip Ethyl, and the melodramatic climax at the fake mine when Malpass kills a mining engineer, strips Virginia half naked, then fights with Virginia's father and they kill each other. Key: old wounds.

Westerner Trueman Rock returns to his old stomping grounds to find former girlfriends all married, but true love on the horizon in ***Sunset Pass*** (1931).[24] Before he can win Thiry Preston, Trueman must overcome the evil influence of Thiry's rustling and murderous stepbrother (it turns out) Ash, one of Grey's most sinister badmen. In main action Trueman hires on at the Preston ranch and proves both detective and politician in order to discover how Ash disposes of hides from cattle he steals and slaughters, and then save Thiry's father from ignominy. Notable features include a costume dance, Trueman's horse Egypt, and irony concerning "law." Key: quicklime.

In the episodic ***Arizona Ames*** (1932), the titular hero roams the Southwest performing good deeds, mostly with his gun, before he wins Esther Halstead and a partnership in the Halstead ranch.[25] Each of four episodes features a romantic interest; Ames first aids his sister, Nesta, then the unhappily married Amy Grieve, then a Mormon and his daughter, and finally the Halsteads. Features include a Grey discourse on "the cowboy," another self-destructing rustler gang shootout, and another lover's (Esther's) inner conflict. Key: game of "Pretend."

English rancher Herrick's sister, Helen, is "strong and rides like a tartar," he says, in ***Robbers' Roost*** (1932).[26] Grey questions the meaning of "outlaw" again in a lawless realm as protagonist Jim Wall battles to rescue Helen from rustler and kidnapper factions among Herrick's ranch hands. Another divided gang, a long trek, descriptions of "Nature at her most awful," and a bloody to-the-last-man battle at the Robbers' Roost hideaway highlight the narrative. Key: violet-eyed goddess.

Molly Dunn of the Cibeque comes to realize that Jim Traft has "brought brains and brawn with him" from Missouri when he comes to Arizona to be his uncle Jim's range foreman in ***The Drift Fence*** (1933).[27] Before he wins Molly, Jim — in the plot's central action — must prove himself to his riders, build his uncle's drift fence, and battle the rustler/kidnappers, the worst being Jocelyn, a Traft cowboy/traitor who abducts Molly. Noteworthy features include Jim's bloody fight with Slinger Dunn (Molly's brother) who tries to "rooster" Jim with spurs, the climactic shootout (Jim now aided by Slinger) which destroys the divided gang, and Molly teaching Jim to hunt wild turkeys. Key: Slinger Dunn.

Grey continues the Traft ranch story with ***The Hash Knife Outfit*** (1933), introducing a famous, but disintegrating gang.[28] Jim's sister, Gloriana, joins him in Arizona after an unhappy affair with a con-man, Darnell, who has stolen from her. She becomes part of a double romance, pairing up with cowboy Curly Prentiss while Jim has to re-win Molly Dunn. The complicated plot involves confrontations between the gang and Jim's cowhands, including the kidnapping of both Gloriana and Molly by the outlaw Croak Malloy. Highlights: breakup of the gang and the comic completion of Gloriana's western education as Jed Stone, with Molly's help, poses as a "real old West" desperado. Key: Jed Stone.

Like Gloriana Traft, Georgiana Stockwell brings a past of flirtation when she joins her sister Mary at the Tonto Basin ranch of the Thurmans in ***Code of the West*** (1934).[29] In yet another double love plot, Mary marries Enoch Thurman and Georgiana Enoch's brother Cal, the novel's action centering around Cal's "taming of the flirt." Features include two Tonto courting-time dances, beautiful Tonto scenery, the fists of ex-Marine Tuck Merry, and — aided by Tuck — Cal's Petruchio-like overpowering of Georgiana to make her his bride. Key: taming.

A beaver sees strange water ripples and leaves the valley in ***Thunder Mountain*** (1935), foreshadowing ominous events.[30] In a plot with, for Grey, some unusual twists, the novel centers on the efforts of Lee "Kalispel" Emerson to overcome the villainy of claim-jumpers Borden and Leavitt in the mining town of Thunder City which springs up around a gold strike he and his brothers originally make. ***Thunder Mountain*** highlights Kalispel's giving up the eastern beauty, Sydney, to marry the loyal western dancehall girl, Nugget; a long trek with exotic descriptions of nature; two trials rigged by the corrupt judge, Leavitt; and the Frank Norris-like melodramatic slide of Thunder Mountain which buries Leavitt clutching bags of gold. Key: nugget.

Featuring a cattle drive from Texas to Dodge City in 1871, ***The Trail Driver*** (1936) consists of one long trek during which an ideal Grey cowboy, Texas Joe Shipman, wins the love of western orphan Reddy Bayne, who, disguised as a boy, hires on for the drive.[31] Incidents revealing obstacles to the drive's success constitute the action: cattle rustler-induced stampedes, swollen rivers with quicksand, hail and electrical storms, a buffalo stampede, and Comanche Indians. Highlights include herd owner Adam Brite's adoption of Reddy, a cowboy ambush against Indians, and a disturbing conclusion in which three of the cowboy trail drivers kill each other after successfully completing the drive. Key: Reddy Bayne.

The disjointed plot of ***The Lost Wagon Train*** (1936) opens during the Civil War; with U. S. troops mostly occupied, Stephen Latch joins Kiowa chief Satana in ambushing pioneer wagon trains and destroying the remains in a hidden canyon to leave no trace.[32] In the first part of the narrative Latch and Satana's rum-filled braves massacre a wagon train except for the beautiful Cynthia, saved, abducted, and stripped by a lecherous gang member. She turns out to be Latch's old sweetheart, and Latch has a gang member marry them. Latch leaves his bride at his ranch, is wounded, and returns years later to find Cynthia dead but a seven-year-old daughter, Estelle, there instead. In the second part, trail driver Corny Cornwall rescues Estelle (now sixteen), and smitten, assumes the name Slim Blue and saves Latch from an old enemy-turned-rustler, Leighton. Features include bits of Western Americana, the wagon-train massacre, and "Latch's Field" — a ranch originally started by Latch as a front for his raids. Key: "Tullt & Co. No. 1A" (gold-laden lost wagon).

Pecos Smith has to rescue southern beauty Terrill Lambeth from the river to discover she's a woman in ***West of the Pecos*** (1937).[33] In central action, Pecos encounters settler Lambeth, his daughter, and two ex-slaves heading West, leaves them for a time in order to sell unbranded calves with two partners who cheat (they secretly change brands), and after watching a shootout between Indians and a white lynching party after his former partners, he again encounters Terrill, father now dead, the ranch drained by rustlers. He stays to build up the ranch, marry Terrill, and kill the rustler Sawtell who rips off Terrill's clothes. Highlights include Sambo and wife Mauree, horse Cinco, and a humorous wedding scene. Key: Judge Roy Bean.

Grey resurrects Buffalo Jones for a minor role in ***Raiders of Spanish Peaks*** (1938), but a cowboy triumvirate led by Laramie Nelson has center stage in another ranch rescue, this time of easterner Lindsay, come West with, appropriately, three daughters.[34] This plot ploy issues in a triple romance: Laramie and Hallie, Lonesome and Lenta, Tracks and Flo, and lets Grey employ various familiar motifs: abduction (Lenta) and chase, a dissenting gang, lynchings, and nature's awakening call in a heroine. In main action, Lindsay is first cheated in the ranch sale, then has his cattle rustled by the crooked Arlidge and gang until Laramie and his pards catch up to them. Key: Three Musketeers.

"The wust times air yet to come," says Cap Britt, Colonel Lee Ripple's foreman in ***Knights of the Range*** (1939).[35] Two years later, Ripple is dead, his eighteen-year-old half-Spanish daughter Holly runs the ranch, and the outlaws have arrived. In central action gunman Renn Frayne hires on to lead Holly's tough cowboys against the depredations of rival rancher/rustler Sewall McCoy, and wins Holly's love over loyal cowhand rival Brazos Keene. Highlights feature cowboy hijinks, including Negro cowboy "Ride-em" Jackson's riding a bronc while biting his nose, Holly's giant party with speeches by Holly, Brazos, and Frayne, and a shootout with lynching. Key: Brazos Keene.

Grey uses a first-person narrative in ***Western Union*** (1939).[36] New Englander Wayne Cameron, unable "to stay indoors and study," comes West in 1861 to work for the Western Union. Like *The U.P. Trail* and *The Trail Driver*, ***Western Union*** portrays a long cross-country push overcoming various obstacles to the goal, in this case the transcontinental telegraph line. Grey adds one more double romance and kidnapping. Obstacles include cattle, prairie fire, Indians, buffalo stampede, and continual harassment by rustlers and all-around bad hombres Red Pierce and Black Thornton, who plan a final robbery of a mining town near the line's end. Before Wayne prevails with caravan owner Sunderland's daughter Kit, and pard Vance Shaw with dance-hall girl Ruby, Wayne and his pards must rescue Ruby from the dance hall, fight off a massive Indian attack, and then find and rescue Ruby again because Pierce has abducted her during the Indian attack. Special features: hiding Ruby "blackface" in the pards' wagon, Shaw's saving idea to survive the buffalo stampede, and the final search and shootout. Key: Ruby.

In part a study of a pioneer woman's endurance and fight against loneliness and loss, ***30,000 on the Hoof*** (1940) records the bitter struggle of Logan Huett, ex-Army scout, to realize a dream.[37] In main action Logan, after capturing the Indian Matazel, quits the army, sends for a former sweetheart, marries her, and sets out to homestead the idyllic and isolated Sycamore Canyon. With three sons and a foundling daughter, Barbara, Logan battles cougars, wolves, hawks, the elements, rustlers, and finally a con-artist who steals his fortune. Matazel takes ironic revenge by forcing Logan's wife during the rancher's absence; the result, the narrative hints, is son Abe, who wins the love of Barbara. The three sons enter World War I, and two are killed, but, on an upbeat note, Abe returns to end the novel. Special features include Lucinda and sons fighting off a wolf attack, a grasshopper plague stopped by wild turkeys, a wild brawl at a dance, and ironic references to the "Indian" and "savage" qualities of Abe. Key: Matazel.

After riding off from Holly Ripple and her knights (*Knights of the Range*), Brazos Keene stars in ***Twin Sombreros*** (1941).[38] Brazos escapes being lynched for the murder of Allen Neece and proceeds to do some detective work to track down the real killers, hired by rustler Raine Surface so Surface can take over Twin Sombreros Ranch. After restoring the ranch and stolen money to its owners, Brazos has a tough choice between the beautiful Neece twins, June and Janis. Highlights include Brazos' flirtation with the female outlaw, Bess Syverson; a shootout where Brazos wounds Bess and kills her two partners; Brazos' retreat to nature; and the surprise ending where one of the twins tracks Brazos down and marries him. Key: birthmark.

Oregonian Lance Sidway and his super-horse Umpqua go to Hollywood and encounter coed Madge ("Majesty") Stewart and some black-car gangsters in ***Majesty's Rancho*** (1942).[39] In the central action, Lance spots the black-car gangsters again on his way to Arizona, takes a temporary job driving a gangster truck thus learning about modern rustling methods, and subsequently hires on at the Stewart ranch. With friend Ren Starr, Lance rescues Gene Stewart from bankruptcy by outwitting the gangster/rustlers. Highlights: rustling by truck, Majesty's colorful university friends who spend the summer, erotic threat from gangster Uhl who kidnaps Majesty, Lance's repeated rescues of Majesty including a shootout in the hills, and another double romance: Lance and Majesty, Ren Starr and Bonita Mains. Key: Honey-Bee Uhl.

Coerced into marriage with Guerd Larey and miserable after four years at her grandfather's desert waterhole, Ruth Virey runs away in desperation and is rescued by Adam Larey in ***Stairs of Sand*** (1943), sequel to the earlier *Wanderer of the Wasteland*.[40] Nature plays an unusually strong role, even for Grey, as Adam and his friend Merryvale wait for an opportunity to liberate Ruth and foil the villains' — Guerd and crooked sheriff Collishaw — plot to get the waterhole rights in advance of a rumored railroad. Highlights include a familiar abduction, the desert's "inscrutable design," and Adam's reward for two novels' worth of Good

Samaritan deeds when, captured and bound, he and Merryvale escape as the gang self-destructs because Adam years before killed a man who wronged their guard's wife. Key: stairs of sand.

"All same just another bloody rustler!" says Sterl Hazelton in ***Wilderness Trek*** (1944), Grey's western transplanted to Australia.[41] Central action is a super cattle drive — 3000 miles across Australia — in which American cowboy pards Red Krehl and Sterl sign on, work to outsmart the bushranger (rustler) Ormiston, and end up in a double marriage with Australians Beryl Dann and Leslie Slyter, daughters of two of the cattle drive owners. Australian lingo aside, "bloody" fits, as sixteen men and one woman of the original party die, including a lynching and a suicide. Abos (aboriginals) replace Indians, dingoes supplant coyotes, but the scenery reminds the Americans of Utah and Arizona, and the action is familiar, including the kidnapping of Beryl. Highlights: the character of Stanley Dann, a less-forceful version of August Naab (*Heritage of the Desert*), sinister Abo presence and attack, and the final chase and shootout as Sterl and Red save Beryl. Key: "Friday" (black guide).

Gunman hero Wade Holden faces three main problems before he marries Jaqueline Pencarrow in ***Shadow on the Trail*** (1946): how to escape Texas Rangers, ease his conscience about the money he has from a bank robbery, and rescue the Pencarrow ranch from rustlers.[42] About a third of the somewhat complicated action has Wade on the run after a bank holdup in which dying Slim Bell admits he is Wade's real father. Wade is saved by young Jaqueline Pencarrow who takes off her blouse to prevent Rangers from searching her tent. Five years later, Wade rides up to the Pencarrow ranch, hires on as foreman, and subsequently hires tough young Hogue Kinsey and his pals to fight the rival rancher/rustlers and their gunmen. Features include a double romance (Hogue and Jaqueline's sister, Rona), Wade's long trek escaping the Rangers, the double lynching (two times) of outlaw Blue, and Ranger Mahaffey riding off after a visit with Wade, Jaqueline, and their infant, leaving Wade at peace. Key: "Rustler" (sign on Blue's lynched body).

Panhandle Smith meets his childhood sweetheart and childhood rival in ***Valley of Wild Horses*** (1947).[43] After a boyhood spent loving horses, Panhandle roams as a cowboy, then tracks down his family to find them cheated out of a homestead by boyhood enemy Hardman, who is also after Lucy Blake. In the central action, Panhandle, old pard Blinky Moran and two other pals team up to trap wild horses as a start for a move to Arizona. They have to rescue dance-hall girl Louise Melliss, their horses, and finally Lucy from the clutches of all-around rustler and badman Hardman before the double romance — Panhandle and Lucy, Blinky and Louise — ends happily. Highlights: description of Louise, crooked sheriff Matthews' disgrace by the western "Code," and the rescue of Louise after she knifes Hardman. Key: The Five-Minute Marriage.

Battered in the face by an exploding cannon's breechblock, embittered Oregonian veteran Keven Bell returns from an army training camp hospital to find his father dispossessed of his store by cannery owner Brandeth and his own reputation soiled by lies of Brandeth's equally corrupt foreman, Atwell, former major, in ***Rogue River Feud*** (1948).[44] With illegal nets the "rustlers" here steal fish instead of cattle. Keven and a pard, Garry Lord, try to earn a living catching fish despite threats of crooked cannery fishermen until they uncover the truth. When Keven and Garry are caught boat netting illegally, Keven stabs the no-good, Mulligan, and in the fight, pal Garry drifts out to sea. In remaining action, Keven escapes upstream and meets old flame Beryl Aard; he stays — regaining his health, working for Beryl's father, fishing for steelhead, and falling in love. "Gosh, it's a fairy story," Keven says, while honeymooning. It is. All turns out well. Highlights: escape downriver, Keven's later escape and trek upriver, fishing action, and descriptions of splendid Rogue River country. Key: greed.

In ***The Deer Stalker*** (1949), the Grand Canyon strips bare "the truth of her heart" for New Yorker Patricia Edgerton.[45] For Patricia's new friend, Sue Warren, it's her blouse that's nearly stripped, as she and Patricia agree to a Canyon tour with two cowboy guides and are surprised by badman Dyott. Sue flees, encounters Ranger Thad Eburne, and Thad rescues the other three. They spend an idyllic ten days at Eburne's cabin. Aside from the double romance — Patricia and Thad, Sue and guide Nels — the central action involves an unusual plan to save overpopulated deer by means of a drive to another area. Sabotage and a blizzard spoil the drive, but not the romance, as Patricia finally accepts Thad's fourth proposal. Special features: description of the canyon country, problems of deer management, Thad's proposal at sunset on the canyon rim, and the Hollywood-attended great deer drive. Key: conservation.

"She's got hell's fire in her veins," says Vince, cowboy pard of Lincoln Bradway in ***The Maverick Queen*** (1950).[46] He means Kit Brandon, the "Queen," of course. Main action of this most detective-like western has Linc return to South Pass, Wyoming, to try to uncover the mystery of pard Jimmy Weston's murder and to clear his friend's name. The trail leads to an unusual range war between cowmen and cowboys and, ultimately, to the key, rustling backed by the Maverick Queen, in this ironic narrative where "good" and "bad" characters operate from the same motives and the meaning of "law" once again blurs. Special features include a powerful western Code rule about silence with regard to accusing women; Linc's hurried, secret marriage with Kit's niece, Lucy, and the dramatic climax — a shootout and lynching of Kit (whose character is based on the real life "Cattle Annie"). Key: KIT brand.

"This heah man won't show up, an' if he does you can marry him. Ha! Ha!" laughs a cowboy near the opening of ***The Dude Ranger*** (1951).[47] The cowboy proves prophetic and the last laugh belongs to Ernest Selby, the "dude" who inherits the Arizona Red Rock Ranch and comes from Iowa to find out why the cattle and profits have disappeared. Central action involves yet another double romance and has Ernest (using the name Ernest Howard) and new pard, Nebraskie, winning Anne Hepford and Daisy Brooks. Ernest hires on at Red Rock, proves his mettle, battles lecherous cowhand Dude Hyslip, and exposes ranch manager Hepford's crooked dealings. Special features: positive use of a lawyer, Daisy's sexual helplessness before Dude Hyslip, and Ernest's stealing of Hepford's tell-tale blue book and elopement with Anne. Key: the heart-shaped bootmark.

Mary Newton's pen proves at least as good as a sword in ***Captives of the Desert*** (1952), and leads to her worthless husband's death.[48] Central to the somewhat confusing plot are the efforts of John Curry, chief of cowboys at Black Mesa Trading Post, and Hi-Lo, one of the cowboys, to expose the illegal running of whiskey to the Indians by Wilbur Newton and his partner, Hanley. For Curry, in love with Mary, a parallel goal is her liberation. The conclusion is another double marriage, Curry and Mary, Hi-Lo and the Indian, Magdalene. Highlights include a romantic Hopi Indian festival race, Magdalene's pregnancy by and revenge on Newton, the role of New Yorker Katherine Winfield, and irony concerning the title with its multiple implications for "captive." Key: desert magic.

Tough young Andrew Bonning, who "tore the varsity line to pieces as a freshman," heads west at the same time as another easterner, equally tough runaway Martha Ann Dixon, hitchhikes for Wyoming to find her rancher uncle, Nick Bligh. They meet on the road, Andrew rescues Martha from some hoboes, and they're destined for romance in ***Wy-***

oming (1953).[49] In the main plot, Andrew hires on at Bligh's ranch — failing due to rustlers — and with the help of Texas Haynes and Bligh's only ranch hand, crippled Jim Penner, exposes rival rancher/rustler McCall. Special features include Martha's kicking a would-be masher to a bloody mess when she hitchhikes, Andrew's one-man assault on an entire crew at a rodeo, Tex's calling out of McCall and crooked sheriff Slade, and Martha spying on Andrew through a peephole in his cabin. Key: Wyoming MAD.

Both Arizona desert and archeologist Philip Randolph awaken New Yorker Janey Endicott in ***Lost Pueblo*** (1954), a comic captivity narrative filled with hijinks and farcical episodes.[50] Janey's father, eager to get Janey away from New York fortune hunters, persuades Phil to kidnap her. He does, taking her to Beckyshibeta, site of the dig where he hopes to find a lost Indian pueblo. Action consists of a series of visitor-induced episodes including one with fake outlaws Black Dick and Snitz Jones, one with comical eastern suitor Bert Durland and his mother, and a more serious one with cowboy Ray who, jealous of Phil, threatens to lynch him. Highlights: descriptions of mystical nature, Janey's discovery of the lost pueblo, and Janey's "revenge" — hiring Black Dick and Snitz to kidnap Phil and put him on the train with her. Key: Beckyshibeta.

Bitter Seeps, its "great pale pool like an evil eye," hints at the wrongdoing of trader Belton, villain of ***Black Mesa*** (1955).[51] Kansan Paul Manning, grieving from a ruinous love affair, rescues Texan Wess Kintell from jail and buys in with Belton to raise cattle. Belton's evil includes a bigamous marriage forced on Louise, artificial embittering of the waterhole with chemicals, and rustling the ranch cattle and selling them back to Paul as new stock — all resolved before Paul can claim Louise and her baby and ride off with them accompanied by faithful Wess. Special features: the other wife, a trek after rustlers, nature's effect on character, and the dramatic end of Belton over a precipice. Key: "Sister" (Belton's legitimate wife).

Dying prospector and former Hole in the Wall gang member Bill Elway lays a heavy challenge on Kent Wingfield in ***Stranger from the Tonto*** (1956); he is to find the gang's hideaway and rescue Lucy Bonesteel.[52] In the central action, Kent makes a long trek and finds the Hole in the Wall gang's idyllic retreat, hides out and wins Lucy's love, then braves the gang and foments an intrafactional blowoff in which the gang self-destructs while Kent and Lucy escape through a secret waterfall entrance revealed to Lucy by her father. Special features: Lucy's super-horse, Spades; nature description including the idyllic hideaway; irony concerning "justice" in connection with the revelation of Bonesteel's "other life" as Utah rancher Cheney; and the lovers' escape on Spades and Clubfoot. Key: Paradise Lost and Found.

Texan Bruce Lockheart survives pursuing Texas Rangers, two gangs of outlaw enemies, and a complicated and sometimes confusing plot before being chased down by foundling Trinity Spencer nee Melrose in ***The Fugitive Trail*** (1957).[53] Twin plot threads eventually intertwine: Bruce changes clothes with his no-good brother, Barse, to save him from capture after a robbery, then rides off as an outlaw hunted by Rangers; after an adventurous long trek, he hires on at the Melrose ranch to help fight rustlers. Meanwhile, Trinity sets out after him, learns her real identity, and finds a new home with her father, Melrose. Captain Maggard finally tells Trinity that Bruce is "square" with him, and the lovers are free. Highlights: Bruce's long escape and trek, a wild shootout between rustlers and a Ranger-cowboy coalition, and Trinity clutching Ranger Maggard's arm so he won't shoot Bruce if he recognizes him. Key: Captain Maggard.

Bad hombre Buck Hathaway "beats hosses an' kicks kids," a young lad tells Dodge Mercer at the opening of ***The Arizona Clan*** (1958).[54] One look at Nan Lilley convinces Dodge that he has to get involved in the Hathaway-Lilley trouble to rescue Nan and save the Lilley ranch. In the central action, Dodge locates a Hathaway still — they have nearly ruined the Lilleys with "white mule" — then aided by half-Apache, Coplace, repels an attack by a Hathaway-Quayle group and sets off in pursuit to finish the job, taking Nan along. Buck kidnaps Nan briefly, but Dodge trails her and they marry with the parson Buck has brought. Special features: liquor's effects on the Lilley family, Dodge's trek with Uncle Bill in search of a still, and the hurry-up cabin wedding while the unwitting Buck stands talking outside. Key: white mule.

In ***Horse Heaven Hill*** (1959),[55] set in Washington state, part Nez Perce Lark Burrell and Stan Weston meet while riding and share a sweeping hilltop view, a sure sign of romance. At novel's end, now married, they pause at a divide, gazing down at Lark's Idaho ranch. In between, main action centers on a great drive of wild horses to be sold in Montana as chicken feed. Lark has come to live with her cousin, Marigold Wade, Stan's fiancee; action must free both Stan and the captured horses. Special features: the cruel maiming of horses caught in the greedy captor's trap, Lark's secret release of the horses, Marigold finally telling off the villain Hurd Blanding, and Lark shooting Hurd in the arm to save Stan. Key: Lark.

Californian Lynn Weston proves a one-man dynamo for ***Boulder Dam*** (1963).[56] An ex-football star, Lynn hears the desert call when he comes to work on the dam. Main action interweaves three plot threads: a gangster/Communist scheme to both blackmail and yet blow up the dam, gangsters' white slave designs on Anne Vandergrift, and Lynn's progressive mastery of the construction process by working his way up from pick and shovel through eleven phases of the work. Special features: extensive description of the construction, Lynn's rescue and subsequent hiding of the nude Anne, Lynn's daring exploits saving dam workers, and his second rescue of Anne in a wild melee with a darkened room full of gangsters. Key: hospital wedding.

Notes

Introduction

1. Grey's career as a writer was long and distinguished and eventually made him a wealthy man. This volume, however, makes no attempt to synthesize Grey's life. For a short but informative biographical sketch, see Lawrence Clark Powell's *Southwest Classics: The Creative Literature of the Arid Land* (Los Angeles: Ward Ritchie Press, 1974), pp. 202 – 215.

I: The Formula

1. Russel Nye, *The Unembarrassed Muse* (New York: Dial Press, 1970), p. 303.
2. Don D. Walker, in "Notes Toward a Literary Criticism of the Western," *The Popular Western,* Richard W. Etulain and Michael T. Marsden, eds. (Bowling Green, Ohio: Bowling Green State University Popular Press, 1974), p. 89.
3. Cynthia S. Hamilton, *Western and Hard-Boiled Fiction in America: From High Noon to Midnight* (London: Macmillan, 1987), p. 80.
4. See, for example, "The American Literary West and its Interpreters: The Rise of a New Historiography," in *Pacific Historical Review,* Vol. 45, No. 4, pp. 311 – 347; *The Western: A Collection of Critical Essays,* James K. Folsom, ed. (Englewood Cliffs, New Jersey: Prentice-Hall, 1979), pp. 157 – 58, 167, 170. Kenneth W. Scott's *Zane Grey: Born of the West, A Reference Guide* (Boston: G.K. Hall, 1979) is basic. All these sources provide an excellent starting point for bibliography. See also listings in *Western American Literature.*

Two recent works on the western with special emphasis on Grey are Christine Bold's *Selling the Wild West* (Bloomington: University of Indiana Press, 1987), and Hamilton's *Western and Hard-Boiled Detective Fiction in America*; both contain extensive bibliographies. See also "Essays on Sources" in Robert G. Athearn's *The Mythic West in Twentieth-Century America* (Lawrence: University Press of Kansas, 1986), pp. 276 – 309. Candace C. Kant's *Zane Grey's Arizona* (Flagstaff, Arizona: Northland Press, 1984) examines Grey from a biographical point of view as a popularizer and promoter of the West and is an excellent resource.

5. Nye, *The Unembarrassed Muse,* p. 294

6. See, Don D. Walker's "Can the Western Tell What Happens?" in *Critical Essays on the Western American Novel*, William T. Pilkington, ed. (Boston: G. K. Hall, 1980), pp. 93 – 108.

7. In *The Western: A Collection of Critical Essays,* p. 160.

8. "History and Theory of The Popular Western Novel," *Southwest Review,* vol. 51 (1966), pp. 11 – 28, in *Critical Essays on the Western American Novel,* p. 41.

9. Athearn, *The Mythic West in Twentieth-Century America*, p. 168.

10. John Cawelti, *Adventure, Mystery, and Romance: Formula Stories as Art and Popular Culture* (Chicago: University of Chicago Press, 1976), p. 240.

11. "Nature" is the slipperiest of terms. See, Arthur G. Kimball, "Silent Walls: 'Nature' in Grey's *The Vanishing American,*" *South Dakota Review,* Vol. 26 (Spring 1988), pp. 78 – 90.

12. Hamilton, *Western and Nard-Boiled Fiction,* p. 33.

13. Carlton Jackson, *Zane Grey* (New York: Twayne Publishers, 1973), p. 66.

14. "Notes Toward a Literary Criticism of the Western," *The Popular Western,* p. 87.

15. In *Critical Essays on the Western American Novel,* p. 41.

16. Hamilton, *Westerns and Hard-Boiled Fiction,* p. 10.

17. Cawelti, *Adventure, Mystery and Romance,* p. 209.

18. *Ibid.,* p. 233.

19. See, William Bloodworth, "Zane Grey's Western Eroticism," *South Dakota Review,* Vol. 23 (Autumn 1985), pp. 5 – 14; Bold, *Selling the Wild West,* p. 84; Cawelti, *Adventure, Mystery and Romance,* p. 241.

20. The reader can easily find the review citations for the years indicated in Scott, *Zane Grey.*

21. "Zane Grey Dies," *New York Herald Tribune,* October 24, 1939, p. 18.

22. "Zane Grey, 64, Dies Suddenly on Coast," *New York Times,* October 24, 1939, p. 23

23. Roscoe Burton, "Opie Read and Zane Grey," *Saturday Review of Literature,* November 11, 1939, p. 8.

24. *Arizona and the West,* Vol. 12 (Autumn 1970).

25. Ann Ronald, *Zane Grey* (Boise, Idaho: Boise State University, 1975), p. 13.

26. Gary Topping, "Zane Grey: A Literary Reassessment," *American Literature,* Vol. 13 (Spring 1978), pp. 51 – 64. See also the Pocket Western reprint of *Boulder Dam* (New York, 1967), p. 198; in a postscript, "Ohio's Writer of the Purple Sage," Erwin A. Bauer maintains, "Beginning in those first novels, Grey set a pattern for his heroes that never varied."

27. Frank Gruber, *Zane Grey: A Biography* (New York: World Publishing Co., 1970), p. 87.

28. See Scott, *Zane Grey,* pp. 1 – 3.

II: The Land

1. John Milton, *The Novel of the American West* (Lincoln: University of Nebraska Press, 1980), pp. 89, 111.

2. Cited in Gruber, *Zane Grey: A Biography,* pp. 68 – 69.

3. See, Kant, *Zane Grey's Arizona.*

4. Mary Alden Hopkins, "A Poly-Angular Novel," *Publishers Weekly,* January 20, 1917, p. 210, cited in Scott, *Zane Grey,* p. 44.

5. See, Scott, *Zane Grey,* p. 44.

6. Ronald, *Zane Grey,* p. 38.

7. Matthew 20:16, II Thessalonians 1:11, King James Version.

8. See William Bloodworth, "Zane Grey's Western Eroticism," pp. 5 – 14.

9. Gruber, *Zane Grey: A Biography,* p. 59.

10. *Ibid.,* p. 151.

11. Cawelti, *Adventure, Mystery and Romance,* p. 233.

12. Milton, *The Novel,* p. 111.

13. *Ibid.*

14. Ronald, *Zane Grey,* pp. 15 – 16.

15. *Ibid.*

16. See, Arthur G. Kimball, "Silent Walls: 'Nature' in Grey's *The Vanishing American,* and Arthur G. Kimball "My Navajo Oasis:

Irony in Grey's *Heritage of the Desert," South Dakota Review,* Vol. 28 (Summer 1990), pp. 34 – 51.

17. Ronald, *Zane Grey,* p. 16.

18. Gruber, *Zane Grey: A Biography,* p. 87.

19. Kenneth W. Scott, "*The Heritage of the Desert:* Zane Grey Discovers the West," *The Markham Review,* Vol. 2 (February 1970), pp. 10 – 14.

20. Jackson, *Zane Grey*, pp. 33, 37.

21. *Ibid.,* p. 37.

22. Ronald, *Zane Grey,* pp. 14, 16, 17.

23. Bold, *Selling the Wild West,* p. 82.

24. Hamilton, *Westerns and Hard-Boiled Fiction,* pp. 22, 103.

25. Richard Slotkin, *The Fatal Environment: The Myth of the Frontier in the Age of Industrialization, 1800 – 1890* (New York: Atheneum, 1985), p. 15.

26. Richard Slotkin, *Regeneration through Violence: The Mythology of the American Frontier, 1600 – 1860* (Middletown, Connecticut: Wesleyan University Press, 1973), p. 17. See also p. 412.

27. Hamilton, *Western and Hard-Boiled Fiction,* p. 80.

28. Bold, *Selling the Wild West,* p. 44.

29. See, Slotkin, *Regeneration Through Violence,* passim; see also Arthur G. Kimball, *Rational Fictions: A Study of Charles Brockden Brown* (McMinnville, Oregon: Linfield Research Institute, 1968), esp. pp. 191 – 228.

30. I want to acknowledge the hazards of any attempt to deal with a slippery concept like "nature." As the novel indicates, Grey's use of the word is often confused and confusing, as when he says (p. 158), desert is "hard and cruel, inevitable as nature itself," and "The storms are fierce, sudden, violent, like the nature of the desert." For a bibliographical start, see *The Encyclopedia of Philosophy,* Paul Edwards, ed., 6 vols. (New York: Macmillan, 1967), *s.v.* "Nature."

31. Bloodworth, "Zane Grey's Western Eroticism," p. 13.

32. John D. Nesbitt, "Uncertain Sex in the Sagebrush," *South Dakota Review,* Vol. 23 (Autumn 1985), p. 21.

33. *Ibid.,* pp. 21, 24.

34. Bold, *Selling the Wild West,* p. 83. The idea is interesting and deserves further study. Nophaie's canyons are certainly insulated, but he must leave them, of course, and does so one time in order to enter the war. Bold, incidentally, says Grey is "at his most mature" in *The Vanishing American,* and that it contains "the formulaic

or mythic shape, the dramatization of a social issue and the formal requirements of a complex plot, without making one carry more weight than the others (pp. 89 – 90)."

35. Gary Topping, "Zane Grey: A Literary Reassessment," p. 62.

III: The Lovers

1. In "My Answer to the Critics," cited by Jackson, *Zane Grey,* p. 144.
2. Bloodworth, "Zane Grey's Western Eroticism," p. 14.
3. Cited by Jackson, *Zane Grey,* p. 49.
4. Hamilton, *Western and Hard-Boiled Fiction,* p. 90.
5. Bold, *Selling the Wild West,* p. 88.
6. "Ten-Gallon Hero," in *The Western,* pp. 15 – 30.
7. Hamilton, *Western and Hard-Boiled Fiction,* p. 86.
8. Jackson, *Zane Grey,* p. 112.
9. Bloodworth, "Zane Grey's Western Eroticism," pp. 5 – 6.
10. Bloodworth, "Zane Grey's Western Eroticism," mentions only *Wanderer of the Wasteland, The Heritage of the Desert, Riders of the Purple Sage, The Call of the Canyon, The Reef Girl, The Day of the Beast,* and a short story, "Canyon Walls." Of *Betty Zane, The Spirit of the Border,* and *The Last Trail* he says in passing, "sexuality is generally a negative feature." Similarly, most of Nesbitt's article ("Uncertain Sex in the Sagebrush") focuses on *Riders of the Purple Sage* and *To the Last Man,* with brief mention of *The U.P. Trail* and, in passing, *The Light of Western Stars* and *Knights of the Range.*
11. Bloodworth, "Zane Grey's Western Eroticism," pp. 8,14.
12. Nesbitt, "Uncertain Sex in the Sagebrush," p. 26.
13. *Ibid.,* p. 21.
14. *Ibid.*
15. "Foreword," *To the Last Man,* (New York: Harper's, 1922) written in "Avalon, California, April, 1921."
16. Cawelti, *Adventure, Mystery and Romance,* p. 235.
17. Jackson, *Zane Grey,* p. 63. For reviews, see Scott, *Zane Grey,* pp. 41 – 42.
18. Ronald, *Zane Grey,* p. 26. Frank Gruber (*Zane Grey: A Biography*) gives the novel high praise, but deals almost entirely with the story of "Henry Plummer and his road agents," real life characters who evidently fueled Grey's imagination for his "Border" men; see pp. 122 – 124. Bold (*Selling the Wild West*) does not

discuss *The Border Legion.* Hamilton does, stressing that Grey places his women "in a position that heavily reinforces traditional concepts of sex roles," and that Joan articulates their dilemma; see pp. 81 – 82; 85 – 89.

19. Slotkin, *Regeneration Through Violence.* See especially Chapter 4: "Israel in Babylon: The Archetype of the Captivity Narratives (1682 – 1700)." As my discussion will indicate, I am much indebted to Slotkin for features of the myth.

20. Among them, e.g., "beast," "power," "devil," "hunger," and important appearance-reality variants like "blindly."

21. Slotkin, *Regeneration Through Violence,* p. 35, and see his Index, *s.v.* "Faust."

22. Compare, *The Tragical History of Dr. Faustus (1588 – 89),* Scene XIII, pp. 90 – 96.

23. Slotkin, *Regeneration Through Violence,* pp. 101 – 102.

24. *Ibid*, p. 109.

25. *Ibid.*, pp. 28 – 29.

26. Ronald, *Zane Grey,* p. 25.

27. See, *The Sovereignty and Goodness of God, Together with the Faithfulness of His Promises Displayed: Being a Narrative of the Captivity and Restauration of Mrs. Mary Rowlandson* (1682). See, Slotkin, *Regeneration Through Violence,* pp. 94 – 115.

28. See, Henry Nash Smith, *Virgin Land* (Cambridge: Harvard University Press, 1950), Chapter XXI.

29. On the demise of the "savages," see, Richard Drinnon, *Facing West: The Metaphysics of Indian-Hating and Empire Building* (New York: New American Library, 1980), and Slotkin's *The Fatal Environment.*

30. Suggesting the link between the frontier idyll/dream and capitalism, Slotkin says, "If we approach this Myth with an awareness of its function as a rationalizer of the process of capitalist development in America, we can begin to see some of the special characteristics of American ideology that link, us to — and distinguish us from — the political culture of Europe." (*The Fatal Environment,* p. 34.)

31. Compare, Sacvan Bercovitch, *The American Jeremiad* (Madison: University of Wisconsin Press, 1978), p. 141; the Jeremiad functions in ways akin to the captivity and, in light of the latter, Grey's novel.

32. Slotkin, *Regeneration Through Violence,*, p. 411.

IV: The Law

1. Hamilton, *Western and Hard-Boiled Fiction,* p. 2.
2. Cawelti, *Adventure, Mystery and Romance,* p. 193.
3. Hamilton, *Western and Hard-Boiled Fiction,* pp. 80 – 81.
4. Cawelti, *Adventure, Mystery and Romance,* pp. 193 – 194.
5. Alexander Pope, "An Essay on Man," Epistle II, lines 107 – 108.
6. Cawelti, *Adventure, Mystery and Romance,* p. 233.
7. Quoted from the D. Appleton edition, 1926, p. 149.
8. Hamilton, *Western and Hard-Boiled Fiction,* p. 83.
9. W. H. Hutchinson, "Virgins, Villains, and Varmints," in *The Western,* p. 35.
10. I presume Grey's use of disparaging terms like "nigger," "greaser," etc., was an attempt at authentic dialogue. In his novels overall he portrays black Americans and Mexicans in both "good" and "bad" roles (e.g., Mercedes in *Desert Gold;* "Ride-em" Jackson in *Knights of the Range,* both "good").
11. As of this writing, a current Seattle murder trial suggests the relevance for contemporary law/justice; the defense for the admitted double murder rests on "temporary insanity," which is to say that the defendant was "driven to" the deeds. See *The Seattle Times* and *Seattle Post Intelligencer,* week of June 9 – 15, 1991.
12. Hamilton, *Western and Hard-Boiled Fiction,* p. 83.
13. *Ibid.,* pp. 87, 89.
14. The recent Persian Gulf War would seem a case in point on an international scale, despite the appeals to "law" in the form of U.N. mandates, arbitrarily applied.
15. See, Daniel G. Stone, *April Fools: An Insider's Account of the Rise and Collapse of Drexel Burnham* (New York: D. I. Fine, 1990).
16. Patricia Nelson Limerick, *Legacy of Conquest: The Unbroken Past of the American West* (New York: Norton, 1987).
17. Annette Kolodny, *The Lay of the Land* (Chapel Hill: University of North Carolina Press, 1975).
18. Loren Grey, in "Foreword," *The Maverick Queen* (New York: Harper's, 1950) p. vii.
19. See, Denis McLaughlin, *The Encyclopedia of the Old West* (London: Routledge and Kegan Paul, 1977), s.v. "Watson, Ella."
20. Jackson, *Zane Grey,* p. 108, errs regarding the death of Jimmy Weston.

21. Milton, *The Novel,* p. 21.

22. Topping, "Zane Grey: A Literary Reassessment," p. 63.

23. Cawelti, *Adventure, Mystery and Romance,* p. 239.

24. Hamilton, *Western and Hard-Boiled Fiction,* pp. 18 – 19, 23 – 24.

25. Jackson, *Zane Grey,* p. 58.

26. *Ibid.,* p. 59.

27. Gary Topping, "Zane Grey's West," *Journal of Popular Culture,* Vol. 7 (Winter 1973), pp. 43 – 44.

28. *Ibid.,* p. 41.

29. Cawelti, *Adventure, Mystery and Romance,* pp. 237 – 238.

30. Jackson, *Zane Grey,* p. 62.

31. Slotkin, *Regeneration Through Violence,* p. 5.

32. *Ibid.,* p. 179.

33. For more on Slotkin's thesis on the ideology of law and the hunter myth, see *The Fatal Environment*, pp. 49 – 80, 126 – 136.

34. Edwin Fussell, *Frontier: American Literature and the American West* (Princeton: Princeton University Press, 1965).

35. Slotkin, *Regeneration Through Violence,* p. 565.

36. See, Roberto M. Unger, *The Critical Legal Studies Movement* (Cambridge: Harvard University Press, 1986); Stanley Fish, *Doing What Comes Naturally: Change, Rhetoric, and the Practice of Theory in Literary and Legal Studies* (Durham: Duke University Press, 1989); Sanford Levinson and Steven Mailloux, eds. *Interpreting Law & Literature: A Hermeneutic Reader* (Evanston: Northwestern University Press, 1988); Robert A Ferguson, *Law and Letters in American Culture* (Cambridge: Harvard University Press, 1984).

37. See, H. L. Hart, *The Concept of LAW* (New York: Oxford University Press, 1962), p. 6, cited by Fish in *Doing What Comes Naturally,* p. 503.

38. See, Ferguson, *Law and Letters,* Chapter I, "In America the Law is King."

39. Hamilton (*Western and Hard-Boiled Fiction*) is an exception.

40. See Fish, *Doing What Comes Naturally,* pp. 503 – 524.

41. *Atlantic Monthly* (October 1915), p. 509, cited in Scott, *Zane Grey,* p. 40. *The Lone Star Ranger* derives from two shorter works, "The Last of the Duanes," and "The Lone Star Ranger," both published in 1914.

42. Hamilton, *Western and Hard-Boiled Fiction,* p. 83.

43. *Ibid.*

44. That is: Why do innocents suffer? Are they always unfit? Why do the "bad" guys get killed? Some of them are greased lightning on the draw and have survived a long time; Why does their "turn" come? etc.

45. See, Scott, *Zane Grey,* pp. 37 – 41.

46. Jackson, *Zane Grey,* pp. 112 – 113.

47. M. Crevecoeur, *Letters from an American Farmer* (London, 1782); I quote from the convenient Dutton paperback (New York, 1957), p. 49.

48. See Fish, *Doing What Comes Naturally,* pp. 503 – 524.

49. Rene Girard, *Violence and the Sacred* (Baltimore: Johns Hopkins University Press, 1977), pp. 20 – 21.

50. *Ibid.,* p. 21.

51. *Ibid.,* p. 25.

52. Slotkin, *Regeneration Through Violence,* p. 564.

V: The Dream

1. Slotkin, *Regeneration Through Violence,* p. 281.

2. Smith, *Virgin Land,* pp. 123 – 132.

3. Milton, *The Novel,* p. 88.

4. Ronald, *Zane Grey,* p. 13.

5. Cawelti, *Adventure, Mystery and Romance,* p. 218.

6. *Ibid.,* pp. 240, 244.

7. Hamilton, *Western and Hard-Boiled Fiction,* pp. 90 – 91.

8. Kant, *Zane Grey's Arizona,* p. 40. Kant's study is extremely useful in tracing characters, themes, and places which later emerged in Grey's Arizona-based novels. For bibliography of Grey's quarrel with the Game Commission, see p. 167, n. 25.

9. Hamilton, *Western and Hard-Boiled Fiction,* p. 89.

10. *Ibid., p. 21.*

11. Scott, *Zane Grey*, pp. 50, 56.

12. Compare, Bold, *Selling the Wild West,* p. 88.

13. See Kant for the model for Nas Ta Bega. For the folly of referring to "The Indian," and for Indian-white relations in the West, see, "The Persistence of Natives," in Limerick, *Legacy of Conquest.*

14. Jackson, *Zane Grey,* p. 118.

15. Hamilton, *Western and Hard-Boiled Fiction,* p. 23.

16. Cawelti, *Adventure, Mystery and Romance,* pp. 238, 240.

17. "The Practical Spirit: Sacrality and the American West," in *Western Writing*, Gerald W. Haslam, ed. (Albuquerque: University of New Mexico Press, 1974) pp. 129 – 142.
18. Hamilton, *Western and Hard-Boiled Fiction,* p. 74.
19. "Ten-Gallon Hero," in *The Western,* p. 18.
20. Gruber, *Zane Grey: A Biography*, p. 180.
21. Cawelti, *Adventure, Mystery and Romance,* p. 213.
22. Slotkin, *Regeneration Through Violence,* p. 34.
23. Cawelti, *Adventure, Mystery and Romance,* p. 233.
24. In *The Western,* p. 24.
25. Athearn, *The Mythic West,* p. 76.
26. Hamilton, *Western and Hard-Boiled Fiction,* p. 90.
27. Cawelti, *Adventure, Mystery and Romance,* p. 239.
28. "Introduction" to *The Western,* p. 11.
29. Bold *Selling the Wild West,* pp. 83 – 84.
30. Jackson, *Zane Grey,* p. 68.
31. Topping, "Zane Grey: A Literary Reassessment," p. 62.
32. Hamilton, *Western and Hard-Boiled Fiction,* p. 9.
33. Topping, "Zane Grey: A Literary Reassessment," p. 62.
34. "Introduction" to *American Dreams, American Nightmares,* David Madden, ed. (Carbondale: Southern Illinois University Press, 1970), p. xxvii.
35. See Kimball, *Rational Fictions.*
36. James Fenimore Cooper, *The Spy: A Tale of the Neutral Ground* (New York, 1821), pp. vi – vii.
37. (New York, 1828), *s.v.* "law." During this writing, Congress considered a Supreme Court nomination; "natural law" came under discussion.
38. Milton, *The Novel,* p. 1.

Appendix

1. New York: Grosset & Dunlap, n.d. Originally published by Harper's (New York: 1910). Harper's remained Grey's publisher of book-length novels throughout his career. Cited below are the editions consulted for *Ace of Hearts* which reflect the pagination referred to in this volume. Date of original publication by Harper's follows.
2. New York: Grosset & Dunlap, n.d. (1912).
3. New York: Pocket Books, 1969 (1913).
4. New York: Walter Black, n.d. (1914).

5. New York: Pocket Books, 1969 (1915).
6. New York: Pocket Books, 1961 (1915).
7. New York: Pocket Books, 1957 (1916).
8. New York: Grosset & Dunlap, n.d. (1917).
9. New York: Pocket Books, 1956 (1918).
10. New York: Pocket Books, 1985 (1919).
11. New York: Grosset & Dunlap, n.d. (1920).
12. New York: Walter Black, n.d. (1921).
13. New York: Pocket Books, 1971 (1922).
14. New York: Grosset & Dunlap, n.d, (1923).
15. New York: Thorndike Press Large Print Edition, n.d. (1924).
16. New York: Walter Black, n.d. (1925).
17. New York: Pocket Books, 1982 (1925).
18. New York: Pocket Books, 1976 (1926).
19. New York: Pocket Books, 1974 (1927).
20. New York: Bantam Books, 1946 (1928).
21. New York: Walter Black, n.d. (1928).
22. New York: Grosset & Dunlap, n.d. (1929).
23. New York: Pocket Books, 1984 (1930).
24. New York: Walter Black, n. d. (1931).
25. New York: Walter Black, n.d. (1932).
26. New York: Pocket Books, 1977 (1932).
27. New York: Walter Black, n.d. (1933).
28. New York: Walter Black, n.d. (1933).
29. New York: Pocket Books, 1963 (1934).
30. New York: Pocket Books, 1972 (1935).
31. New York: Pocket Books, 1959 (1936).
32. New York: Pocket Books, 1964 (1936).
33. New York: Walter Black, n.d. (1937).
34. New York: Grosset & Dunlap, n.d. (1938).
35. New York: Grosset & Dunlap, n.d. (1939).
36. New York: Walter Black, n.d. (1939).
37. New York: Pocket Books, 1982 (1940).
38. New York: Pocket Books, 1976 (1941).
39. New York: Pocket Books, 1980 (1942).
40. New York: Pocket Books, 1981 (1943).
41. New York: Grosset & Dunlap, n.d. (1944).
42. New York: Walter Black, n.d. (1946).
43. New York: Pocket Books, 1959 (1947).
44. New York: Grosset & Dunlap, n.d. (1948).

45. New York: Pocket Books, 1965 (1949).
46. New York: Pocket Books, 1982 (1950).
47. New York: Pocket Books, 1981 (1951).
48. New York: Pocket Books, 1977 (1952).
49. New York: Pocket Books, 1962 (1953).
50. New York: Pocket Books, 1965 (1954).
51. New York: Pocket Books, 1960 (1955).
52. New York: Walter Black, n.d. (1956).
53. New York: Pocket Books, 1963 (1957).
54. New York: Pocket Books, 1966 (1958).
55. New York: Walter Black, n.d. (1959).
56. New York: Pocket Books, 1967 (1963).

Bibliography

Robert G. Athearn *The Mythic West in Twentieth-Century America* (Lawrence: University Press of Kansas, 1986).

Sacvan Bercovitch, *The American Jeremiad* (Madison: University of Wisconsin Press, 1978).

Christine Bold, *Selling the Wild West* (Bloomington: University of Indiana Press, 1987).

Douglas Branch, *The Cowboy and His Interpreters* (New York: D. Appleton and Co., 1926).

John Cawelti, *Adventure, Mystery, and Romance: Formula Stories as Art and Popular Culture* (Chicago: University of Chicago Press, 1976).

James Fenimore Cooper, *The Spy: A Tale of the Neutral Ground* (New York, 1821).

Richard Drinnon, *Facing West: The Metaphysics of Indian-Hating and Empire Building* (New York: New American Library, 1980).

Paul Edwards, ed. *The Encyclopedia of Philosophy,*, 6 vols. (New York: Macmillan, 1967).

Richard Etulain and Michael T. Marsden, eds., *The Popular Western,* (Bowling Green, Ohio: Bowling Green State University Popular Press, 1974).

Robert A Ferguson, *Law and Letters in American Culture* (Cambridge: Harvard University Press, 1984).

Stanley Fish, *Doing What Comes Naturally: Change, Rhetoric, and the Practice of Theory in Literary and Legal Studies* (Durham: Duke University Press, 1989).

James K. Folsom, ed. *The Western: A Collection of Critical Essays,* (Englewood Cliffs, New Jersey: Prentice-Hall, 1979).

Edwin Fussell, *Frontier: American Literature and the American West* (Princeton: Princeton University Press, 1965).

Rene Girard, *Violence and the Sacred* (Baltimore: Johns Hopkins University Press, 1977), pp. 20 – 21.

Frank Gruber, *Zane Grey: A Biography* (New York: World Publishing Co., 1970).

Cynthia S. Hamilton, *Western and Hard-Boiled Fiction in America: From High Noon to Midnight* (London: Macmillan, 1987).

Gerald Haslam, Ed., *Western Writing* (Albuquerque: University of New Mexico Press, 1974).

Carlton Jackson, *Zane Grey* (New York: Twayne Publishers, 1973).

Candace C. Kant *Zane Grey's Arizona* (Flagstaff, Arizona: Northland Press, 1984).

Arthur G. Kimball, *Rational Fictions: A Study of Charles Brockden Brown* (McMinnville, Oregon: Linfield Research Institute, 1968).

Annette Kolodny, *The Lay of the Land* (Chapel Hill: University of North Carolina Press, 1975).

Sanford Levinson and Steven Mailloux, eds. *Interpreting Law & Literature: A Hermeneutic Reader* (Evanston: Northwestern University Press, 1988).

Patricia Nelson Limerick, *Legacy of Conquest: The Unbroken Past of the American West* (New York: Norton, 1987).

David Madden, ed., *American Dreams, American Nightmares* (Carbondale: Southern Illinois University Press, 1970).

Denis McLaughlin, *The Encyclopedia of the Old West* (London: Routledge and Kegan Paul, 1977).

John Milton, *The Novel of the American West* (Lincoln: University of Nebraska Press, 1980).

Russel Nye, *The Unembarrassed Muse* (New York: Dial Press, 1970).

William T. Pilkington, ed. *Critical Essays on the Western American Novel* (Boston: G. K. Hall, 1980).

Lawrence Clark Powell, *Southwest Classics: The Creative Literature of the Arid Lands, Essays on the Books and Their Writers* (Los Angeles: Ward Ritchie Press, 1974).

Mary White Rowlandson, *The Sovereignty and Goodness of God, Together with the Faithfulness of His Promises Displayed: Being a Narrative of the Captivity and Restauration of Mrs. Mary Rowlandson* (1682).

Ann Ronald, *Zane Grey* (Boise, Idaho: Boise State University, 1975).

Kenneth W. Scott *Zane Grey: Born of the West, A Reference Guide* (Boston: G.K. Hall, 1979).
Richard Slotkin, *The Fatal Environment: The Myth of the Frontier in the Age of Industrialization, 1800 – 1890* (New York: Atheneum. 1985).
_____. *Regeneration through Violence: The Mythology of the American Frontier, 1600 – 1860* (Middletown, Connecticut: Wesleyan University Press, 1973).
Henry Nash Smith, *Virgin Land* (Cambridge: Harvard University Press, 1950).
Daniel G. Stone, *April Fools: An Insider's Account of the Rise and Collapse of Drexel Burnham* (New York: D. I. Fine, 1990).
Roberto M. Unger, *The Critical Legal Studies Movement* (Cambridge: Harvard University Press, 1986).

Periodical Literature

William Bloodworth, "Zane Grey's Western Eroticism," *South Dakota Review,* Vol. 23 (Autumn 1985).
Roscoe Burton, "Opie Read and Zane Grey," *Saturday Review of Literature,* November 11, 1939.
Richard Etulain, "The American Literary West and Its Interpreters: The Rise of a New Historiography," *Pacific Historical Review,* Vol. 45 (Winter 1976).
_____. "A Dedication to the Memory of Zane Grey, 1872 – 1939," *Arizona and the West,* Vol. 12 (Autumn 1970).
Arthur G. Kimball, "Silent Walls: 'Nature' in Grey's *The Vanishing American,*" *South Dakota Review,* Vol. 26 (Spring 1988).
_____. "My Navajo Oasis: Irony in Grey's *Heritage of the Desert,*" *South Dakota Review,* Vol. 28 (Summer 1990).
John D. Nesbitt, "Uncertain Sex in the Sagebrush," *South Dakota Review,* Vol. 23 (Autumn 1985).
New York Herald Tribune, October 24, 1939, p. 18.
New York Times, October 24, 1939, p. 23.
Kenneth W. Scott, "*The Heritage of the Desert:* Zane Grey Discovers the West," *The Markham Review,* Vol. 2 (February 1970).
Gary Topping, "Zane Grey: A Literary Reassessment," *American Literature,* Vol. 13 (Spring 1978).
_____. "Zane Grey's West," *Journal of Popular Culture,* Vol. 7 (Winter 1973).

Index